Therapeutic Education

D0209236

Despite much research into the role of therapy in schools, many professionals agree the needs of troubled pupils are often not being adequately met by their educational institution. Considering the number of students in full-time education with significant emotional and behavioural difficulties, some strategies and skills used by therapists can be usefully shared by teachers. Schools can develop therapeutic approaches to learning.

This fascinating book traces a substantial four-year research and school development programme that practically applied the principles of 'therapeutic education', and exposes how current educational contexts actually contribute to disaffection and the disruption of young people's learning.

The authors present a well-tested practical model of school and curricular experience, based on therapeutic relationships, that has led to outstanding positive results in school development. With suggestions throughout for tried and tested strategies that really work, this book can help professionals transform troubled young people's experience of education – from the nightmare it can be into an adventure with positive results for lifelong learning.

Teachers, educational psychologists, counsellors and anyone working with children or young people will find this important book an enlightening and invaluable read.

John Cornwall is Principal Lecturer in Special Educational Needs at Canterbury Christ Church University College, UK. He is also an Education Consultant and Research Psychologist.

Craig Walter is the Principal of Westwood School, a non-maintained special school in Kent, run by NCH, and is focused on developing new therapeutic approaches to education.

Therapeutic Education

Working alongside troubled and
troublesome children

John Cornwall and Craig Walter

Routledge
Taylor & Francis Group

LONDON AND NEW YORK

First published 2006 by Routledge
2 Park Square, Milton Park, Abingdon Oxon OX14 4RN

Simultaneously published in the USA and Canada
by Routledge
270 Madison Ave, New York, NY 10016

Routledge is an imprint of the Taylor & Francis Group, an informa business

© 2006 John Cornwall and Craig Walter

Typeset in Bembo by
Keystroke, Jacaranda Lodge, Wolverhampton
Printed and bound in Great Britain by
MPG Books Ltd, Bodmin

British Library Cataloguing in Publication Data
A catalogue record for this book is available from the British Library

Library of Congress Cataloging in Publication Data
Cornwall, John, senior lecturer
Therapeutic education : working alongside troubled and troublesome
    children / John Cornwall & Craig Walter.
        p. cm.
    Includes bibliographical references and index.
    ISBN 0–415–36661–5 (hardback : alk. paper) – ISBN 0–415–36662–3
(pbk. : alk. paper) 1. Children with social disabilities–Education–Great Britain.
2. Problem children–Education–Great Britain. I. Walter, Craig. II. Title.
    LC4096.G7C69 2006

    371.93'0941–dc22

    2005023936

ISBN10: 0–415–36661–5 (hbk)
ISBN10: 0–415–36662–3 (pbk)
ISBN10: 0–203–01929–6 (ebk)

ISBN13: 978–0–415–36661–8 (hbk)
ISBN13: 978–0–415–36662–5 (pbk)
ISBN13: 978–0–203–01929–0 (ebk)

Contents

List of figures   viii

List of tables   ix

Acknowledgements   x

1 Introduction: the 'human face' of education   1

Changes over the years or simply more of the same? 2

Therapeutic education: challenging academic tradition and social 'norms' 7

Roots, principles and paradigms 8

Contesting and developing notions of therapeutic education 11

2 Behavioural graffiti: ignoring the writing on the wall   19

Broadening the perspective and debating practice 20

Mapping holistic theories on to the reality of schooling 22

What characterises therapeutic education? 28

Mapping therapeutic education on to current practice 32

3 Education – adventure or nightmare?   38

Predictability, flexibility, coherence and values are 'seen' by young people 39

One size does not fit all: the child is at the centre of the learning process 41

The human element: everybody exhibits challenging behaviour 42

Troubled children growing into troublesome adolescents and adults 48

*Self-efficacy, one key to successful personal development, change and
   growth 51*

4 Who am I? Identity, agency and resilience   54

An activating approach: self-efficacy and human agency 55

Moral, social and emotional 'agency' as a result of self-efficacy 61

Discrimination and identity: self-worth and self-development 65

Vulnerability and resilience, key factors in personal growth and learning 68

5   **A curriculum for life?**   71
    Therapeutic education and behavioural, emotional and social development
        (BESD) 72
    Developing therapeutic relationships in learning and teaching 74
    Are we making a difference? The nature and scope of BESD provision 77
    How do we measure the quality of teaching and learning, quality of
        relationships and quality of life? 83

6   **The case study and grounded research**   90
    Introducing the school-based research programme 90
    Data sets, synthesis and analysis of data 94
    Brief summing up 105

7   **Measuring the effectiveness of holistic and ecosystemic**
    interventions   107
    Demonstrating that therapeutic approaches are effective in a school
        context 108
    Applying the basic features of human agency and self-efficacy 110
    Social and emotional skills: learning to behave, behaving to learn and
        learning for life 117
    Keeping it all together: it is experience that counts in the end 121

8   **A real alternative to an 'alternative curriculum'?**   123
    The interactive curriculum and young people's behaviour in the school
        context 124
    Importance of a school's 'statement of purpose' (policy statements) 124
    Theoretical and legislative precursors to creating a therapeutic environment 130
    Implementation and management of the behaviour policy 132
    Operational procedures and methods of promoting good behaviour 134
    Handling conflict and potentially violent situations 137

9   **Achievement and lifelong learning: A 'principled' approach**   141
    Therapeutic education: arguing for new solutions to old problems 141
    Introducing empowerment concepts into the school ethos 144
    Reviewing the problems of young people in education 146
    Developing effective and empowering practices and a humanistic ethos 148
    Monitoring and developing a learning environment that is 'therapeutic' 150

10 **Putting it all together, together**   157
    From criminality, control and coercion to cooperation and consensus 158

*From retribution and recidivism to ecology, relationships and learning
  behaviour 160*
*Interpersonal relationships and human agency in the facilitation of
  learning 166*
From curriculum to relationships, personal growth and lifelong learning 168

Appendix 1: Evaluating areas of therapeutic working   172

Appendix 2: Therapeutic education assessment for shared values   175

Appendix 3: Proactive and pro-social management of behaviour   179

Appendix 4: The points system   182

Appendix 5: Handling difficult and violent situations   186

Appendix 6: Case-study data and preliminary analysis   189

Appendix 7: A schedule for observing and assessing a therapeutic
approach   207

Appendix 8: Behaviour and PSHE profile   210

Notes   222
References   224
Index   232

Figures

2.1   Example of graffiti art from a wall in Budapest   19
2.2   Example of graffiti art in the United Kingdom   20
2.3   Schools do not exist in a vacuum   23
2.4   Behaviour management, inclusion (academic and social)
      achievement and lifelong learning: a conceptual framework   30
2.5   Does this diagram from *Every Child Matters* indicate a UK model
      of therapeutic education and associated activities?   35
4.1   An adaptation of Kolb's simple model of experiential learning   55
4.2   The feedback loops involved in learning   56
5.1   Goddard's 'interlinked four-part curriculum' model   75
5.2   The interactive curriculum model at Westwood School   76
8.1   Operational aspects of the 'interactive curriculum'   125
9.1   Troubled and troublesome children: identified needs in terms of
      care and support   149
10.1 Breaking the cycle of retribution and recidivism   165

Tables

2.1   Illustration of the breadth of activities that could be termed
therapeutic education (from a US example)   35

2.2   Comparison of therapeutic and educational principles   36

3.1a   Give some examples of *your* recent challenging behaviour   44

3.1b   What were your thoughts at the time?   44

3.1c   What were your feelings?   44

8.1   Stages to the 'life-space interview' in the event of a serious
incident or problem   136

9.1   Summary of vulnerability and resilience factors and their impact
on children and young people   153

10.1   Summary of activities at different levels indicating support in a
therapeutic learning environment   161

Acknowledgements

The authors would like to thank the staff and pupils of Westwood School and NCH National Children's Charity, without whom this book would not have been possible.

Chapter 1

Introduction

The 'human face' of education

The postmodern era has brought with it an acceptance of a technocratic and accountancy model of education that favours statistics and measurable outcomes above human values of learning and the interactive processes that make it work. This book aims to encourage and support teachers in helping pupils engage with their peers and adults – to participate in schooling and gain access to relevant knowledge and, with that, some of the skills that will truly help them to cope with and have some success in their lives. Learning and teaching is not an end result but a continuous interactive and humanistic process. This human process is not constrained by professional peccadilloes, fashions or accounting procedures. We, the authors, wish to promote an environment and practice that encourage learning behaviour and learning relationships and in turn supports participation, engagement and access to learning opportunities with young people who are sometimes regarded as intelligent, often very creative and regularly challenging. It suggests that educational practice should be evidence based and defined by those who actually do the work. It should not be dictated by those who do not understand the interactive processes involved, who have no real tested experience in the field and who are driven by a social and political agenda alone. Poor evidence bases for professional knowledge and political interference in schools have demoralised and depressed professionals whose job it is to create encouraging and effective learning environments within state education in the United Kingdom and some aspects of public school education in the United States.

This book is a commentary on the development of practice in creating a therapeutic environment for pupils who have been excluded, or are at risk of being excluded, from educational opportunity. It is also an examination of the social context, theoretical underpinnings and principles involved in working with young people who are 'troubled and troublesome' or 'vulnerable and challenging'. It is a treatise on the background theory and research that underpin practice in 'therapeutic education' or 'therapeutic approaches to learning' or the 'development of a therapeutic environment in an education setting'. It is also a toolbox, derived from practical work by the authors in an educational setting for pupils who have been excluded (and excluded themselves) from school and from available educational opportunities at school. Our intention is that the material in later chapters and in the appendices will provide professionals in this field with something to consider in terms of their practice. But the book is also an attempt to cultivate and contribute to a sound theoretical and evidence base in this most challenging and interesting work with young people who are both troubled and troublesome.

Changes over the years or simply more of the same?

Over the past twenty years, education has been beleaguered by an ethic that gives emphasis to procedural competence, end results and the mechanical transmission of a tightly prescribed curriculum. We are now seeing a scramble to make curricula more flexible in order to meet the needs of young people, particularly for the age group 14–19 years (for example, see Scottish Executive, 2001). According to the *Annual Survey of Trends in Education* (NfER, 2003), the main increase in the apprehension of headteachers in the United Kingdom in this year concerned National Curriculum assessment, which was seen as a priority by about one-third of the headteachers surveyed. This is the highest figure reported for this area in any of the nine surveys in this series and illustrates the pressures headteachers are facing in meeting Key Stage targets. Headteachers were also asked how many members of the teaching staff had a post-experience qualification in special educational needs (SEN), and the number ranged from none to four, with 60 per cent of the schools reporting that they had no teachers with a post-experience qualification in SEN and a further 25 per cent reporting having only one teacher with such a qualification. This woeful state of affairs in UK education flies in the face of local and national government initiatives to increase the number of pupils with SEN in mainstream schools, including those who are socially and emotionally vulnerable and challenging. It also contrasts with the situation in the United States, where generally teachers in special education are expected as part of their licensing procedures to study a specialism at Master's degree level. It is fairly typical of the top-down driven educational system in the United Kingdom, where planning for change (in this case inclusion) invariably takes place after the changes have happened.

The UK government's new guidance, *Every Child Matters* (Treasury, 2003), has some main planks that are consistent with our view of therapeutic education and a more holistic approach to learning. It sees the following as necessary for children's well-being:

- *being healthy:* enjoying good physical and mental health and having a healthy lifestyle;
- *staying safe:* being protected from harm and neglect;
- *enjoying and achieving:* getting the most out of life and developing the skills for adulthood;

- *making a positive contribution:* being involved with the community and society and not engaging in antisocial or offending behaviour;
- *economic well-being:* not being prevented by economic disadvantage from achieving one's full potential in life.

However, there are also some major differences; but it makes little sense to argue about such fundamental and incontestable wishes for children and young people in our society. Nevertheless, there is once again enormous inconsistency between a position that states such obvious wishes, as if these have not always been the aspirations of children's services (children didn't matter before 2003?), and yet relies on under-resourced and struggling services to put into practice these laudable sentiments. What is clear from working within these services for many years is that the range of expectations and demands placed on professionals and workers in these services is enormous. It has taken successive governments more than sixteen years to realise that the demands of the National Curriculum were not realistic in the face of the reality of teaching children. Once again, the emphasis in *Every Child Matters* is on 'driven' change through expectations (e.g. working in multidisciplinary teams around schools or developing common assessment frameworks). It is not as if professionals have not been trying to do this for many years, but they have been hampered and restrained by organisational and management structures within children's services. These are not impossible goals, but radical change within the structures is needed. One positive step is the creation of a Young People's Fund with an initial budget of £200 million and increasing investment in child and adolescent mental health services (CAMHS) to deliver a 10 per cent increase in CAMHS capacity each year for the next three years. It remains to be seen whether a 'target-based' economy can produce such fundamental changes as those expected in the simple five statements of the White Paper. The most recent 'inclusive' legislation in the United States, 'No Child Left Behind' (NCLB), has split opinion between those who subscribe to legislation aimed at 'driving up' standards, much as UK governments have done, and those who have large reservations about both the intentions of the legislation and its funding basis. The four pillars of NCLB are stronger accountability for results, more freedom for states and communities, proven education methods, and more choices for parents. It is aimed at driving out the gap between middle and upper socio-economic groups and deprived or disadvantaged groups in terms of educational success. The difference in attainment between, for example, children from black and Hispanic inner-city populations, rural poor, Native Americans and the inhabitants of more affluent leafy suburbs, more predominantly white, has been the subject of contention and discussion for some time. Those who have concerns (e.g. the state of Connecticut) about 'No Child Left Behind', with its heavy emphasis on testing and its failure to address some of the underlying causes of the achievement gap, have found themselves caught by its demands and expectations.

Over the past month, the state has battled with the federal government over President Bush's signature education legislation, with the state saying that the No Child Left Behind law was inflexible and that not enough money has gone into it. The nation's largest teacher's union, the National Education Association, is challenging the law in court, claiming it is under-funded. Connecticut has also threatened to file a lawsuit on similar grounds.

(Salzman, 2005)

Whether or not Connecticut's objections to the law are valid, the state's achievement gap has made it vulnerable to criticism. The essential underpinning is that children must achieve and be successful in education, no matter what their socio-economic background. This is very similar to the weight of legislation and guidance in the United Kingdom, where the inspection process for the past twelve years has been concerned with driving up standards of educational attainment along the narrowly defined lines of literacy, numeracy and science. The question of whether driving up these limited academic 'standards' will really have the social effect that both UK and US federal governments desire is one still to be answered. The record of social change contingent on educational successes in both countries is not a very healthy one so far.

In the words of Raven (1991), 'The assessment of the results of good educational practice defies conventional measurement.' The application of so-called 'standards' and a 'driven' educational economy has resulted in the growth of target setting and the measuring of that which is easily measured rather than that which is possibly more important in educational terms.

Seymour Papert introduces 'constructivism' as a means to reform the educational process. He reviewed existing standards and curriculum agendas and questioned their validity in an ever-changing world. Dr. Levine, et al. [1992], argue that schools ignore the students' whole learning experience and instead focus on ways of obtaining statistical results. They express that schools need to be 'learning communities'; places where our children can gather in social activities and experience the process of learning. Whereas, most of our educational system is in fact based on a model of quantitative results instead.

(Kay, 2000: ch. 2)

Replacing the mechanistic view of education and change with a more human face would more appropriately define it as the transmission of culture and a search for personal growth and development within a community, where excellence is recognised as much by participation and progress as by attainment and exams. Applying human principles in learning means focusing equally on the predictive capacities and creative abilities of children and young people, not just on their ability to soak up factual and easily measurable curriculum content. It should not, either, be measured by their ability to cope with large, inhuman 'institutions' or to conform to irrational or unchallenged or conventional group pressures and competitive classroom cultures. We should not ignore the fact that educational exclusion is clearly related to both social and cultural exclusion, and that education does have a pivotal role (Bradshaw *et al.*, 2004; Parsons, 1996, 1999; Cornwall and Tod 1998; Cornwall, 2000; Sparkes, 1999). More specifically, the role of education has been linked with many social problems such as crime, antisocial behaviour and just general disaffection with learning institutions. However, it is also clear from social research (Bradshaw *et al.*, 2004; Sparkes, 1999) that failure and exclusion in education are pivotally related to social factors and less obviously to emotional factors and educational disadvantage (e.g. Cornwall and Tod, 1998), mainly because of a lack of research focus on this perspective. There also exists in our society an 'underclass' (Murray and Phillips, 2001) that comprises not just a group of people who are poor in material terms but people who are at the margins of society – people whose social behaviour in terms of child rearing (Waldfogel, 1999), education and family life may mirror similar behaviour by persons in other strata of society (i.e. the 'overclass' described by Murray and Phillips, 2001) but for whom the life consequences of their behaviour can quickly become far more disastrous (Murray and Phillips, 2001). We share some of the frustrations expressed by Murray (Murray and Phillips 2001: 6) in recognising that while figures for homicide and robbery were higher in the United States than in the United Kingdom in 1993, between 1996 and 2001 the levels of property crime, sexual offences and robbery had become double those in the United States. Just as frustrating is the lack of socially positive changes in our society.

> Young males are dropping out of the labour market, violent crime has risen drastically, the illegitimacy ratio is at 38 per cent and climbing. Trends that in 1989 couldn't possibly continue for another ten years have continued for another ten years. But so what? Trying to get people's attention about the underclass these days makes me identify with Jeremiah. The economy is humming, stock portfolios are bulging, and, many readers may ask, if this growing underclass is as big a problem as Murray says it is, why has British life changed so little?
>
> (Murray and Phillips, 2001: 12)

The principles described through the practice developed and portrayed in this book directly challenge the current politicisation and commercialisation of education as well as its use as a tool for social engineering. Much of the terminology around education over the past two decades has become 'business-like' (e.g. the target-setting culture exemplified by Lloyd and Berthelot, 1992) and has more to do with concepts of 'efficiency' and corporate identity than with the nurture and development of young lives. For example, people are seen as 'human currency', either as participators in society or as achievers (serving to boost statistics and achieve pre-set political targets), or as components of a social context with all its cultural norms and socio-cultural objectives (economic, social, political, civil, and religious or spiritual). These are critical in determining relationships between learners and the institutions that provide education, or training as it is in danger of becoming. Knowledge transfer has become a transaction, in which currencies and goods are prioritised, and thus the terms of inclusion are defined:

> social exclusion remains an ill-defined, contested concept. . . . It proposes that inclusion hinges on participation in social relationships enacted through a variety of 'transactional processes', where currencies are assessed and goods distributed or withheld accordingly. 'Currencies' are human as well as financial, providing evidence of human or social capital – what people do and are as well as have. Although transactions can be for different purposes and of different types – free market or social rights-based, formal or informal – a broad generic process can be described.
>
> (Witcher, 2003: 1)

To follow Witcher's (2003) arguments further, she explains that inclusion is defined by those who administer the institutions and that what is held to be valuable in a human being is also defined by administrators who allocate resources and who also define socio-cultural objectives such as wealth creation, skill acquisition, religious codes, employment figures, exam results, and so on. On this basis, it could be argued that the broader the definitions of 'social currency', the more inclusive a society becomes. Conversely, the narrower these socio-cultural definitions become, the more exclusive a society becomes. Or it could be argued that 'inclusion' is just another way of getting people to conform to the middle-class values of education and achieve esteem through recognition by respectable institutions that are accepted as arbiters of attainment and achievement. When job markets, financial success and exam success dominate a society and its education provision, then the greater will be the number of people excluded, either by dint of their own predispositions or because they choose to define their own lives by other intellectual, cultural, social or emotional parameters.

A teacher or a nurse in our modern society is generally rewarded less than a company director, software engineer or an armaments salesperson. Are they therefore valued less? The concept of 'human currency' is a fashionable one in planning the socio-cultural developments of our times and impacts no less on education than elsewhere (e.g. health provision) in our society. The reality of a profit-based society is that, despite the use of education for social planning and engineering, the so-called 'human currency' or value placed on people in our society is not necessarily consistent with the value placed on culture and learning in different communities. In addition, the current promise of 'inclusion' in society through educational testing and attainment does not match up to the reality for a significant proportion of young people. The current ethos in education, where pupils are treated as units of 'human currency', flies in the face of a humanitarian or even a common-sense approach.

Therapeutic education: challenging academic tradition and social 'norms'

This book is not articulating a soft approach to the difficulties that teachers and other professionals face in dealing with the social, behavioural and emotional problems in schools and services. Nevertheless, it does suggest that the hard-edged punitive and competitive ethos that characterises much secondary provision in both the United Kingdom and the United States has not been successful in reducing disaffection or the extent of social and educational exclusion taking place. According to figures set out in *Every Child Matters* (Treasury, 2003: 15), out of 11 million children in the United Kingdom, 3–4 million are regarded as vulnerable, 59,700 are children looked after, 25,700 are on child protection registers and 50–100 per year die from abuse or neglect. The terms 'vulnerable children' and 'looked after children' also hide a plethora of complex social and emotional conditions and circumstances. Clearly, with over a quarter of children regarded as being vulnerable, this is a significant situation that requires attention. What it does suggest is that the very challenging and sometimes extreme behaviour exhibited by some young people may well be a perfectly natural response (one that any of us might make) to a most horrific and depressing set of life circumstances.

The concept of discipline in schools should be based not on a punitive or control ethos but on an ethos of well-defined expectations, a positive learning environment (e.g. Rogers, 1991) and well-organised, child-centred teaching and organisational practices (the student is the stakeholder). This is not 'soft' but hard work and requires careful conception and planning in order to engage, motivate and enthuse learners, and provide an environment in which they can flourish. It should not be an 'additive' to have strategies, resources and facilities that are geared towards supporting a young person having difficulties. It should be part of the very fibre of a school. This surely has to be the aim of all schools? But it requires more skill and personal resources on the part of the adults involved. It also requires well-informed (by the professionals) material and conceptual support by funding agencies.

Childhood behaviour indicators show that problems at school lead to 'adult malaise' (Hobcraft, 2000). In *Every Child Matters*, once again, the UK government is catching up with progress in professional and service knowledge by describing a 'continuity of anti-social behaviour from 5 to 17'[1] in which a young child progresses from being oppositional and defiant at 5 years through to being a career offender, unemployed and misusing drugs, at 17 years. It has long been recognised by workers in this field that there can be a downward path that starts early in life.

It should also be recognised, however, and perhaps researched as much as the 'negative cycle' model, that there are a good many more young people who are 'resilient' and self-determined, and manage to get through their education despite adverse circumstances. We, the authors, subscribe to a positive psychology viewpoint (exemplified in this book by Bandura's positive social psychology through the constructs of self-efficacy and self-determination). Therapeutic education should above all empower the young person to take responsibility for themselves and develop the kind of change that will develop in them sufficient 'resilience' (e.g. Pilling, 1992) to enable them to overcome setbacks and to get through their education and life experiences.

The concept of 'adult malaise', as opposed to simple socio-economic analysis, is very important because it hides a multitude of human factors that are developed in this book and outlined later in the chapter. Further evidence of the complexity of the problem can be seen in the relationship between potential inclusion (or success in education) and mother's and father's interest in their child's education, summaries of educational test scores and of frequent school absences at ages 7, 11 and 16, and of three different reports of contact with the police by age 16 (Hobcraft, 2000). We not only propose that the notions attached to therapeutic education should be incorporated generally into education, but suggest that they are already taking hold in schools through many initiatives and demands from children, parents and teachers for a recognition of the 'human face' of education.

Roots, principles and paradigms

Albert Bandura's (1977b) social cognitive theory stands in clear contrast to theories of human functioning that overemphasise the role of purely environmental factors in the development of human behaviour and learning. Behaviourist theories, for example, show scant interest in self-processes, because theorists assume that human functioning is caused by external stimuli. Social cognitive theory is rooted in a view of human agency in which individuals are agents proactively engaged in their own development and can make things happen by their actions. Central to this sense of personal effectiveness or agency is the fact that, among other personal factors, individuals possess self-beliefs that enable them to exercise a measure of control over their thoughts, feelings and actions, that 'what people think, believe, and feel affects how they behave' (Bandura, 1986: 25). Creating a learning environment which supports the principle of 'self-efficacy' should influence the very fabric of schools practice and not be regarded as something that applies only to those in obvious difficulty. It is time that the superficial slogan (hiding a traditional punitive and competitive attitude to learning) 'no pain, no gain' was laid to rest once and for all. Humans instinctively search out new experience as if it were woven into our very beings (Kelly, 1955; Bannister and Fransella, 1986) and just as instinctively know that satisfaction, enjoyment or simple pleasure are vital components of a productive learning environment. Subsequent chapters in this book will elaborate on these constructs and ideas and then develop the principles on which the practices investigated are founded.

This is not to say that a learner or young person cannot and should not, through learning, transcend their difficulties, nor does it make the learner passive. On the contrary, active learning is necessary to achieve a state where academic success or self-actualisation (Maslow, 1968) is even possible. The learner has to become responsible for their own actions in this respect in order to participate and progress at all. This book and the approaches we examine in detail later clearly expound the view that it is foolish, short-sighted and downright dangerous to ignore the broader holistic nature of the learning and teaching relationship and the ecology of the learner's situation. An ecological view of the child concerned implies that the problem never resides solely within the individual; it resides in the relationship between that individual and their surroundings and experiences. Once this has been established, therapeutic education becomes a process whereby a therapeutic environment is developed in order to provide an alternative to the very environment that has triggered off the problems in the first place. More than that, it suggests that if the learning environment of mainstream education were to be radically altered, then the problems encountered by many young people would be lessened and the general learning environment in schools would become much more 'human' and 'humane' for everyone. 'Behaviour is often taken as evidence of identity or capability and this is how confidence and competence are destroyed in the classroom' (O'Connor and Seymour, 1990: 90).

There is a vast difference between what seems to be accepted these days under the broad umbrella of therapeutic education and what was at one time called 'Planned Environment Therapy', pioneered by Dr Marjorie Franklin (1968; cited in Bridgeland, 1971) as a young junior medical officer in the Portsmouth Borough Mental Hospital in the early 1920s. She developed the relationship between mental illness and the patients' environment. She observed the improvements that occurred in response to a cheerful, encouraging environment and sympathetic nursing, but also, in some cases, the dramatic improvement of the psychotic condition linked to the onset of severe physical illness. She concluded that the 'therapeutic environment' triggered by the physical illness benefited the patients' mental condition also. This approach was very much embedded in therapeutic medical practices and probably coincided with the further development of psychodynamic approaches applied to education. This book is not solely based on medical theories, psychodynamic principles or on any one of the more exclusive definitions proffered by any single group of professionals or legitimised by any single area of professional practice over and above others. Early experiments were led by psychiatrists and were characterised by trying to achieve 'social adjustment' through a planned therapeutic environment, the use of creative arts and individual remedial teaching. The Children's Social

Adjustment Society at Arlesford Place (mentioned in Bridgeland, 1971) was planned as a continuing experiment in that it was intended to measure, by testing and observation, the effect of a particular method of re-education on maladjusted children. The 'experiment' was to be conducted by psychiatrists, who were largely responsible for selecting the children and organising the treatment policy. Wardens and other staff were responsible for constructing and maintaining the environment, and psychologists, both inside and outside the establishment, assessed the results. Certain practical difficulties of the Ashford Place venture cast some doubt on the effectiveness of the approach, but were mainly due to disagreements among the professionals involved. Nonetheless, the principles invited further study, and various constructs around 'therapeutic education' have thrived since then.

We intentionally use the term 'therapeutic education' because it most closely fits the theoretical and practical basis on which a specific provision for young people who have been socially and educationally excluded has developed. We define it in much broader terms than those implied in the modern psycho-dynamic versions of the early therapeutic education and planned environments described previously. This book and the project on which it is based share some of the characteristics of those earlier attempts to develop a 'therapeutic environment' in which vulnerable and challenging young people can thrive and learn. It is our endeavour to share genuinely reflective and professional practices through structured analysis of changes in organisation and pupil progress in the project environment. However, we do not accept the term 'maladjusted' with its implications, and focus on individual social and psychological deviance. The intention is to challenge previous definitions of 'therapeutic education' as being either limited by disciplinary boundaries or currently criticised (or even ignored by educational academics) because it does not concern itself with social or educational dimensions but centres on an individual, rather than a 'collective', approach.

These days the more traditional 'therapeutic' approaches (where they exist) in schools seem to be rooted in both psychodynamics or individual interventions through counselling and in the medicalisation of behavioural symptoms by the administration of drugs, such as in attention deficit hyperactivity disorder (ADHD). This book intends to offer a complementary set of practices focusing on young people in the latter stages of their school careers.

Environmental therapists must initially have had a concept of 'maladjustment' that lays stress on the environmental causes and on the impact on the social and emotional development of young people. The 'environment' may be widely interpreted to include the whole-life experience, but particular emphasis has usually been placed on experience within the family. The 'maladjustment' (as historically described) may be largely the product of social factors, which can be dealt with by the experience of living together in a tolerant and sympathetic community, or may be of more deep-seated emotional origin related to the quality of love which the child has received.

Theoretical support for this position derives originally from the work of Suttle (1952), D. W. Winnicott (see Bridgeland, 1971), Anna Freud (1946) and others, who stress the importance of loving relationships within the family as the prerequisite of mental health. More recent developments have seen more socially 'nurturing' (Bennathan, 1998) or positive behaviour management (e.g. Rogers, 1991) approaches in which early social development and interactive approaches to behaviour have become equally important. This is in stark contrast to medical interventions involving the use of drugs to alter behaviour, which can be useful in the short term but in the 1980s was not proven to be of value in the longer term. The very positive 'nurture' movement (Bennathan and Boxall, 2000) focuses on younger children and early years educational experience, and thus makes possible a much wider range of social and emotional interventions than the rather short-term, though apparently immediately effective, drug therapies. There are still sharp contradictions in the education system between a proposed 'one size fits all' inclusive social culture and an intensely individual medico-legal treatment process typified by counselling and medical interventions through drugs or intense behaviour modification.

Contesting and developing notions of therapeutic education

Barron (1969) epitomises a protective stance in this quotation from an article in *Therapeutic Education*:

> So many charlatans have claimed to be therapeutic educators and have got away with it because the concepts are complicated and difficult and cannot be readily checked and assessed in the way in which a training approach can be assessed, that we are in danger of associating a therapeutic approach with woolliness of thought, laziness of practice and an irresponsibility towards the seriousness of our children's disorders.

We would like to think that our own work in a small way reflects the struggle epitomised by early pioneers in therapeutic education practices and in developing 'planned therapeutic environments'. We too are struggling to change perspective from a punitive, blame-based, unfairly competitive and deviant-defined culture of educational and social practice to one that celebrates diversity and cultural differences, and, above all, shows a positive regard for young people who are struggling with social, emotional and behavioural difficulties.

It is easy, with hindsight, to criticise traditional medical practices for seeing the problem as centred within the individual, rather than being a result of cultural or social circumstances. However, it is important to acknowledge that, historically, the move from punishment-based approaches to medicalisation is all part of the gradual process of illumination and growth in approaches for working alongside young people in trouble and disengaged from both education and, often, their own communities. These difficulties, far from being entirely centred within the individual (as a traditional medical model would have it described as maladjusted), are, as we have said, often a very normal and adaptive response to the extraordinary life circumstances that a significant minority of young people find themselves. Hence the adoption of a bio–psycho–social paradigm, the nature of which will become clearer through subsequent chapters. We intend that the case study of this school and the engagement in a rigorous five-year research programme will enable us to turn away any criticisms as regards 'woolliness of thought or laziness of practice'. On the contrary, we have taken very seriously our responsibility to young people who are both vulnerable and challenging, and we have a sincere wish to share and develop a more humane and therapeutic approach to education and learning generally. This book also sets out to share a view of therapeutic education that not only is based on theoretical paradigms and educational principles but rests also on the ongoing life experiment and the rigour of action research.

Therapeutic education values the social and emotional transactions involved in learning, and this includes the psychology of learning, the process of teaching and learning, personal growth, life skills and the transfer of a humanitarian culture. It acknowledges the human element in learning and the human face of the education process:

> such disadvantage at school can be seen to be strongly linked to disadvantage at home. Looking forward, it may be predicted that the disadvantage is likely to perpetuate itself through educational under-achievement and a greater likelihood of economic marginalisation and social exclusion.
>
> (Innocenti Report Card No. 4: 3)

This is far more complex than the simple socio-economic breakdowns that have currently emphasised a simplistic curriculum model and basic skills teaching as a means of enforcing appropriately focused learning. For example, there seem to be strong gender differences in the relative importance of parental interest in education, with 'father's interest proving more salient for males and mother's interest for females, perhaps suggesting the importance of same gender role models' (Hobcraft, 2000: 33).

Learning is not just about economics, basic skills or financial resources. The factors involved are much more complex, requiring acknowledgement of more diffuse human characteristics. A therapeutic approach takes into account the totality of a young person's experience, but it is more than just environmental or medical: it is holistic and encourages a young person to take responsibility for themselves, their behaviour and their learning. Therapeutic education is the commitment to setting up an environment that enables and empowers a young person to do this. There is a current global movement called 'health-promoting schools' (HPS), which is described by Parsons (2000: 7) as a contested, collective, multi-faceted term embracing the Healthy Schools Schemes established in the UK, and the Comprehensive School Health Education movement found in the USA . . . conceptualised as information giving and exhortation about not engaging in hazardous behaviours or developing health threatening lifestyles.

The notion of therapeutic education is still contested in educational circles (not to mention health circles) and we hope that this book will contribute towards helping therapeutic education make progress towards becoming a more firmly based construct for schools, much as the HPS initiatives have become established, with their benefits gradually becoming apparent. In common with our conception of therapeutic education, examined in this book, is a 'settings approach' (Parsons, 2000) that brings with it broad-based organisational commitments about the structure, processes and relationships in our educational institutions. Historically, and perhaps still today, a general conception is that therapeutic education is about educating young people about health, providing mental health services (counselling, therapy) and possibly family support. These are all important aspects of therapeutic education. Health education is relatively embedded in school provision, and supports self-determination and control over one's life in general, whereas mental health services and family support are the domain of different agencies outside school both in the United Kingdom and in the United States. An important element of therapeutic education is the establishing of joint working and management practices between agencies, and in this respect it coincides with the expectations of *Every Child Matters*, mentioned earlier. In France, on the other hand, counselling and social or family support services are often found centred within a school. In addition, US elementary schools are often large enough to warrant having their own dedicated psychologists and therapists, or at the very least these professionals will be shared between two schools. This international comparison does highlight the still rather fragmented and under-resourced services encountered in the United Kingdom.

Relationships are a key factor in engaging and supporting young people who have rejected or withdrawn from attempts to include them in the education process. John Dewey (1897) expresses very clearly the relationship of the learner to his or her social environment and applies this to all education, as do we:

> true education comes through the stimulation of the child's powers by the demands of the social situations in which he finds himself. Through these demands he is stimulated to act as a member of a unity, to emerge from his original narrowness of action and feeling, and to conceive of himself from the standpoint of the welfare of the group to which he belongs. Through the responses which others make to his own activities he comes to know what these mean in social terms.

The strength of therapeutic education lies in part in its focus on relationships, and the importance of relationships is supported by much research over a long period of time, as will be explored further in the next chapter.

Whenever people interact with each other, a relationship develops between them, a bond is created. Some relationships will be based on strong social and emotional bonds and the people concerned will feel committed to that relationship, while other relationships will be based on weak emotional bonds and the people will feel 'distant'. If any positive progress is to be made by the young people, it is important that they are able to form strong social and emotional bonds with one or more adults. If this can be achieved, it can form the basis of the social and emotional development of the young person as they develop a sense of acceptance, belonging and being cared for.

The most central of these influences is the relationship between a teacher and a young person. When a teacher sees behaviour, judges it to be unacceptable and intervenes to stop it, it is the relationship between that teacher and the young person or young persons involved that will determine the success of that intervention (Elton, 1989: 64).

Hattie *et al.* (1997) conducted a meta-analysis of adventure programmes, an undertaking they found to be complex and multifaceted. They found that, in general, adventure programmes had a positive impact on self-esteem, leadership, academic work, personality and interpersonal relations, with self-esteem change being most significant. These changes were shown to be more stable over time than the changes generated by more traditional educational programmes. The broad definition of therapeutic education includes programmes that are based on creative activity as well as challenging through social learning, rather than specifically outdoor or (as in the United States) 'wilderness' projects, but the intentions and outcomes are similar. Therapeutic programmes can revolve around the social context and group activities rather than a specifically individual process. Such research indicates that programmes that are primarily focused on social (and emotional) challenge can effectively facilitate academic learning or more simple basic skills learning when a young person has become disaffected.

We recognise that therapeutic education is a contested notion and that it has not been fully established in terms of academic research, although we have cited substantial evidence of the links between disaffection, conflict at school and educational failure, and a whole range of social, emotional and environmental factors. This chapter has already cited and developed a considerable evidence base for the usefulness and necessity of a therapeutic education perspective, and the book itself is an action research testament to the strategies offered under this broadly used designation. However, there are specific critiques and challenges to some of the underlying principles and their practices which cannot be ignored because they serve to keep the ship on course and will lead to useful critical self-examination. The discussion is often about the boundaries between education and therapy, or about an individual perception of what education is all about. For example, Ecclestone (2003), in a concerted attack on the whole construct of self-esteem (or rather, on the way that it is interpreted and used), accuses educationalists of disempowering young people in further education:

> Yet such responses miss the way in which a pseudo-psychological twist is now evident in debates about inclusion and exclusion. This depicts deep-seated problems as an emotional or psychological dysfunction that people 'suffer from', and which need professional intervention in the form of guidance, counselling, mentoring and teaching. Such interventions are not seen as a problem. Instead, a radical and progressive strand in post-16 education over the past 25 years has successfully created professional expertise and credibility in inclusive pedagogy, which legitimises an interest in people's emotional wellbeing.

Therapeutic education is not an inclusive pedagogy but a whole set of commitments to organisational and environmental change. It is not limited to individual and disempowering interventions, such as those criticised by Ecclestone and discussed earlier in the chapter, but is characterised by a holistic view of the learner. This is not the 'pseudo-psychology' dismissed out of hand by such critics, but is firmly based on research and on a tradition of exploration and self-examination, not found in those who cling to a traditional and retrospective view of what education is about. Research cited in this and following chapters clearly supports the notion that social and emotional factors are involved in learning. Good teachers have always been intuitively aware of this. What Ecclestone challenges is the rather pitying view of self-esteem and the fallacious link between educational success (euphemistically called 'inclusion' – see the discussion on human capital earlier) and the industrial view of inclusion in teaching encouraged by government. She rightly questions the linking of the psychological construct of self-esteem with a kind of vague notion of 'identity capital'. She is right in questioning the linking of psychological constructs with broader political and social values and with the contrived links between social and educational endeavours and business terminology that have characterised the past twenty years of political interference with education. It also shows how sociological research has been hijacked by a political and economic (i.e. commercial and business) agenda. We, the authors, see therapeutic education as above all a 'humanist' approach to education, and not a passivity-inducing medical or clinical intervention in education. We see this model as proposing an active and challenging set of strategies dedicated to exploring new ideas and cultures and permitting dissent through skilled interaction, rather than repressing dissent through either punitive strategies or pseudo-medical interventions – sometimes facetiously termed 'the liquid cosh'. The many examples in the United States of 'adventure' and 'challenge' programmes testify to the active and exciting practical application of psychology and education, based on grounded theory (e.g. Hattie *et al.*, 1997; Berman and Davis-Berman, 1995; Sanders, 1997; Aspen Education, 2004). It does come down in the end to what one's view is of the purpose and outcomes of education. We have worked for many years with young people who are disaffected, very challenging and very vulnerable. They are 'vulnerable' not because we have labelled them so, but because of the consequences for their own lives of their behaviour and the behaviour of others.

Other critics point out that focusing on individuals' problems overlooks structural causes of deprivation and inequality. Yet this chapter clearly focuses on significant research emphasising the social context as being absolutely crucial, and a competent awareness of this context as vital to teaching generally, and particularly when one is teaching young people at risk of social exclusion. There is a vague and generalised criticism of its being the work of people who miss the 1960s or who wish to engage in a mass production of the New Age person. Further criticisms revolve around the setting up of a 'gulag mentality' whereby we aim to 'correct dysfunctional and worrisome thinking' (Wuerthele, 1997), rather like an attempt to condition young people into conformity or else consign them to a social Siberia if they will not conform. We, by contrast, feel that this is nearer to what is happening under a harder-edged and punitive educational regime where the social boundaries are drawn too tightly and enforced inappropriately in the learning environment. And finally, criticisms also revolve around the taking over of parental responsibility by professionals, or the state. We leave it to readers to make up their mind about such criticisms after reading the rest of this book. Unfortunately, the critiques offered do not appear to be supported by substantial research of any kind, but are based on rhetoric, argument and (usually) logical discussion – all of which are nevertheless very valuable and should be engaged upon regarding any ideas proffered in education. We feel that we have made our position clear and have attempted to make sure that the evidence and concepts proffered will bear scrutiny, and we welcome further discussion on the issues involved.

There is no doubt that young people who have been excluded or are at risk of exclusion are both vulnerable and challenging. They have been rejected by, or have themselves rejected, regular and mainstream education and associated training and work-related projects operated by schools and support agencies and, at a later stage, by Connexions and the mainstream of the Youth Service. Therapeutic education offers a genuine alternative to mainstream and regular projects, and the alternative strategies applied are supported by research undertaken over the past twenty years, including more recent publications on positive behaviour management and therapeutic approaches to education, training and subsequent employment. In both the United Kingdom and the United States there are many new projects, professionals and agencies searching for new and creative ways to approach the education of young people who are in difficulties or are finding it hard to make the most of what educational opportunities are on offer. Such young people are not able to benefit from regular education. Some are not able to benefit even from special education services or from outpatient mental health services, and may even be in need of hospital mental health treatment, which is not always available to them. They may be experiencing extremely challenging and difficult life circumstances and be at risk of being segregated into residential care or secure situations, but they can be helped by appropriate community-based programmes in an educational context. This can only happen when the programmes have a focus such as therapeutic education or one clearly focused on long-term solutions through empowerment and enabling the learning of the young people who are struggling, disaffected or simply confused and at a loss with how to deal with their life circumstances.

Further defining what we take to be therapeutic education is the task of the book as a whole and its research, but there are a number of important outcomes or consequences that are worthy of note. Taking into account the social and community factors makes partnership with parents a vital component, along with enabling a young person to develop useful life skills. Often the nature of special education support means resourcing effective classroom assistance for learning and making proper use of experiential learning. Of paramount importance is taking the learning relationship seriously and not either undermining this or assuming its existence without careful consideration and planning. Above all, though, what is important is to bring fun, enjoyment and recreation back into skill development and personal or moral growth. This is more often achieved by gearing up, activating, energising and exciting participants, rather than delving into emotional literacy (Priest, 1999).

There are also many young people who confront adults responsible for delivering education, or find themselves in conflict with schools or other authorities, because they reject either the values and aspirations of respectable institutions or the conformity expected in schools. This book does not argue about the morality of dissent, or attempt to dissect the moral values (often widely differing) that provide the social context within which education takes place in the United Kingdom and the United States, but it does argue about the ways in which we respond to the problems we have described. We argue very firmly that a punitive and hard-edged response to the challenges faced by teachers, schools, child workers and professionals and the many agencies involved will not provide the long-term answers required in order to grow and develop our culture. We argue that therapeutic education provides a framework in which these problems can be approached in the long term, and that it is not rejecting responsibility for academic learning, nor is it a 'soft touch' approach. A young person's access to educational opportunity is absolutely crucial, and the whole approach developed in this book demands a high degree of professional skill and personal resources in the formation of positive relationships – higher than that generally accepted as the relationship between teacher and pupil typified by an exclusively 'academic' approach to education. By this we mean that which may be situated solely in academic (or attainment) outcomes, rather than the importance of the learning relationship and process. We see this kind of blinkered academic approach as expecting a high degree of learner conformity and passivity on the one hand, and as setting up a confrontational blind alley for teachers who work in the less well resourced and less affluent sectors of society. This link between lack of success in education and affluence (and lack of it) is clearly illustrated in the UK National Pupil Database figures for 2002 in transition from primary to secondary school by differences in attainment at ages 7, 11 and 14. In the United States the figures reflect the same story as in the Connecticut example mentioned previously in this chapter.

This chapter has been very critical of the social and political context in which we, the authors, work and of the remote, technocratic and accountancy model of education which favours statistics and measurable outcomes above human values of learning. It has set the scene for questioning an outdated and anachronistic curriculum that has developed over the past fifteen or so years and suggests instead that we should be encouraging professionals to help pupils engage with their peers and teachers, to participate in schooling, and gain access to relevant knowledge and, with that, skills that will truly help them to cope with life, if not succeed in material terms. Unfortunately, the education system is in the grip of those who will not acknowledge that learning and teaching is a process, not an end result. It is constrained by those who will not appreciate that learning is not a mechanical or purely academic process but a human process involving participation, engagement and access to learning opportunities. It is being driven by too many people who do not understand the interactive processes involved in learning and teaching and who have no real, tested experience in the field. The appropriation of educational and learning opportunity by those with a limited social and political agenda has demoralised and depressed professional expertise in the teaching profession. For too long, schooling has been driven by a 'macho', business-like model based on simplistic outcomes and blindness[2] to the complexities of human learning and successful self-actualisation (Maslow, 1968). Finally, we invite readers to speculate on how many of the strategies, concepts, values and processes described in this book under the umbrella of therapeutic education could usefully be adopted in education generally and are integral to John Dewey's (1938) earlier vision of what education is about. Therapeutic education has a distinctly 'human face'.

Chapter 2

Behavioural graffiti
Ignoring the writing on the wall

Everywhere in Britain, graffiti is visible. It is visible as we travel to work, walk in the park or take a ride through any city. It is most visible when one takes a train ride, for example into London. It is an intriguing phenomenon and poses many questions if one takes the time to make a serious inquiry into the reasons for its existence. The more one looks, the more it really becomes a whole culture in itself – or, as some see it, an alien subculture or even a subversive subculture. It is also a worldwide phenomenon, and there is a global subculture in most developed countries of the world and in many Third World countries. This worldwide movement has been termed 'urban art'. A brief search on the Internet will lead the reader fairly quickly to a substantial range of information, articles and particularly 'art', and many examples of it, worldwide.

Urban art is also called 'graffiti', a term coined by the Romans to describe people who write on city walls. One of the authors has seen for himself examples of Roman graffiti on the walls of the city of Pompeii and preserved when it was destroyed in the volcanic eruption of AD 79 that also destroyed Herculaneum. Its writer, or *graffito*, was indeed expressing some dissatisfaction with the current political and social milieu. What is clear is that there is a struggle to make this kind of art (or, in some cases, social comment) visible to the world in general. For example, Mayor Rudolph Giuliani spent millions of dollars to control the outpouring of 'urban art' in New York, and his actions are not popular with some people such as Lederman (2005), who complain about public access issues. In addition to the urban art, the free speech protest and the expression of youth culture in general, there is the perhaps less creative use of graffiti by street and urban gangs to mark their territory and leave warnings for rival gangs.

Figure 2.1 Example of graffiti art from a wall in Budapest. (Source: http://www.graffiti.org/, or visit the A.R.T.I.S.T. website: http://www.openair.org/alerts/artist/nyc.html.)

What is it that energises this massive global movement or subculture predominantly among young people in so many countries? Is it the inherent physical danger of spraying paint near a railway line that attracts the young graffiti artists and writers? Is it the lure of provoking an authoritarian reaction to what the 'challenger' may feel is a perfectly reasonable position to hold? What does it mean? Is there some kind of unconscious need to precipitate a conflict situation – a need for excitement? Is it simply delinquents disrespecting their environment or is it a shout for help and recognition by young people whose culture and position in society are being ignored? Is it a basic biological instinct to mark one's territory, or is it a sophisticated statement of disaffection and disillusionment with a society that ignores the plight of significant minorities who do not sub-scribe to middle-class aspirations, attend respectable institutions and aspire to climb the corporate ladder? Is it an attempt to dominate the immediate environ-ment and maintain a sense of security? Or perhaps, in the final analysis, is it just 'art', a reflection of the natural human instinct for self-expression?

Broadening the perspective and debating practice

In the previous chapter we challenged and questioned current approaches to challenging behaviour in schools, and in particular an approach that reduces teachers and parents to passive bystanders by 'medicalising' the problem. All too often the debate about challenging behaviour, social and educational exclusion has been narrow and blinkered. That is, it revolves solely around conflict in the classroom environment or is focused purely on the individual and has become 'medicalised', requiring the intervention of 'experts' and disabling a positive social or emotional response. This 'medicalising' of behaviour difficulties also serves to divert attention from a focus on parenting, child care and early development as being very much responsible for the difficulties encountered later at school.

A therapeutic approach, by contrast, implies action and activity on the part of all those involved as well as a radical approach to organising the environment (in its broadest sense) around the child or young person. The many questions that arise from the exploration of what we have called in this chapter 'behavioural graffiti' suggest that a broadening of perspective is needed in order to under-stand fully what is happening in schools and in society. It is not sufficient to keep on falling back on old ideas, such as the current and politically desirable but

Figure 2.2 Example of graffiti art in the United Kingdom.

dead-end conception of 'school discipline'. School discipline is a narrow conceptualisation of what is a far more complex phenomenon. Just as urban art and graffiti have become a global and international phenomenon, a similar phenomenon in school is apparent.

The notion that challenging behaviour in school and disaffection with education requires a new conceptualisation is supported by the range of research cited in Chapter 1, and other research currently emerging on behaviour and learning (e.g. Powell *et al.*, 2004). Behaviour is a more abstract and less obvious form of self-expression than graffiti but it is also the means by which humans interact with their environment to maintain health, security, self-efficacy and social contact or communication. What is it that drives both the subculture involved in challenging school authority and simply the behaviour in schools that teachers find so challenging and difficult? Is it a subculture, is it an expression of something that young people have in common or is it simply (as we are being led to believe) a small number of semi-deranged young people who go off the rails to varying extents? This is what the more sensationalising media would have us believe about behaviour in schools. This obsession with the individual is evident, for example, in the case of more extreme events such as the killing of students by two of their peers at Columbine High School in Jefferson County, Colorado, on Tuesday 20 April 1999. Looking into this extreme situation in more detail reveals a very complex set of circumstances where the apparently obvious 'madness' becomes a little less obvious. The high school culture, the availability of firearms to young people in the home and the powerful effect of Internet websites encouraging emotionally disenfranchised young people to find extremely negative role models all form part of a powerful cocktail that erupted in an extreme form of behavioural self-expression or 'behavioural graffiti'.

Thankfully, this kind of extreme behaviour is still very rare, but a range of behaviours from the merely annoying through to highly challenging confront teachers in schools every day. Readers would not have to search far for a whole range of sensationalising media articles about behaviour in schools that explore only superficial aspects of the problem.[1] Many young people's lives and educational opportunities are radically affected by both their behaviour and the response of teachers and schools to that behaviour. It is not usually headline-grabbing but is nevertheless very significant and affects substantial numbers of young people every year. What has also become of increasing concern is the 'fallout' in school of the 'behavioural graffiti', or what is termed challenging behaviour and mirrored in society generally as 'antisocial behaviour'. That is, the impact on other children and their learning opportunities within the school and classroom is far greater than the actual proportion of young people who show 'challenging behaviour' in school, like the considerable impact felt by the public of a small number of young people who persistently behave in an extremely violent or antisocial manner.[2]

We have called this chapter 'Behavioural graffiti' simply because the culture of urban art and the use of graffiti for self-expression or territorial self-preservation resonates very strongly with the phenomenon of challenging behaviour in the context of education. It raises many questions pertinent to the development of therapeutic education; it polarises opinions as to its nature, usefulness and desirability; and, finally, it raises the debate as to how teachers as individuals and schools as institutions should respond to the challenging behaviour of young people. Although behaviour is not a physical representation of culture or disaffection, or even sometimes an expression of disaffection or even psychological difficulty, as urban art or graffiti may be, it is an abstract representation of a similar phenomenon. This book does no more than raise questions that any sentient adult asks themselves when faced with a young person whose behaviour is challenging. Despite massive social and technical developments over the past fifty years, the ethics and practice of teaching and learning and the structure of education systems have not changed to keep pace with modern life. The basic activity in the classroom and the 'experience' of the average classroom remains much the same as in the past hundred years, despite the bolting on of technology and modifications for pupils with additional educational needs. The contents of this book challenge anachronistic, hard-edged and competitive views of education. Giving due attention to the human factors involved in educational transactions is the best way to change what seems to have become an intransigent social problem.

Mapping holistic theories on to the reality of schooling

At the very least, a broader view of academic learning, incorporating some of the realities of life itself, should serve to increase choices and open out other possibilities for positive action (rather than punitive), as well as clearly defining the human and material resources that need to be marshalled. Figure 2.3, the work of McGuiness (1993), illustrates the broader view of a single incident of conflict in a school. Appendix 1 represents a practical planning tool derived from this model.

Aggression and arguments are not uncommon in schools, and yet these are regarded by teachers as less disruptive than a consistent personal challenge to their authority in the form of rudeness and minor disruptions to the business of teaching (Elton, 1989). A single incidence of challenging behaviour is rarely just a matter of conflict originating solely between two people at that one moment in time. There is nearly always a range of background factors (social, educational and personal) involved. This is not to suggest that at each incidence of conflict or challenging behaviour, there is time to analyse the current political climate or to engage in deep psychological analysis. However, strategies that are purely based on dealing with that incident, without cognisance of the contextual factors, may provide short-term gains more but often than not are doomed to longer-term problems. A therapeutic environmental approach suggests that there is a positive regard for the person; the specific behaviour is challenged, but challenged by suggesting, enabling or developing new behaviours.

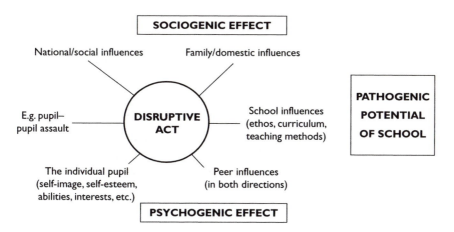

Figure 2.3 Schools do not exist in a vacuum. (Source: McGuiness, 1993.)

So, a working knowledge of the possible additional influences (see Appendix 1) is necessary in order to be able to 'pick the bones out' of a specific problem and to develop an environment in school that does not mirror, exacerbate or incorporate the problems experienced outside school. We, along with McGuiness, do hold the view that schools do not work in a vacuum, nor do staff work in a climate unaffected by the larger, different worlds within which we and our young students live. Appendix 1 offers a way of assessing the other potential factors and the way in which they might manifest themselves in school. Part of this recognition leads to the acceptance of a model of education that takes into account the social, cultural, moral and emotional 'environment' inhabited by the learner, as well as the environment in which learning is planned to take place (e.g. the school). There may be factors inherent in the way the school is run or there may be things happening to a child that contribute to the situation (such as bullying or harassment). An inflexible and boring curriculum could be one of the important factors influencing behaviour, and McGuiness (1993) calls this the 'pathogenic influence of school' itself.

As long ago as 1983, Phillips and Jones suggested from their research that simply representing difficulties in school as the difficulty of one pupil's adjustment is an inadequate perspective. Their view is in keeping with a more social model of action and heralded a move away from the medical model of maladjustment and treatment of an individual. Instead, the focus should be on school strategies and should be part of a systematic and ecological approach, more recently called an 'eco-systemic approach (e.g. Molnar and Lindquist, 1989). It is possible that the reality of a narrowly defined curriculum, often supported by either a 'punitive' or a competitive institutional ethos (or both), has contributed to sharp increases in, and concern about, the number of young people excluded from school in the United Kingdom (Parsons, 1996, 1999; Parsons *et al.*, 2002a).

Despite the commendable intentions of *Every Child Matters* (Treasury, 2003), there is insufficient multiplicity in the educational system at present to cater for a wide diversity of needs in the school population, not to mention the diversity of parental expectations and desires for their children. Similarly, discussions between educators in the United States over 'No Child Left Behind' recognise that there are political agendas afoot in the attempt to drive up standards and that education is being used for social engineering purposes. Nor do we, the authors, accept that educational progress should be measured within the narrow confines that determine 'attainment' in the current school model.

The influence of factors outside the school or the effect of family life on a child, McGuiness (1993) calls the 'sociogenic effect'. There is no doubt, on an intuitive level, that a young person's home and community circumstances will affect their ability to take advantage of learning opportunities, although it should also be said that on occasion adverse circumstances can drive ambition and engagement as a means to transcend current difficulties. According to Mills (1943; quoted in O'Sullivan, 1980: 138), the concept of 'social pathology' and the ideally adjusted man

> conforms to middle class morality and motives and 'participates' in the gradual progress of respectable institutions. . . . His mother and father were not divorced, nor was his home ever broken. He is successful, at least in a modest way – since he is ambitious.

It could be argued that current views of 'social inclusion' are still no more than an expectation of conformity to middle-class values and aspirations, and we would certainly argue that there are many 'value judgements' at play in such a woolly concept as inclusion. The conception of social inclusion has become synonymous in many areas of education with success at school, having suitable social and economic ambition and generally conforming to an accepted view of appropriate social behaviour. This conformist view of behaviour management is not necessarily anything to do with 'behaviour for learning' or even inclusion, but is more to do with inarticulate assumptions about what is 'acceptable'. O'Sullivan's (1980) research, carried out more than twenty-five years ago, suggested that teachers' unconscious predispositions towards pupils with working-class or diverse backgrounds are a complicating factor in the learning–teaching interaction. At an institutional level, recent research (Parsons *et al.*, 2004) indicates that UK schools are discriminating inordinately against black Caribbean boys and the children of travellers, and this supports O'Sullivan's theory. On an intellectual, academic and logical level, the idea of 'sociogenic factors' impacting on behaviour and success at school is also borne out by the considerable social research cited in this and the previous chapter.

Exclusion arises from the 'rupture of the relationship between the individual and society' (Gore *et al.*, 1995: 2; see also Room, 1995). People may be excluded from or by societal relationships, whether this exclusion is based on an expectation of adherence around assumed 'norms', or happens because a young person has deviated from a more explicit contractual framework, or is the consequence of the distribution of a 'fixed pot' of resources to which the young person does not have access. In short, young people can fail to access or participate in educational opportunity or engage with school because they do not accept or understand such 'norms'; they are not convinced that the contract of 'learn at school and succeed in life' applies to them and may also be starting from a highly disadvantageous point from the outset. This, however, is not a fixed situation and says little about how societal relationships are enacted. By using the lens of 'therapeutic education', these kinds of societal relationships can be challenged, by challenging what are seen as the traditional exchange of resources (i.e. knowledge and skills) and 'customary activities' (i.e. assumptions about the social demands of schooling).

Young people who are excluded from school are viewed as members of an 'underclass', with different behavioural norms, aspirations, expectations and morals, which threaten to undermine those of mainstream society (e.g. Levitas, 1998; Morris, 1994). In effect, this amounts to a 'them and us' approach, arguing that the young person has ruptured their relationship with society or the community by failure, or perhaps inability, to adhere to socially approved norms. This again perhaps explains why the emphasis so often reverts back to an individualistic, either medicalised or blaming (punitive), approach rather than a therapeutic (personal and emotional) or environmental (e.g. social) one.

Exclusion is also seen as the result of unemployment (Paugam, 1993; Levitas, 1998). Inclusion, therefore, becomes identified with employment, just as it is with success at school – a stance promoted by much of New Labour's social security policy. Certainly, in our society success at school (or at least engagement with schooling) and subsequent employment opportunities count as key 'customary activities' and the main way through which material resources are acquired.

There is an invisible divide between what is proposed as a benevolent policy intended to save young people from exclusion and one that becomes social engineering in order to satisfy economic requirements and has little to do with education. It is therefore necessary to reiterate that therapeutic education is not synonymous with current vague and often paradoxical notions of inclusion, but has more to do with personal efficacy, responsibility, growth, identity and change. All these things are contingent on the societal or community environment within which young people find themselves.

In describing the 'psychogenic effect', McGuiness (1993) (Figure 2.3) is alluding to the factors within the young person that immediately impact on functioning socially and academically in school, including the way the learner sees themselves in the learning context. This area is more in keeping with much of the past and current activity in relation to challenging and aggressive behaviour in society, at school and in the home. In other words, the problem resides in the individual. There is something wrong with the individual. Again, we do not deny that there may well be inherent problems within an individual, but we differ (or move on) from current 'customary practices' and from previous notions of therapeutic education. We propose that this is only part of the story and should therefore be only part of the response. We further propose that positive notions of self-efficacy are more purposeful, fulfilling and, in the final analysis, practical than the negative psychology that has hitherto been applied to this area of study. We make no excuse for the development of Bandura's (1996) work in this book, which is aimed at developing a positive sense of 'self', confidence and self-belief. All these notions have been assiduously avoided by behaviourists, psychologists and educationalists over the past twenty-five years because they cannot be simplistically defined, easily measured or simply enacted in a school environment. Yet to ignore these broader concepts of human learning, social and emotional interaction and interpersonal transactions in learning is to ignore the 'writing on the wall'.

Over a period of years, one of the authors has collected hundreds of statements from teachers and classroom assistants during workshop and reflective activity in undergraduate and postgraduate courses regarding their own experiences in education. These memories and the effect they had on the young person's feelings of self-worth and efficacy were so powerful that they remained as vivid memories with many people over forty years later. Here are just a few of the feelings they expressed where their self-efficacy was reduced:

- 'Overpowering and chaotic environment, feeling at a loss . . .'
- 'Being forced to eat school dinners.'
- 'Being put down by teacher or adult and made into a public spectacle.'
- 'Being put under pressure, socially etc., makes you forget what you know, you know . . .'
- 'Didn't know what was required . . .'
- 'I was terrorised by the teacher's unpredictability and moods.'
- 'Being told off unfairly in front of others – getting a bad reputation . . .'
- 'Playtimes were hell!'
- 'Standing on a chair – punishment/humiliation . . .'
- 'Being compared to (more able?) others – guilty, not bright . . .'
- 'Being made to look stupid in front of others – particularly in spelling "westerly" . . .'
- 'Being told you're stupid – wanted to avoid getting the cane – unfair – angry/upset . . .'
- 'Not being encouraged/given feedback – useless, unsure'
- 'Home contact devalued – guilty feelings . . .'

Conversely, the same groups of people also came up with inspiring and uplifting experiences (although they usually say that these are not so powerful in their memory). The following statements, selected from many more, illustrate the kinds of things that made young people feel strong, worthy and capable:

- 'Praise – for good reason from a significant (to me) person.'
- 'Having work put on display.'
- 'Having pride in own achievement . . .'
- 'Being "chosen" – for responsibility or taking part . . .'
- 'Adult takes time to acknowledge and encourage . . .'
- 'Getting it right; praise – lifted, encouraged . . .'
- 'Included in play/friendship groups . . .'
- 'Getting a prize and feeling good about myself (gobsmacked!).'
- 'Being given responsibility – important, good, more choice . . .'
- 'Belonging to a group – warmth, confidence . . .'
- 'Happier in "stream" – group at own level . . .'
- 'Friendships were good and I was able to enjoy social activities.'

Even a cursory glance at these statements would lead one to conclude that the problem does not lie simply within an individual but relates to two further very important notions:

- The relationship between teacher (or adult) and student is crucial and should not be ignored as a factor in so many people's learning processes.
- The ambience of the class or ethos of the school deeply affects academic learning and, through it, expectations for compliance with what are sometimes very arbitrary social rules.

This is a view reflected in the work of Carl Rogers, the strength of whose approach lies in part in his focus on relationship: 'The facilitation of significant learning rests upon certain attitudinal qualities that exist in the personal *relationship* between facilitator and learner' (1967: 305).

The 'writing on the wall', a recurrent theme in this chapter, is associated in the chapter heading with the idea of 'behavioural graffiti', and perhaps we should explain this extension of the analogy with behaviour in schools and the phenomenon of exclusion in society. A few years ago a school inspector said to one of us that research indicates that most incidents of school exclusion can be traced back to a confrontation between a teacher and a young person at an early stage in the exclusion process, usually the incident that triggered off the whole process. Some people assume that young people's challenges to authority are the main or sole reason for these conflicts that lead to exclusion. However, this book, and a holistic approach to working with young people, as in therapeutic education, do not accept a simplistic view such as this. What was also implied in the statement by the inspector was the role that the teacher too played in the conflict situations – that is, whether they aggravated the situation by their own unskilled or persistently hostile responses to these challenges or whether they consistently managed the situations in a skilful and empathetic manner. More-over, the inspector went on to point out that often a young person will be sent on a continuing downward spiral into exclusion once an initial conflict has taken place. The causes for this downward spiral are often complex but are as much about the response of the school as about the continuing behaviour of the young person once they have become labelled in this way. We have experience of many young people who have been 'branded' by a single incidence of conflict with authority or with individual teachers and who are subsequently unable to shed this branding, almost no matter what they do. Or worse still, once this reputation has been acquired, they are then put under such negative scrutiny and 'labelling' (Quicke, 1999) that redemption is impossible. This tends to reinforce McGuiness's (1993) notion of schools as an integral part of the social and emotional context in which they exist and the multiplicity of factors involved.

One implication of this trend is radical support for a new, coherent and longer-term view of teacher training and continuing professional development (Cornwall, 2005b). The 'writing on the wall' is simply a warning that if we continue to supply and attempt to implement simplistic behavioural or punitive solutions to what are complex human problems, then many lives will be blighted and there will continue to be an undercurrent of disaffection in education. We are not suggesting that therapeutic education is the only answer, but we are suggesting that it should be part of a more skilled and complex response as befits a sophisticated society. While developing basic skills of literacy and numeracy is no doubt important in our modern world, it is not in any way proven that literacy and numeracy are the salient factors in education that make a difference to life chances; there are many other such factors. While research indicates that qualifications are important (Sparkes, 1999), the persuasive weight of evidence cited in this book suggests that these are only a part of success in life. This chapter suggests that the solutions require a broader and deeper search for salient factors to reduce disaffection, disruption and exclusion, and deal with the challenges that face schools.

What characterises therapeutic education?

Hattie *et al.* (1997), in their research cited in the previous chapter, also develop some significant areas for consideration in generating learning experiences that are likely to make a lasting difference to young people who are at risk of exclusion and punishment. They signify a distinct change of educational culture, of the kind that has been suggested throughout this chapter – a change from a rather inflexible and hard-headed approach to young people, particularly in the teenage years, to one that acknowledges a young person's abilities to take responsibility for themselves and to plot their own way through the education system. In our experience, young people out of school and in trouble often have had little opportunity in their lives to make decisions, take responsibility, examine their own behaviour (or that of others) or challenge their own thinking and experience positive learning environments. In fact, they have more often survived by unconscious adaptation to threatening situations, including those in the classroom. These following observations, while not exhaustive, are entirely consistent with our study of therapeutic education and the evidence bases developed in this book. They give some indication of a departure from accepted practice based on tradition and assumption and a positive promotion of personal growth and development:

- Making personal growth and personal responsibility *as important as* conforming social behaviour is an important departure from a culture in which externally applied rules and regulations have become the means by which behaviour is mediated in our society.
- Improving self-awareness and self-understanding by setting personal goals and having the confidence to explore new positive behaviours *rather than* be subjected to rigid rules and punishment will enable the young person to carry their own code of conduct with them wherever they are.
- Developing problem-solving and decision-making skills *as well as* static knowledge bases will develop the ability to deal flexibly with new and challenging circumstances, rather than fall back on previously learned and less successful strategies.
- Increased awareness of the human dynamics of the classroom situation among politicians and the public generally (*not* ignorance or making assumptions about learning in assuming it to be a simple transfer of knowledge) will enable teachers to become more involved in the transaction and have more professional standing in enabling learning.
- An enabling and supportive school (or learning) environment will permit a young person to embark on journeys of self-exploration and success *in addition* to confronting self-defeating thoughts and behaviours.
- Education thus becomes the therapeutic tool in itself *instead of* simplistic behaviour modification within school, or psychotherapy 'bolted on' somewhere else.

Teachers are mentors and facilitators, not prison officers or sergeant majors. The role of mentor, teacher, guide and facilitator is not consistent with that of an iron-hard disciplinarian, and there are not many teachers who see themselves in that role. If anything, they are generators of self-discipline, self-awareness and self-regulation. Whilst self-defence and security for teachers are clearly necessary, there should be very little need in most schools for control and restraint. When it is needed, this is often because the 'writing on the wall' has been ignored. In therapeutic education, care and control are not seen as separate components, but viewed as a whole. There is little point in controlling young people who do not feel 'cared for' as well. At the same time, young people cannot feel 'cared for' unless the situation they are in is safe and secure. The concepts of care and control are intertwined. There is a delicate balance between them that must be maintained if there is to be a positive outcome for a young person at the point of learning.

This concept is in clear contrast to the behavioural approach adopted by schools over the past twenty years, and perhaps the time is now ripe for a radical change in the educational ethos from coercion to cooperation. Such a change would only be right, and in response to many, many developments and initiatives that are growing all over the United Kingdom. For example, the 'behaviour for learning' programme based on EPPI research (Powell *et al.*, 2004) currently emphasises 'learning relationships' (Tod, 2005). This is illustrated by Figure 2.4, where the learner is seen to have a relationship with the teacher and peers (participation), with the curriculum (access) and with themselves (engagement). Despite research over many years, the complex and interactive nature of learning is still not sufficiently recognised in the content of teacher education, and most students instinctively realise this. The Elton Report (1989) was a clear signpost to pave the way for a radical change in the way that behaviour for learning was perceived, and yet it has taken nearly twenty years for some of the recommendations to be revived in the DfES (2004) Primary Behaviour Strategy for schools in the United Kingdom. Sadly, although Maslow's life work is recognised in the shape of his levels of motivation model (as mentioned in a note to Chapter 1), the DfES (2004) seems unable to uphold an 'evidence-based practice' approach, as it neglects to put in proper references to his specific work and publications, allowing teachers to follow this through. More recent research into learning relationships, in which one of the authors has been involved from the beginning, clearly develops the importance of relationships in learning and the notion of 'behaviour for learning', and this will have an impact on teacher training.

It should go without saying that the teacher's role is not simply that of deliverer of curriculum or classroom manager, but also that of designer of the learning environment, manager of group dynamics and complex relationships, and facilitator of social interchange. Nonetheless, an inordinate amount of time and effort are given over to the sheer mechanics of curriculum development in

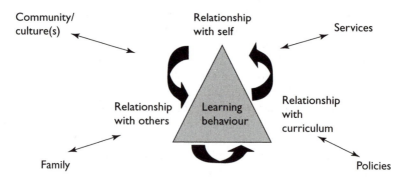

Figure 2.4 Behaviour management, inclusion (academic and social) achievement and lifelong learning: a conceptual framework. (Source: Powell *et al.* 2004.)

teacher training. There has been a serious dearth of responsible consideration given to how teachers, while being trained, are prepared for inclusion programmes in school (Garner, 2001). Teaching is a complex and subtle process, and over the past twenty years it seems that more attention has been given to outcomes than the actual transactions and interactions involved. One consequence of this is both a fear of, and an inability to deal with, challenge and conflict in the classroom. Learning inevitably involves challenge and conflict because of the changes in the structure of the personality involved in developing new constructs (Kelly, 1955). According to Barrett-Lennard (1998: 184), Rogers was offering some tentative hypothesis on learning, based on his long years of work on 'client-centred therapy' and 'student-centred teaching', as illustrated in these three quotations:

1   *'We cannot teach another person directly; we can only facilitate his learning.'* The model of teacher as facilitator implies that the teacher is part of the process of mediating and interpreting knowledge, skills and information. This more useful notion puts the teacher at the centre of the process and further implies a range of facilitation activities. This is in contrast to a model that describes the teacher as the deliverer of curriculum and the producer and arbiter of outcomes. It is arguable that different government recommendations for teachers are contradictory, for example, the Qualifications and Curriculum Authority, commenting on the quality of the learning environment, describes the teacher as crucial in:

   • creating effective learning environments;
   • securing young persons' motivation and concentration;
   • providing equality of opportunity through teaching approaches;
   • using appropriate assessment approaches;
   • setting targets for learning.

                                                                                                (QCA, 1999)

   Apart from the vague notion of 'effective learning environments', the implication in guidance is that 'setting targets' is a teacher activity. In our experience, setting targets is a pupil or student activity, and in this way the 'young person's' motivation and concentration' are 'secured'. Starting from where the learner is has become an increasingly difficult, well-nigh impossible, task for teachers, given the demands for National Curriculum targets and superficial snap judgements from external bodies such as OfSTED, the United Kingdom's Office for Standards in Education.

2.   *'The organization of the self appears to become more rigid under threat.'* Almost without exception, the young people at risk of exclusion have experienced the learning environment as a social or personal or academic 'threat' and have responded by either rejecting it or withdrawing from attempts to engage and involve them. Threat as a construct is well defined by Kelly (1955) and can be conceived as a realisation that the core structures of the

personality are unable to deal with the current situation. Unlike behavioural approaches, it is necessary to acknowledge and deal with personality and what Kelly (1955) calls 'core structures' (of the personality). This is a much deeper and more complex approach than that which has characterised many educationalists' and schools' approach to challenging behaviour up to now. Even so, it should be perfectly within the interpersonal and communication skills and abilities of teachers to deal with the dynamics of the personalities in their classes. After all, this is something that people do in their everyday lives and is part of the human transaction involved in teaching. A key feature of therapeutic education is to remove the 'threat' involved in learning and develop successful risk-taking behaviour.

3. *'Significant learning occurs when a differentiated perception of the field of experience is facilitated (we are helped to see things differently).'* The implication is that in order to see things differently, there must be a change in what is offered, and in order to be perceived as differentiated (i.e. not more of the same), it must be delivered in a different way. Therapeutic education is an 'alternative environment' and an 'alternative curriculum' in every sense and as such offers the young person a carefully planned learning environment that enables them to see their own learning in a new and more successful light. Changing the environment around the young person as a learner is a very powerful tool in engaging and working with disaffected learners but provides an alternative to more medically based approaches that attempt to intervene in emotional development directly. It is not good enough for the teacher, educator or provider to feel that they are offering something different; the offering must be perceived by the receiver, the learner, the young person as different. This is where many attempts to develop alternative approaches fall down. Insufficient attention is paid to how the learner sees the situation and interprets efforts at communicating or teaching.

Mapping therapeutic education on to current practice

The therapeutic process often requires a tougher, more committed and more rigorous approach to teaching, as it does require particular skills and personal resources on the part of adults attempting therapeutic approaches through learning or any other therapeutic medium. It is not a superficial approach and it does not pass the buck by allocating blame solely to the young person or seeing it as an individual problem. The adult also takes responsibility for their part in the interactive process and should not sweep their own behaviour and actions under the carpet. While positive regard will accept a person with their blemishes and faults, this kind of false separation of a person from their behaviour may not be conducive to helping them take responsibility for their behaviour. The question is, at what point does the person become challenged to change? In this 'behavioural' way a young person will change their behaviour to suit different circumstances; their behaviour becomes 'environment specific'. This is a regular occurrence in behaviourist regimes, and progress is regularly reversed by a new set of challenging circumstances. Thus, a young person may behave in a disrespectful or antisocial manner when the circumstances either allow or encourage that response. In contrast to this, a therapeutic education approach, with positive regard for the young person, contains more subtle and positive messages as well as developing a set of internal concepts and beliefs which the young person can carry with them. These things we instinctively know, but for reasons of simplicity they seem to have slid out of sight in the systematic but superficial management of young people's behaviour in schools. Furthermore, young people who find it hard to access learning opportunities are sometimes completely ignored by those who feel that education is an intellectual activity worthy only of those who are capable of surviving the social and emotional demands of the institution. More often than not, this view epitomises a traditional, elitist and selective attitude to education and learning. In both the 'systematic' behavioural interventions and the elitist academic ethos, there is a tendency to devalue the thoughts and feelings of the young person, as the focus is on behaviour and performance only.

The concept of 'therapy' as such has become diversified over the years, with commonplace applications in a vast array of human circumstances from the facetious but often convenient 'retail therapy' to 'physical' therapy or more exotic forms such as 'aromatherapy'. The question is whether recent conceptions of 'education' can ever be seen in the same frame as notions of 'therapy'. We contend that in practical teaching terms, education is therapeutic. Skilful teachers and youth workers form relationships with young people that not only enhance their learning but are also, more often than not, crucial to it. Professionals who feel they have been specially trained in either discipline may see therapy and education as separate and distinct activities. The truth is that the edges are not fixed or even real and that the principles and practices of teaching, learning and therapy have always been significantly intertwined. This is not to dismiss or demean the importance of training in either discipline, or the respective practices involved. It simply recognises that reality is not as simple and clear-cut as we try to make it by separating children's lives into the various components of professional endeavour. It does suggest, though, that the training of professionals in the two disciplines should have common elements. Added to this, the recipient of education and therapy does not experience these activities in isolation but will put them together in a holistic way in their own thinking and apply them on their life. If they are not able to do this, then often the teacher and the therapist will be wasting their time. There will be no carry-over from one context to another or into life generally.

There are new and exciting therapeutic education programmes growing up, particularly in the United States. Whereas adventure schemes may not on the surface seem therapeutic, there is no doubt that research (e.g. Priest, 1999; Sanders, 1997; Berman and Davis-Berman, 1995) shows therapeutic education's effectiveness not only in challenging deep-set and habitual conflict-laden behaviours but also in developing a sense of trust and a growing ability to form positive relationships. It is what used to be called 'character building', and perhaps a little more acceptable than attempting to delve into emotional problems and become psychologists or counsellors rather than teachers.

Further exploration of notions of therapeutic education has led us to the conclusion that it is as wide as it is long, and as deep as the purveyors or deliverers make it. It can range from a very medical or clinical approach, for example in educating people about (their) illness and health, to the kinds of adventure programmes already mentioned. For example, therapeutic recreation is the provision of treatment services and the provision of recreation services to persons in order to improve health and well-being. Therapeutic recreation is provided by professionals who are trained and certified, registered and/or licensed to provide therapeutic recreation in the United States (e.g. ILRTA, 2003). Therapeutic recreation is a recognised profession and is defined by the US Department of Labor as a form of treatment for persons who are physically, mentally or emotionally disabled.[3] The American Therapeutic Recreation Association (ATRA, 2005) has affiliates all over the United States whose activities are aimed at improving the physical, cognitive, emotional and social functioning of persons disabled as a result of trauma or illness. The concept of emotional disability may be a useful one in the United Kingdom if it leads to better consideration of pupils who have, perhaps through abuse in the family, experienced social and emotional trauma. The concept of 'activity' as a therapeutic medium in this context is not new but is not yet accepted in the United Kingdom. The usual recourse is to counselling, with variable results for young people. In other words, in the United Kingdom there are limited creative responses to social and emotional difficulties.

Another good example from the United States that exemplifies the breadth of activities under the auspices of therapeutic education can be seen in the web advertising of a licensed community mental health centre serving south-west Kansas. It describes itself as dedicated to providing mental health care, treatment, education and supportive services in an efficient, effective and compassionate manner to individuals, families and communities, and, it states, it strives to enhance quality of life through the highest standards of professional care. An outline of its activities set out in Table 2.1 illustrates what kinds of things could come under the broad definition of therapeutic education.

In the United Kingdom, there is a developing model based on *Every Child Matters* (Treasury, 2003) in which a multi-agency approach is encouraged, an approach that sets the child at the centre of the professional activities in many spheres. This is an attempt to produce joined up working between professionals and agencies. However, the experience of researchers in the United States and in France, where there are different systems, seems to suggest that there needs to be a more systematic and profound change in the way services are provided before these aims will be achieved.

Table 2.1 Illustration of the breadth of activities that could be termed therapeutic education (from a USA example):

Psychological evaluations	Behaviour disorders	Rocky Mountain High Camping Program
Individual psychotherapy	Parent education	Child and adult case management
Chemical dependency assessments	Domestic violence offenders programme	Law enforcement consultations
Divorce workshops	Stress management	Hospital consultations
Monthly interagency meetings	Care facility consultations	
Juvenile Justice Authority	School systems liaison	

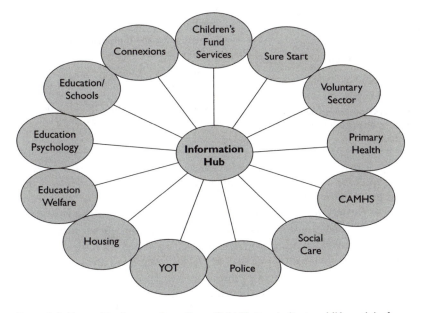

Figure 2.5 Does this diagram from *Every Child Matters* indicate a UK model of therapeutic education and associated activities? (Note: YOT, Youth Offending Team.) (Source: DfES, 2003.)

Table 2.2 suggests some of the characteristics that cross over between education and therapy. It also provides a summary of therapeutic education approaches as applied to young people who need support and help in order to be able to engage and participate in education, training and work-related programmes (Cornwall, 2004: 38).

Table 2.2 Comparison of therapeutic and educational principles

Therapeutic **education**	**Therapeutic** education
Maintains and raises self-esteem and self-awareness	**Therapy is:**
	Client-centred and led
Uses social and emotional literacy or intelligence	Intent on healing, making better or happier
Values young person's views and gives them responsibility – helps them to manage themselves	Understanding the problem as far as possible and achieving solutions
Proposes that effective teaching starts from where the learner is	Giving time for individual expression and attention
Makes explicit what skills young people need in order to learn in school settings	Using the client's own expression output to work with and develop or shape
Includes ideas of nurture, growth and development – develops nurturing strategies	Sometimes objectified with 'targets' but more often not (e.g. music, art, aromatherapy)
Deals with curriculum issues by integrating and complementing content	'Hands on' by the therapist, who takes part fully in the process
Protects from undue conflict and stress – uses assertive strategies	A transaction between individuals or in small groups
Gives teachers and young persons the confidence to engage with each other and the curriculum	Challenging to existing conditions, habits, responses or circumstances

In this chapter we explored whether the behaviour of a young person is trying to make a point or tell us something about their experience of education. A number of factors are involved in the complex mixture of the origins of disaffection and social disenfranchisement and they beg the question as to why they impact so heavily on education. By broadening the perspectives on what education is about and debating practice, we have attempted to answer questions about what characterises therapeutic education. Sometimes holistic theories are dismissed by practitioners because they appear too complex and the problems of change and resourcing seem insurmountable. They are also often dismissed by politicians and executives in the education system because they are too far-reaching and provide longer-term solutions to the challenges, rather than the short-term political solutions that have become the speciality of successive governments for the past twenty-five years. The so-called 'standards' and 'quality' monitoring in the education system has been characterised by the same old answers to new problems, and this philosophy will be explored further in the next chapter. In answering the question of how different societies determine school expectations and the wider social context in which educational practices take place, this chapter has attempted to map therapeutic education on to current educational practices in the United Kingdom and in United States. 'Exclusion' is a non-professional approach to the difficulties of young people but it is the system that teachers experience. Showing how socially constructed 'scaffolding' in school and community can help young people who are vulnerable is one of the purposes of this book. Such scaffolding is constructed through a therapeutic, holisitic and humanistic approach to learning, teaching and managing the school environment.

Chapter 3

Education

Adventure or nightmare?

This chapter explores some of the reasons why education is an adventure for some and yet a nightmare for others. Perhaps it is too big a project to attempt to determine the numbers involved, and we have not yet tracked down salient research into the emotional legacy of years of education. Rather, there are quantities of social and educational research papers cited already that look at schooling from the social, rather than the personal, viewpoint.

Yet it is not uncommon to come across a range of people who describe their whole education experience as a 'nightmare'. In many cases the person involved has also experienced one of many defined special educational needs, such as dyslexia, dyspraxia or another specific learning difficulty. Their difficulty may not have been recognised at all, or may have been recognised too late, after the individual had undergone too many negative educational experiences. In other cases, young people experience a wide range of social and emotional difficulties that interfere with their education and often experience negative, controlling or aggressive responses to their behaviour rather than the support that they often crave and desperately need. In other situations, young people experience social and emotional pressures either from home or from school (or both) that militate against their being able to access the educational opportunities on offer (see McGuiness, 1993; see also Chapter 2 and Appendix 2). We hope readers will bear with us while we surmise the possible causes for such a 'nightmare' experience on the basis that it does illuminate the psychological discomfort that many experience in school. For some, this psychological discomfort becomes so extreme that they can no longer tolerate being at school. Others react emotionally and behaviourally, sometimes causing as much, if not more, discomfort in others.

The most obvious cause of negative experience, and one that is often quite rightly drawn attention to in the media, is bullying. In some schools, bullying has almost become an ingrained and barely visible part of the overall school culture. Large secondary schools often have physically isolated locations on their premises and a variety of subcultures present on the campus. These can lead to bullying in 'out of sight' places.

Some schools are subject to the influence of the 'gang cultures' that are present in the community around the school. One of the authors has himself recently interviewed staff in two UK city schools that have had incidents and conflicts stemming from surrounding neighbourhood conflicts. He has also given public presentations in St Louis, Missouri, on the effect of conflict and violence in school on teachers and other students as part of a sponsored reduction of gang violence project. There are too many examples of tension and conflict-laden cultures in schools, and most particularly secondary or high schools, to keep on viewing them as isolated incidents or using the term 'discipline' as a simplistic remedy. Unfortunately, the recent public debate on discipline in UK schools[1] is likely to continue to revolve around the same insolvent and ineffective approaches to discipline, based on rewards, sanctions and intolerance.

Predictability, flexibility, coherence and values are 'seen' by young people

In the first two chapters there was much discussion about the current characteristics of our education system overall and the social policy that drives it. In order to move forward and examine some of the reasons why some young people find the process of education an absolute nightmare, it is obligatory to look now at the role of the adults involved and how schools develop an ethos for providing a successful learning environment. A key cornerstone of any successful team approach is an expression of shared values. Both the UK and the US education systems comprise a very varied mixture of values and intended outcomes, ranging from the very impersonal and competitive through to a highly personalised view of individual nurturing. An initial step is to consider the values shared by any particular group of teachers. Differences in values can be a major stumbling block. That is not to say that everyone has to think the same, but that sharing views and developing a coherent, ethically based approach is a keystone of effective practice. Appendix 2 is a therapeutic education assessment of shared values, and one that raises salient issues in terms of staff and adult values. It is intended to give an assessment tool with which to check the shared values of staff. The following list is a view of the formalised or projected image of education. Is education all things to all people, as it sometimes feels like, or can we define it more closely? At the very least, the question arises as to what any particular group of individuals in any given school see as their educational values. Which of these characterisations of education do you prefer:

- competition for success in life – linked to passing exams and gaining recognition/accreditation;
- social engineering to produce 'worthy' citizens;
- training to make sure that enough people have sufficient 'basic skills' for work;

- education to give young people skills to succeed in life and cope with society's demands;
- self-actualisation – to achieve personal potential and liberty;
- personal growth and fulfilment that encourage lifelong learning.

Teaching approaches that are all stick and very little carrot are doomed to work only with those children who are extremely resilient. Inspiration, motivation, engagement, enjoyment and inclusion are all important characteristics of therapeutic education. The overall aim of this chapter is to provide a rationale and context for work with pupils and students who, for whatever reasons, may lack inspiration, motivation and engagement, and to do so in an informed and positive way. To achieve this we need to define a number of specific purposes that relate to the way in which teachers can:

- recognise and contextualise the learner's characteristics and work more effectively with them;
- be more sensitive to learners' individuality (and humanity) and listen better;
- develop strategies that will better inform daily lesson delivery and planning;
- use positive relationships to counter the insecurity of current educational 'challenges';
- be more creative and flexible in planning and delivery, challenging constraints to teaching that emanate from a narrowly defined and subject-based curriculum;
- move beyond simple behavioural technologies and into more holistic, nurturing and therapeutic approaches.

In brief, this chapter puts forward a series of discussions and proposals that may give some insight into the ways in which teaching practices and school management can develop them into a more humanistic and successful model for working with young people. This means young people who are in difficulties and at risk of exclusion, prosecution, self-injury and developing antisocial behaviour patterns. But we would emphasise again that adopting a more therapeutic approach is beneficial to all pupils. It simply recognises the human element in learning. Relying on simple behavioural approaches (e.g. rewards and sanctions), even when they are applied on a whole-school basis, is not enough. It will not deal with a significant proportion of children's difficulties, nor will it develop confidence on its own. Furthermore, therapeutic education is not about turning teachers into therapists but about developing and making explicit therapeutic strategies that teachers have used ever since the concept of 'teaching' began.

One size does not fit all: the child is at the centre of the learning process

Debate often centres on groups of people prone to exclusion, such as people who are unemployed, disabled, elderly, or from ethnic minority communities (e.g. Silver, 1994). Exclusion may be concentrated in certain geographical areas, often with a disproportionate demographic representation of people with such characteristics. It is often described as a process of interconnected outcomes. For example, a young person may be experiencing ill health, poor housing, low educational attainment, unemployment, and direct or indirect financial hardship. These tend to 'cluster' in a downward spiral, one provoking the other and combining together to drive the kind of behaviour that results in exclusion (e.g. Berghman, 1995; Walker, 1995). Poverty tends to be a common thread running throughout. Indeed, it has long been argued that possession of a certain level of material resources is a prerequisite for participation in the activities customary to a given society (Townsend, 1979). Despite the lack of recognition of social factors in the strategies and practices discussed and encouraged by politicians, there are a number of important keys to unlocking this problem, and a more holistic view of the troubles and troubling behaviour of some young people is one of them.

In the past, some local education authorities have sought to remedy these complex difficulties by the creation of large residential schools (Pritchard, 2004), often (but not always) situated in remote locations. For some time there was a strongly held view that institutionalising young people would *cure* them, but even if it didn't, it would at least get them out of our hair for a while. Although such establishments are still present in some areas of the United Kingdom, the government's Green Paper *Excellence for All Children: Meeting Special Educational Needs* (DfES, 1998) made it clear that inclusion was to be high on the agenda for some time to come. The initiative (which is still open to a degree of interpretation) was not intended to bring about the collapse of special schools. However, the paper made it clear that an inclusive framework is based on the ability to support children within their own communities and to use local facilities, resources and expertise wherever possible. 'Special Schools need to be confident outward looking centres of excellence. We want to build on their strengths and ensure that they are an integral part of an inclusive education system for children in their area and perhaps beyond' (DfES, 1998). Indeed, the Special Educational Needs and Disability Act 2001 could, arguably, reinforce this view and further the drive towards inclusion in its purist form. Yet it has been suggested (Forlin *et al.*, 1996) that a critical element in the effectiveness of inclusion derives from the teacher's own beliefs and attitudes towards an inclusive practice, and consequently their commitment to and the ultimate success of such an initiative. As Florian *et al.* (1998) point out, 'Although the concept is part of a broad human rights agenda, many educators have serious reservations about supporting the widespread placement of pupils with SEN [special educational needs] in mainstream schools.' Furthermore, the consequences of such sweeping reform, with or without the full commitment of those with the major responsibility for implementing it, could be significant and far-reaching. The management of change in this process by those with executive functions in both local and national UK government has been far from beneficial to professional development and ownership of the new ideas proposed (Cornwall, 2001). The consequences affect not only the individuals themselves but other children around them, and those who work with and on behalf of those children. Far from exemplifying reform conducive to equality and diversity, this could be regarded as a means of creating an educational environment where individual opportunity and progress are actually inhibited. It seems reasonable that children who are able to excel in a mainstream school should be permitted to do so. However, for a small yet significant proportion of children, superficial access to curriculum materials alone may not be enough. For these children an additional dimension of care and support may be needed. Special units and schools are designed to offer that additional dimension. In the context of therapeutic education, this is achieved in a number of ways that will be examined as this book unfolds.

The nature of specialist provision in both the United Kingdom and the United States is wide-ranging. The specific area of interest here lies with children who are disaffected, and disengaged, and who often exhibit delinquent and socially challenging behaviour. These children are, in England and Wales, likely to have been assessed under the 1996 Education Act and have a Statement of Special Needs produced accordingly. In the United States they will have been assessed and there will be a requirement to produce a legally binding 'Individual Education Plan'. More often than not, their difficulties will be subsumed within the umbrella term of behavioural, emotional and social difficulties (BESD), sometimes qualified with additional descriptions such as 'associated learning difficulties' to signify the impact that their behaviour has had on their academic progress or vice versa. In reality, these children's difficulties and corresponding needs are wide-ranging and complex, often deriving from quite extreme psychological, social and environmental conditions that could have been prevalent from a very early age.

The human element: everybody exhibits challenging behaviour

The strategies and approaches this book proposes are not new but do represent a basic humanistic approach to learning that includes the broad psychology of learning and does not ignore the human element in learning. It is a human transaction, not a mechanical process, and, as such, is prone to inconsistency and difficulty. In that spirit, it makes sense to start with asking the questions of us all – starting with our own evaluation of challenging behaviour and the situations that arise from a spilling over of emotions and an inability to deal with situations and events. In Chapter 1 we quoted Carl Rogers (1967) and it became clear that under stress, humans revert back to previously learned behaviour, sometimes leading to 'rigidity'. That is, when under pressure, people tend to revert back to behaviour they do not have to think about. This applies to emotionally and socially mature adults as well as young people who may be emotionally immature and socially unskilled (in school and learning terms).

So what makes the difference between the kind of challenging behaviour that we all exhibit from time to time and the kind of challenging behaviour that results in young people getting excluded from school and often, later in life, getting into trouble with the police and sometimes ending up with a criminal record? Not as much as one might think. There is a thin dividing line between deliberate aggression and the struggle to control impulses or to revert back to self-protective behaviour. Perhaps the best thing to do is to ask ourselves, and others who are able to express themselves in a mature way that question in order to understand the process better.

This is exactly what one of the authors of this book has done time and again in workshops and training days for teachers and other professionals that he has run over the years. Tables 3.1a–c are a distillation of over thirty workshop and training days involving more than 400 statements from teachers, classroom assistants and other professionals (Cornwall, 2005). This is after the group have accepted that they *do* (as do we all) engage in challenging behaviour from time to time. It is noteworthy that these people are probably more emotionally aware and socially capable on the whole than the young people they work with. Therein lies the lesson of acceptance and exculpation, leading to more positive regard and further justification for the staff assessment found in Appendix 2. This is a vital element of therapeutic education and, in our experience, opens the door to positive outcomes, rather than blame or an emphasis on retribution. Tables 3.1a–c summarise some of the responses.

Drawing lessons from analysing challenging situations and social or emotional responses to these is a very important starting point before launching into discussion strategies and responses to challenging situations that develop in schools and in other learning situations. A brief analysis of Tables 3.1a–c plainly illustrates a number of important factors that apply to *both* adults *and* young people in difficult circumstances and challenging events:

1 Everybody exhibits challenging behaviour at some time in their lives.
2 Challenging behaviour and challenging situations are usually those in which a person feels that they are:

- losing control of the situation;
- losing control of themselves;
- unable to assimilate or deal with the event(s);
- therefore, unable to respond effectively.

3 There is no reason to think that the thoughts, feelings and responses to these kind of challenging situations differ very much from one person to another, whatever their age.

Table 3.1a Give some examples of *your* recent challenging behaviour

This morning feeling frustrated and panicky – verbally abusing a loved one!	Last Saturday in [well-known department store] I waited 40 minutes for my purchase!	Slamming doors and crashing cups to show displeasure but refusing to say what was wrong when asked
Goading partner because I was fed up . . .	Not talking much, and when I did, very brusque	Telling work colleague to **** off because I was under pressure!
Put phone down on friend	Went silent and refused to discuss what was upsetting me	Sulky with husband. . . . Felt justified at the time! Not in retrospect . . .
Cried	Broke phone	Slammed a door

Table 3.1b What were your thoughts at the time?

At a loss as to what to think	Waiting to 'get my own back'	What am I doing here?
How do I get out of this situation quickly?	I'm worthless for not being part of the group	How am I going to make things better?
I'm not part of the group/ accepted	This is an injustice – I'm right	Shut up . . . (anger stopped me thinking at all . . .)
You must be winding me up	Glad to have some power to react . . .	No longer caring how other people see me/think about me
I have had enough, am fed up with the situation	I'm unable to cope with this . . .	Why wasn't I told this earlier?

Table 3.1c What were your feelings?

I felt ignored and not valued and mistreated. I wanted to show that I could be as cold and heartless . . .	Struggled to remain in control – frustration, aggression . . .	Uncaring of how other people cope with my reaction
Leave me alone	Self-righteous	Annoyance, pride, desire for revenge
Confusion, worry, uselessness, hurt	Resentful of others	Stressed
Stubbornness (I'm not giving up here)	Sense of relief and satisfaction	Disillusioned, resigned and helpless . . .

4 A child or young person may not have the 'skills' of an adult in:

- recognising the warning signs of anger as it develops;
- being aware of and coping with powerful emotions;
- drawing on positive past experiences or adult models;
- being able to 'rationalise' their anger (or feelings) afterwards;
- being able to express their feelings appropriately at the time;
- managing their relationship with the other person and patching up or repairing damage to relationships.

5 Often, anger and frustration are justified (i.e. not wrong in themselves) – but there are generally ways of expressing them usefully and effectively.

6 The aftermath of anger, aggression and challenging situations needs to be recognised and always dealt with, not ignored or passed over.

7 Even well-balanced and mature people can resort to physical expressions of anger when their anger becomes overwhelming, but these expressions can be 'shaped' (worked with therapeutically).

8 There is an awareness of the social (or group) effect and consequences, before and after the event.

9 There is often an internal 'struggle', in a threatening situation or when one is faced with aggression from others (verbal as well as physical), to maintain control in the face of bodily (chemical) reactions.

10 The discharge of emotion in these situations often leads to a sense of relief and a feeling of satisfaction – positive reinforcement for an angry person.

11 Threatening situations often cause either an entire blanking out of cognitive (thoughtful) processes (hence impulsive reaction) or a rigidity that comes from reverting to previously learned behavioural patterns.

12 *Everyone has a right to self-defence and to protect themselves from physical, social and emotional threats.*

Insights raised by this analysis are not intended to represent a list of rules, and there is no suggestion that they comprise a particular 'approach' to challenging behaviour. They embody an awareness of the complexity of events and situations that occur both in school and in the community. We propose that this awareness is a different one from that which is currently prevalent in many schools and in society generally, and that influences school ethos. A lack of understanding of the human element is contributing to the number of pupils excluded from school and the problems of social exclusion in society and, on the coat tails of this exclusionary process, difficulties with lawbreaking and other forms of antisocial behaviour.

Earlier in this chapter the question of intention was raised at various points. Teachers often come back to the question of the intentions and determinations of the young person when they are being difficult. This question arises in society generally when the simple solution 'groups' accuse those who wish to examine a humanistic approach of being 'soft'. It is a difficult question, because the criticism of people who are seen to be 'soft' on young people who exhibit challenging behaviour is that they are being taken for a ride. The young person is (in some cases literally) getting away with murder! If they get away with antisocial behaviour, what is there to stop them from doing it again? Why should a teacher put up with insults and aggression from a young person? Teachers often say they don't have the time or resources to cope with each young person's problems or behaviour in school. These are perfectly valid points, but they stem from a total misunderstanding of those who adopt humanistic or therapeutic approaches to teaching as well as to crime and punishment. This misunderstanding probably emanates from a fear of breaking down simplistic and rigid responses to challenge. One could also dismiss it as a laziness of spirit in relying on worn-out solutions that require minimal effort to implement, old solutions to new problems. Despite their prominence in the popular press, the reality is that these kinds of responses have led to more problems, as has been clearly demonstrated by research cited in this book and by the current state of affairs.

This book, in later chapters, outlines strategies, approaches and organisational responses to challenging behaviour in the context of therapeutic education. Nowhere in this book is it suggested that understanding the problems faced by young people who are at risk of exclusion is an excuse for inaction or for not responding clearly and positively to *all* behaviour, particularly when that behaviour is inappropriate. There is positively no suggestion that it is constructive, as a strategy, to totally ignore any significant or repeated behaviour, nor do we suggest anywhere that a young person is not responsible for their behaviour. Tables 3.1a–c and the subsequent analysis only serve to show that a professional, often accompanied by a personal, response is always necessary. The principle that personal responsibility is paramount pervades all that is expounded in later chapters (and is found in Appendix 2). This alludes to personal responsibility on the part of the young person or the learner in that they cannot escape the consequences of antisocial or aggressive action involving others or the environment they share with others.

On the other hand, it is also of vital importance that the adults involved take their personal responsibilities as seriously as they expect young people to. That is, they should not ignore any behaviour that requires a response and they should not pretend that they have dealt with a problem when they haven't. The use of simplistic, rejecting or mechanical (automatic) responses (such as some behavioural regimes) is the antithesis of therapeutic or humanistic approaches. Let us reiterate that this is a thoughtful and strong approach to challenging behaviour and does not seek to sweep the problem under the carpet. Nor does it expect someone else to deal with it. Challenging and antisocial behaviour is everybody's responsibility, and it takes a collective sense of responsibility to deal with it effectively, as well as clear-cut, contingent and carefully thought out collective responses.

All schools are faced with the problem of children's resistance to engaging in learning, because this is inextricably linked to the concept of education itself

(Wilson, 2000). It may apply to any number of children in any classroom in any school at any time and for an undetermined duration. The scale of the problem varies tremendously, but no school could ever consider itself exempt, just as no teacher should consider doing the job without first establishing a system of classroom management and order. Chaos is generally not considered conducive to learning. Some pupils are particularly hard to relate to, motivate or teach. Knowledge and skill cannot just be 'delivered' like a parcel for social and economic survival; it is not an end result, but a complex human process. A system of education should recognise that relationships between people, both adults and children, are fundamental to the process of teaching and learning. Young people will then learn to make judgements about how, when and to what purpose they should use their skills and knowledge. Learners also need to know that their learning has some immediate purpose and personal significance. To separate 'learning' and 'behaviour for learning' from the emotional and social components of learning is akin to ignoring the fact that a ship needs to be watertight before one can successfully traverse the ocean.

Although these factors alone could still be considered manageable in a classroom, they are often coupled with more disruptive behaviour. If a situation like this persists, it is likely to have a negative impact on the education of that child and others around him or her. Mainstream schools operate within 'tolerable limits' in an effort to mirror society's standards and expectations. If a 'troubled and troublesome' child is perceived to have difficulties beyond these limits, then the school's response is often all too predictable: 'While the number of pupils excluded from school still remains small in relation to the overall school population it has risen sharply in recent years: 4000 permanent exclusions in 1991–2, 13,500 permanent exclusions in 1996–7' (Long and Fogell, 1999: 92–93).

Further recent UK statistics (Cooper, 2004) linked to the number of children in England currently experiencing behavioural, emotional and social difficulties (BESDs) make somewhat disturbing reading. At least 10 per cent (936,000) of children have BESDs ('Young Minds' briefing paper No. 1, March 1999, cited in Cooper, 2004), and 1 per cent (93,500) of children are in special schools of various types, including those for BESDs (DfEE figures, 1998). Other recent statistics (DfES, 2002a) show that the number of children in Pupil Referral Units (PRUs) with statements represented approximately 0.7 per cent of the total school population with statements and the number in PRUs without statements represented approximately 0.3 per cent of pupils with SEN without statements. A significant proportion of children with BESDs in mainstream schools have statements. A much higher incidence exists in state special schools and in independent and non-maintained special schools in the United Kingdom. Overall, the UK government's statistical information tends to mask the fact that the number of pupils in PRUs is steadily increasing, as is the number of pupils with special needs in independent and non-maintained special schools. The number of pupils with statements is generally decreasing because of policy changes, but the number in PRUs is increasing. This supports the notion that policy and practice are not generally having a positive impact on the number of children experiencing BESDs.

One must assume that for the children referred to above, some are more 'troubled and troublesome' than others. Of the 1 per cent in special schools, there will be a proportion whose difficulties are severe enough to warrant an even greater level of support, and it is this small group to which this book primarily refers. Laslett (1977: 5) offers a rather raw definition taken from the Handicapped Pupils and School Regulations 1945 that looks specifically at such children identified under the Education Act 1996 and who are most usually referred to special (BESD) schools: 'pupils who show evidence of psychological disturbance or emotional instability and who require special educational treatment in order to effect their personal, social or educational re-adjustment'.

Troubled children growing into troublesome adolescents and adults

Despite the clumsy descriptors, Laslett's definition nonetheless provides a reasonable starting point from which to expand upon the nature of these difficulties and from where they might have derived. In fact, 'troubled' by definition refers to a lack of inner calm experienced, or being prone to emotional conflict or psychological difficulties (*Encarta World English Dictionary*, 1999). The literal definition also refers to experiencing anxiety or distress characterised by problems or adversity. Powell *et al.* (2004) take up the gauntlet by referring to the ability to 'engage' with educational and learning opportunities (through behaving to learn) as a function of a person's relationship with themselves. If that relationship is difficult or strained, as in the case of anxiety, neurochemical problems or social problems that cause further emotional upsets, then that young person will be limited in the extent to which they can 'engage' with others and with the experiences they encounter in school and classroom. In an attempt to conceptualise what behavioural, emotional and social difficulties are, Greenhalgh (1996: 17) draws on the Fish Report (1985; cited in Greenhalgh, 1996) in describing these particular special educational needs as a function of social context. He states that environmental factors in the home and school context are of particular relevance: 'Troubled children bring to school their difficult experiences of home, sometimes acting out dynamics experienced in the family. Children may unwittingly transfer their feelings about their parents onto school staff.'

Powell *et al.* (2004) point out that social interaction is pivotal to cognitive development and influences the development of learning behaviour in school contexts, as the extensive and well-documented work of Piaget (1928) and Vygotsky (1962, 1978) would affirm. Long (2004: 68), however, focuses his attention more on children's emotional needs, and he claims that they provide the energy to drive their behaviour towards specific goals. 'The true meaning of behaviour can only be achieved through an understanding of both their emotional needs and the context in which the behaviour takes place.'

Long (2004) makes the further point that negative life experience, possibly in the form of poor academic success, negative peer relations and difficult peer relationships with adults, will have a dramatic impact on a child's self-esteem. This is likely to trigger a whole range of defence mechanisms such as *projection* ('You're the problem, not me'), *denial* ('I have no problem') and *escapism* (computer games and so on). 'In a world of low self-esteem, pain, anger and sadness they will have little courage to try to change. All their energy is involved in protecting the me as I am' (Long, 2004: 71). In terms of the well-established work of Maslow (1968), mentioned earlier, self-esteem (the need to be valued) is one of five hierarchically ordered biological drives and is crucial for self-actualisation (the need to put one's talents to good use and achieve success). Self-esteem is fuelled by the more basic drives of affiliation (the need to engage with other human beings in reciprocal caring relationships), safety (the need for a secure and predictable environment) and finally physiological (the needs for clean air, warmth, etc.). Put simply, if lower-level needs are not met, then higher-level needs become irrelevant for the person and hence unachievable. Using this theoretical framework, one can start to understand why some pupils fail to engage in learning and also present challenging behaviour. 'Only once healthy self esteem is established can individuals become truly self-directing and operate as autonomous, responsible individuals in a pro-social but independent way' (Cooper, 2004: 58).

'Troublesome' is defined as 'producing annoyance, discomfort or anxiety especially in a recurrent way' or 'causing difficulties or taking a great deal of time' (*Encarta World Dictionary*, 1999). The term as used in this book may suggest or imply blame. The intent, however, is simply to avoid more categorical approaches when describing the range of difficulties experienced by many children and young people. As Cooper (2004: 52) rightly points out in proposing a holistic approach, 'We should be wary about the negative consequences of indiscriminate labelling. It is helpful to think of these categories as applying to social, emotional and behavioural patterns, rather than labels to be applied to people.' This process starts with a better understanding of the range of behaviours some children present, and possible underlying influences and causes. This book promotes a holistic, bio-psycho-social standpoint.

Cooper (2004) describes in some detail the behaviours, patterns of behaviour and manners of self-presentation that 'troubled and troublesome children' may exhibit. He identifies two main categories: 'externalising difficulties' and 'internalising difficulties'.

'Externalising difficulties' are troublesome to others in being disruptive, antisocial and confrontational. They could also include disaffection (antipathy towards formal values), conduct disorder (wilful aggression and destruction), delinquency (lawbreaking) and 'oppositional defiance' (a negativistic, hostile and defiant attitude). All the above can be largely attributed to environmental causes as described earlier, such as unstable and conflicting family circumstances, inconsistent patterns of care, and extensive use of corporal punishment (Patterson *et al.*, 1992). These are also learned behaviours, and as such can be explained through Bowlby's work on attachment theory (1973, 1979; also 1975, cited in Cooper, 2004) Bennathan and Boxall on underlying emotional problems (2000) and Weiner *et al.* on attribution theory (1971, cited in Cooper, 2004). However, another group of 'externalising difficulties' that cover specific developmental disorders such as autism (severely impaired social interaction), ADHD (controlling attention, impulsivity and motor activity) and Tourette's disorder (motor and vocal 'tics') may derive from more biological, neurochemical or possibly even genetic factors.

The second category, 'internalising difficulties', highlights both troubled and troublesome behaviour in the form of truancy, separation anxiety, withdrawn behaviour and elective or selective mutism. These are the result of environmental factors and are learned behaviours, as with the first group of 'externalising difficulties'. A final set of 'internalising difficulties' covers substance misuse and abuse, anxiety disorders and depression, and can reflect negative or stressful social circumstances or life experiences.

If these are seen as some of the root causes of challenging behaviour and their manifestations in society, it would be helpful to establish what the function of these behaviours might be in the context of home life, school life and within the community. The New York State Office of Mental Retardation and Developmental Disabilities (OMRDD, 1998) refers to the concept of all behaviour, even challenging behaviour, as serving a purpose for the individual. OMRDD then expands on this premise by explaining that challenging behaviour usually occurs for one or more of four functional reasons or response classes. These are:

- attention – to attract and engage others;
- tangible – to access an item, service, food or activity;
- sensory – to gain pleasure from look, sound, feel or taste;
- escape – in avoidance of a demand, task or activity.

Clearly, if this communicates something about a person's unmet wants or needs, it could become a very useful tool with which to analyse the behaviour and plan for appropriate responses. Later chapters expand on this through further discussion around using functional analysis as a planning tool, teaching appropriate skills to achieve a person's unmet wants or needs and encouraging self-management and self-regulation.

Self-efficacy, one key to successful personal development, change and growth

Given the extent of personal trauma and disadvantage that many of the children in trouble and excluded from school have suffered, often coupled with the severe nature of their challenging behaviour, what are the conditions under which these children stand the best chance of regaining their self-esteem, developing some control over their lives, and regaining confidence to learn and their ability to succeed? A perspective that puts the young person squarely at the centre of the process, as opposed to one that places either the National Curriculum or the politics of social inclusion at the centre, enables us to develop clearer educational pathways in helping them to gain access to, participate in and engage with their learning opportunities and develop learning behaviours (Powell *et al.*, 2004). The previous chapter expanded on the notion that relationships are key to behaviour for learning, and we propose, along with many others, that relationships are fundamental not only to learning for troubled and troublesome children, but for all children. It is the nature of these relationships that this book is concerned with, and their impact upon young people's learning and upon the character and effectiveness of the education provision for them. The hypothesis that identity is a useful concept and a significant factor in behaviour for learning ties in with much research and emergent theories of 'vulnerability and resilience' (for example, those found in Tizard and Varma, 1992) that take into account, and learn from the many, many young people who face challenging circumstances and adversity in their lives and yet manage to get through and come out of school with ambition and hope. Bandura (1986, 1997) takes a cognitive and affective view in looking at self-belief, self-regulation and self-reflection, which contribute to his theories of self-efficacy. These ideas sit uncomfortably with those who demand simplistic, punitive and often aggressive responses to challenging behaviour in schools. These are sometimes criticised as 'woolly' and complicated by many who hold to simpler solutions, but the fact is that they are generally supported by more research in education, health, psychology and other social sciences than the populist 'behavioural' or simplistic contingent approaches that seem to prevail. Supportive and therapeutic approaches are tougher in their requirements to think, plan and implement effective strategies than depending on immediate solutions and then excluding or dismissing the young person when these fail.

The exclusive culture that schools as institutions are locked into also tends to reflect the scarcity of targeted resources and the blame culture that is endemic to dealing with conflict. An unchallenged and politically expedient culture exists that ignores a wealth of research and evidence bases and prefers to base educational practice on hearsay and tradition. But it goes to a deeper question as to whether the system itself (as well as some teachers within it) really respects the individuality of the learners within it (probably because they are not seen as consumers or stakeholders). Can there be such a thing as systemic 'respect'?

Do some executive players in education simply see pupils as acceptable only when they become part of a conforming mass that is being prepared for a role in populating call centres or are useful in massaging the statistics of educational success and political advancement?

Embedded within Albert Bandura's social cognitive standpoint is the understanding that individuals are imbued with a range of capabilities, and where these are absent, then a young person will struggle. Chief among these are the capacity to symbolise, plan alternative strategies (forethought), learn through vicarious experience, self-regulate, and self-reflect. These resources provide human beings with the cognitive means by which they are influential in determining their own destiny. Much challenging behaviour can be seen as sometimes unconscious, and usually very inept, ways of attempting to gain some influence over events, over the views of others and, from time to time, over the person's actions. It is the self-regulatory components of social cognitive theories that are most applicable to young people who are in trouble in school. It is these self-regulatory mechanisms that provide the potential for self-directed changes in their behaviour. Bandura's theories tend to explain how developing the ability to make sense of their experiences, explore their own cognitions and self-beliefs, and engage in self-evaluation will enable a young person to alter their thinking and behaviour accordingly. For Bandura, the capability that is most 'distinctly human' (1986: 21) is exactly the one that enables a person to control and change their behaviour, and he calls this 'self-efficacy'.

Therapeutic education is not a new idea, nor is it a particularly well-defined concept at the present time. It might seem confusing to take on board a combination of approaches when many teachers are asking for simple solutions. There are no simple solutions to the complex problems that teachers and learning support staff encounter in their classrooms, whether mainstream or in specialist provision. In addition to this, when we analyse what makes up good, inclusive and motivating teaching, we find that it is not a simple transaction of knowledge between teacher and learner. So, education is an adventure for some and a nightmare for others . . . why? This chapter investigates the idea that predictability, flexibility, coherence and values are 'seen' by young people. In short, young people are not just passive recipients of the knowledge and skills that teachers might quite rightly wish to transact with them. They are sentient human beings with their own strengths, and their own emotional baggage in some cases. Some discussion in this and previous chapters has drawn on our experience and research abroad simply because this kind of comparative analysis facilitates consideration of the underlying purposes of education and how it may differ from country to country. The chapter also adopts the firm principle that one size does *not* fit all. A system that places the child and young person firmly at the centre of the learning process must acknowledge difference and diversity and take steps to accommodate them. We reject the notion that schools can be self-serving institutions or that the institution of education is more important than its effects on those who partake of it.

The human relationships involved are not necessarily complicated but they are sophisticated and have an enormous impact on the effectiveness of teaching. This is nothing new to teachers, who have for thousands of years realised that the interpersonal transaction between teacher and learner is enriched by a nurturing and therapeutic ethic. The human element is crucial in developing an ethical and effective approach, and this is exemplified by the fact, already referred to, that everybody exhibits challenging behaviour from time to time. Teaching and learning is not about one (older) group telling the other (younger) group how to behave, but about exploring and sharing the reasons for behaviour and how best to develop self-regulation, personal responsibility and personal growth. Self-discipline is a tool that a person can carry with them, and can guide their lifelong learning. Behavioural compliance is a short-lived and environment-specific pathway to rack and ruin.

We want the best for our pupils. The trouble is that some pupils are easier to form relationships with than others. Some pupils are difficult to reach, to get along with and very difficult to motivate. The cost of not reaching too many young people has already become apparent as troubled children grow into troublesome adolescents and even more troublesome adults who drain the social and personal resources available. Self-efficacy is described as one of the most significant keys to successful personal development, change and growth. It also encapsulates the therapeutic emphasis on a young person taking responsibility for themselves, for their own learning and for their behaviour towards others and the shared environment. Therapeutic education is essentially about the teacher–learner relationship and the various ways that it can be enhanced to improve engagement, motivation and learning for children and young people who are experiencing significant emotional and behavioural difficulties. In short, anyone who has taught young people with these difficulties for any length of time will tell you that the quality of your relationship with that young person has an enormous impact on their ability to learn and access the National or subject-based or any other curriculum and to show what they can really do.

Chapter 4

Who am I?

Identity, agency and resilience

The previous chapter concluded with an emphasis on relationships as being central to a humanistic and therapeutic approach to working with young people who are vulnerable and challenging. We have promoted and proposed a view of education that centres on the nurturing and developmental aspects of education within the context of a humanistic, rather than mechanistic, philosophy of learning. We do not propose a passive or medicalising influence and, on the contrary, emphasised in Chapter 3 the importance of developing notions of personal responsibility with young people. One way of doing this is to 'model' positive attitudes and skilled social behaviour, rather than rely on authoritarian assumptions or punitive systems. Adults working with young people provide role models for those young people, and this is a very underestimated and yet very powerful way of engaging with and encouraging changes in the perceptions of a young person.

This chapter is concerned with developing models and theories of 'agency' and 'resilience' and with exploring how these notions will help to develop a proactive and encouraging approach to the behavioural, emotional and social development of young people in the context of their education. In the spirit of 'positive psychology' (Seligman, 2001), we aim to cultivate a principled base to the practice examined in Chapter 5 which neither strays into a disempowering focus on negative characteristics (without ignoring them), nor retreats into simplistic and often more hard-edged behavioural reductionism.

One thing that becomes eminently clear through the case study in subsequent chapters is that trying to render the true complexities of real life and practice down to a simple empirical framework would be doing the whole project a massive disservice. Consequently, we have no problem with reflective practice but will struggle with these notions and models into practice as all professionals do in the name of more integrative practices in this field. It is the central thesis of this chapter that issues of identity, encapsulated in such concepts as self-efficacy, self-esteem, self-respect and self-regulation, lie at the centre of the emphasis in this book on therapeutic relationships. This chapter now takes up this gauntlet and examines how identity is central to personal growth and 'learning to learn' (Goddard, 1996), and is central to a healthy and resilient approach to the opportunities afforded by the current education system.

Finally, the chapter continues the search for a conceptualisation of a more activating and empowering theoretical base for developing models of practice and strategies for working alongside young people who show challenging behaviour and who live in a domain of social and emotional vulnerability. Identity is an intricate set of concepts, crossing over with personality theories and social psychology as well as the domain of social sciences and cultural studies. A person's identity is a complex amalgam of various influences but it is not a passive thing. Social cognitive theories propose that a person not only shapes their identity, their personality and their behaviour patterns through their actions, but also affects their own neurology and brain development. In short, activity and action, or 'agency', is empowering and a crucial factor in personal growth and change of a young person. It is with the intention of finding activating, motivating and empowering models that this chapter explores the relationships between identity, agency and resilience.

An activating approach: self-efficacy and human agency

The process of action-based learning and learning generally is a feedback loop requiring active participation on the part of the learner. Research on brain development calls attention to the influential role that activity and participation play in shaping and changing structures in the brain (Diamond, 1988; Kolb & Whinshaw, 1998). Kolb's experiential learning cycle seems to be employed in adult teaching these days but appears to have been forgotten by modern pundits of curriculum in schools. Figure 4.1 illustrates Kolb's simple model of experiential learning and emphasises the need for activity and participation.

Why is it that the school curriculum has, if anything, moved backwards away from the 1960s examples of child-centred learning and Nuffield Science era of participation and active investigation and into an era of passive, outcomes-based

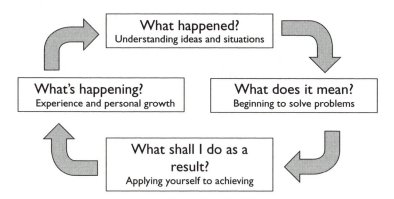

Figure 4.1 An adaptation of Kolb's simple model of experiential learning. (Source: Kolb, 1984)

learning that does not really suit young minds? Is it expediency, lack of resources or just simply lack of effort? One of the authors, as a former OfSTED inspector and headteacher, has had cause to argue on many occasions that researchers such as Kolb, Bandura, Norwich, Cooper, Rogers, Bowlby, Winnicott, Bettelheim, Greenhalgh, Maslow, Kelly and many others who more recently provide the evidence bases for practice in learning and teaching have been largely ignored, whereas the systems that drive education, such as the National Curriculum, the successive OfSTED Frameworks and a significant proportion of the massive amount of government guidance and statutes, have no such provenance. The evidence bases in education are largely ignored in favour of political imperatives, social ideologies and economic expediency, often creating more problems than they solve. Long-suffering teachers have seen the National Curriculum, with its immense rigidity and statutory role, gradually crumble and change as politicians realise that it, and many other politically guided educational initiatives, have proved to be unworkable.

Passive exposure to stimulation does not have the same effect; it is activity in exploring, manipulating, and influencing the environment that counts. In this way the learner becomes an 'agent' (Bandura, 1986, 1997) in the interactive process of learning. Referring back to Figure 2.4 makes it plain that effective behaviour for learning comes about as a result of the relationships the learner is able to develop and sustain with the curriculum (access), others (participation) and with themselves (engagement). Figure 4.2 illustrates the feedback nature of the learning loop as a complex perceptual and activity cycle where 'perceptual sets' and 'emotional triggers' and sifting mechanisms have a clear role in learning. The role of the amygdala (Goleman, 1998) is also represented as having an impact on retrieval of information from long-term memory.

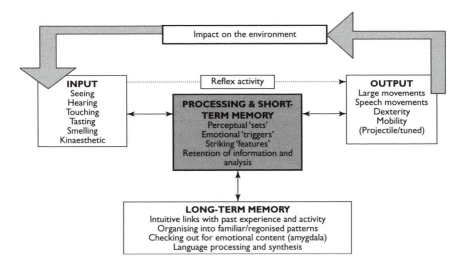

Figure 4.2 The feedback loops involved in learning.

It is this sensorimotor feedback loop and the involvement of other internal perceptual and emotional processes that have given rise to the now common-place, and evidentially supported, practice of multi-sensory teaching. This is probably why modern multi-media presentations and techniques are so powerful in terms of immediate impact but less powerful in terms of memory, consolidation or application in practice. They utilise more of the senses. However, they do not necessarily give rise to activity, and this is the key function in learning in order for the learner to be able to internalise and consolidate what has been learned. A young person may regulate their actions just as much by the thoughts, beliefs and constructs (Kelly, 1955) they hold, as they undergo upward activation by sensory stimulation from outside sources such as teachers and other adults (Sperry, 1993). Young people can intentionally conceive unique events and different novel courses of action and choose to execute one of them. These novel courses of action are not necessarily just generated as an 'impulse' or because the person is a passive actor driven by low self-esteem or 'impulsive' behaviour patterns. Just like other human beings, young people who have experienced great traumas and difficulties in their life will also be making decisions about how to act in any given circumstances, or they may be actually creating situations that suit their purposes and satisfy their need for 'agency' in Bandura's terms. Intentionality and agency raise the fundamental question of how people bring about activities over which they command personal control that 'activate the subpersonal neurophysiological events for realizing particular intentions and aspirations' (Bandura, 2001). A young person who has experienced bullying or physical abuse at home or in family contexts may well create situations in which they will be bullied at school (this being a familiar role), and this in turn will affect their biological make-up (i.e. avoiding becoming physically strong, becoming anorexic or avoiding sporting activity in the physical domain). Thus, in acting on the well-grounded belief that exercise and physical activity might enhance the young person's capability to stand up for themselves, they may avoid these things. Only when the belief system has significantly under-gone some sort of internal change, which also involves new and challenging neural pathways, will there be some permanent behavioural and personality change and some resolution concerning the need to maintain an active role in events.

Our psychological discipline is proceeding down two major divergent routes. One line of theorising seeks to clarify the basic mechanisms governing human functioning. Background knowledge focusing on micro-analyses of the inner workings of the mind in processing, representing, retrieving and using the coded information to manage various task demands, and locating where the brain activity for these events occurs, is often disembodied from interpersonal life, purposeful pursuits and self-reflectiveness. People are sentient, purposive beings. Faced with prescribed task demands, they act mindfully to make desired things happen (Bandura, 2001) rather than simply being passive 'actors' in a contrived context in which external forces will set in motion their own sets of constructs, beliefs and attitudes that may or may not generate solutions. Young people who are in difficulty, no matter how difficult they might find it to express their goals successfully, still

> set personal goals and otherwise motivate themselves to perform in ways that please or impress others or bring self-satisfaction; when they run into trouble they engage in self-enabling or self-debilitating self-talk; if they construe their failures as presenting surmountable challenges they redouble their efforts but drive themselves to despondency if they read their failures as indicants of personal deficiencies; if they believe they are being exploited, coerced, disrespected or manipulated, they respond apathetically, opposi-tionally, or hostilely.
>
> (Bandura, 2001: 5)

The mechanisms linking social, emotional and behavioural drives to action in brain theory and the actual brain or neural activity links to outer visible or inner cognitive (thinking) and affective (feeling) activities are still left largely unexplained. This is despite a number of books that make large leaps of faith and generate all kinds of 'brain-focused' activities when there is still not the evidence base to support any direct linkages with brain changes or neural activity. Our response to this is simply that there remains much work to be done to put many educational practices on sound evidence bases rather than the constant trial and error and 'let's try this to see if it works' or 'that looks useful, let's try that'. Of course the experimenting is an expected part of teachers' approach to working with young people – it is creative and desirable – but there are still too many educational practices and commercial outpourings that make claims that are not supported by evidence bases or current research, and they are not tentative enough in their claims. This is misleading for teachers and other pro-fessionals involved, and is an issue for education generally. There is no current comprehensive theory that will merge the micro-analytical approach to neural (or brain) functioning with an integrated personal (including emotional) and social convergence of the origins of behaviour within a unified and definitive structure. There are some developing hypotheses and proposals (e.g. Dilt's 'unified field theory' in O'Connor and Seymour, 1990: 89) that suggest some of the layers of human functioning underneath the behaviour. It is also apparent that as well as the ubiquitous internal (psychogenic) drives influencing behaviour, there are social contextual factors in operation that will influence and produce behavioural effects. Intellectual and abstract learning is all very well but sooner or later it has to be turned into activity and become interactive with the environment, with others or with the material (possibly curriculum) to hand. By actively adapting their motivation and activities, people produce the experiences that form the functional neurobiological foundations of symbolic, social, psychomotor and other skills. The nature of these experiences is, of course, profoundly dependent on the types of social and physical environments people select and construct in the course of their lives – or, one could say, dependent upon the kinds of experiences that children and young people are subjected to in their lives.

This kind of 'agentic' perspective fosters lines of research that provide new insights into the social construction of the functional structure of the human brain (Eisenberg, 1995). This is a realm of inquiry in which psychology can make fundamental, unique contributions to the bio-psycho-social understanding of human development, adaptation and change (Bandura, 2001). It can be interpreted as meaning that young people do adopt an active role in their lives, no matter what kind of experiences they are subjected to. It is simply that they develop active strategies for coping with the experiences they encounter. In some cases the active strategies are socially and emotionally successful and acceptable to others, and we say that a young person is resilient. In other cases, these strategies are socially unacceptable and emotionally unsuccessful in the long run, and we say that the young person is vulnerable and challenging. It also implies that the kind of simplistic solutions proffered both by critics of therapeutic notions in education and by traditionalists who view education as some kind of academic initiation test into society do not even begin to touch the real nature of the difficulties young people experience in their attempts to access knowledge, participate in learning opportunities and engage with their peers and teachers. In order for the person to change, to take on the challenges of personal growth and to learn how to learn in a school setting, actual physical changes must take place in the brain, brought about by active participation in the learning process. These changes are translated in cognitive and affective terms as changes in core structures of the personality (i.e. beliefs, constructs, perceptions, language and attitude), not an over-reliance on behaviourist and behaviour modification strategies that make the learner a passive (rather than active) player in a highly (and often unrealistically) structured environment.

Social cognitive theories, combined with more recent studies of emotional intelligence (e.g. Ciarrochi et al., 2001), are leading us to a model of emergent interactive strategies where thoughts are not disembodied immaterial entities that exist apart from neural events or behavioural outcomes that are themselves detached from any living context. The very process of learning creates new pathways in the brain, and this creation of new pathways is synonymous with new ways of acting and being. In other words, the process is cyclical and developmental, and does not have simple measurable outcomes but is a process of constant change and growth. The human mind is generative, creative, proactive and reflective, not just reactive.

This is plainly to be seen in the way that some rather challenging young people will not simply react in standard ways to what is put before them but will react according to their past experience and in doing so will generate new situations that require assimilating and dealing with in new and unique ways. This is a great game for some young people and is what can make school interesting for them when they feel inadequate in the tasks that are set or simply disinterested in those tasks. They are used to having to think on their feet and react quickly to adverse (as they see it) circumstances. Often teachers are not so adroit in this sense and are more used to stereotypical reactions to the material they put in front of their students, and the regulatory environment of school requires a considerable degree of stereotypical or conforming social behaviour. It is as if the young person is creating situations that he or she feels more comfortable with, and this then feels extremely alien to the teacher or adult involved. Often this is how conflicts are set up in the school and classroom.

So, young people who are vulnerable and challenging are by no means passive recipients of what is meted out to them; they are planning and thinking as well as acting on impulse. Previously, psychology has consigned vulnerable and challenging pupils to categories such as 'impulse driven', lacking self-regulation or treated them as objects requiring behaviour modification. Without an 'ecosystemic' (Molnar & Lindquist, 1989) perspective, all the problem and blame are loaded on to the young person in trouble. A more 'ecosystemic' approach will also acknowledge the role and function of other participants and actors (in school and at home) who may contribute to those problems encountered. The approach will sometimes also include the professionals involved and their role in perhaps escalating or perpetuating the situation. When we, the authors, mention a 'holistic' approach, it embraces the 'ecosystemic' ideal and goes further of course in acknowledging that a young person is also subjected to the impact of social, political and community forces at work. Perhaps it is nearer the truth to regard young people having trouble and in trouble at school as thinkers of thoughts that exert a resolute influence on their actions? Often over a number of years, they have developed forethought, planful proactive social strategies, aspirations, self-appraisal and self-reflection – but not geared to the goal of achieving conforming behaviour and academic results at school; rather, to the goal of maintaining their social standing and self-respect within their own parameters.

For too long, young people who are experiencing difficulties in school have been consigned to the scrapheap by labelling them in a way that promotes the image of a group of young people as having no control over events and themselves. This can be done by medicalising problems of conduct and using drugs to change behaviour, or it can be done by using disadvantaged social contexts as an excuse, or even by suggesting that they have no 'emotional intelligence'. We reject these simplistic views that make the young person a passive recipient of our beneficent strategies and goodwill. No, rather it is more positive to see the young person as full of capabilities in terms of self-efficacy – that is, being able to think, plan ahead, self-motivate, self-reflect, and self-regulate. This is an approach that builds on Bandura's life work of self-efficacy and agency, and not one that renders a young person as a passive recipient with the aim of inducing conformist behaviour.

Following the direction of the first two chapters, one of the main keys to success is relationships that build on a proactive approach, the opportunity to take on the challenges of personal growth and recognition that lifelong learning is involved. Self-efficacy, self-appraisal and self-regulation can be achieved through a process of learning to learn and learning to behave in such a way as to make learning more possible, more fun and more successful.

Moral, social and emotional 'agency' as a result of self-efficacy

In the previous section the discussion resulted in some conclusions about the ways in which a young person may wish to maintain a feeling of 'agency' or control over events and people around them. Often the focus has been exclusively in understanding the causal factors as to why a young person gets into trouble in school and in the community. These may be important, but they will not necessarily provide educators and teachers with good and effective teaching techniques or ways in which we can enhance the learning opportunities of young people in difficulty. This is very important in terms of understanding why some young people become so disaffected, but the causes of disaffection and challenging behaviour may not, in themselves, provide us with a suitable basis for developing effective, evidence-based and practically realistic strategies for working with young people who are vulnerable and challenging.

So, critics who protest that delving into a young person's social and emotional thinking and behaviour is not acceptable or productive are both right and wrong at the same time. Developing at great length an array of factors that explain why a young person may be in difficulty does not provide a basis for action, nor does it excuse the role of social policy and educational practices in exacerbating the problems that already exist. On the other hand, at least part of the solution resides in understanding how to develop self-regulation, self-reflection, planned pro-social activities, aspirations and self-motivation. This is where the problem with current practice lies, because it is based on what we do *to* a young person, not what they can do for themselves. Developing further Tod's diagrammatic view (Figure 2.4) of the relationships involved in learning behaviour, building these relationships is something that has to be done *with* an individual, not *to* them. This may seem obvious, but the starting point of many behavioural techniques is changing or structuring the environment so that events happen *to* a young person, and these are more often than not doomed to failure because they are not sufficiently internalised.

Nowhere in this book do we suggest that there should not be consequences for a young person's actions if they are significantly antisocial or even aggressive and violent. This is not a process whereby the adults stand around wringing their hands because of the problems that a young person has due to their poor or violent upbringing, for instance. It is an approach that puts the responsibility fairly and squarely back to the young person and expects them to take responsibility for their actions and to take the consequences if these should be negative, and learn from them. It is in this last bit that the approach is strongest. All experiences are a learning opportunity, not just those that are constructed in the classroom. In fact, many young people learn better out of the classroom, as evidenced by the adventure therapy programmes mentioned in Chapter 1. So how does a young person develop social, emotional and moral 'agency' and take responsibility for themselves and their actions?

> Monitoring one's pattern of behavior and the cognitive and environmental conditions under which it occurs is the first step toward doing something to affect it. Actions give rise to self-reactive influence through performance comparison with personal goals . . . rooted in a value system and a sense of personal identity, invest activities with meaning and purpose. . . . By making self-evaluation conditional on matching personal standards, people give direction to their pursuits and create self-incentives to sustain their efforts for goal attainment. They do things that give them self-satisfaction and a sense of pride and self-worth, and refrain from behaving in ways that give rise to self-dissatisfaction, self-devaluation, and self-censure.
>
> (Bandura, 2001: 7)

Setting personal goals has the same pitfalls as 'New Year resolutions' in that they are easy to set indiscriminately but difficult to achieve unless thought is given to them. Unfortunately, the current context for goal setting has been hijacked by yet another simplistically developed strategy from business and commerce, where using SMART targets (Lloyd & Berthelot, 1992) is thought to be the right way forward. This strategy is gradually becoming more disreputable, quite deservedly being criticised for measuring what is convenient and not what is important. In order for self-developed goals to activate and influence internal cognitive and affective processes, they need to be specific to that individual, provide a suitable level of challenge and be realisable in a time span that the individual can clearly see and desires. Goals that are more immediate are more likely to mobilise self-influences and direct what one does here and now. The more distant goals are worthy in setting a general course of events but are not likely to provide effective incentives or guides for immediate action in competition with other competing activities usually found in a young person's life. Progress towards valued futures is best achieved by self-developed and carefully structured goal systems combining long-term aspirations with more immediate self-guidance. Goals embodying self-engaging properties serve as powerful motivators of action (Bandura, 1991; Locke & Latham, 1990).

Moral agency – acting in accordance with a set of beliefs and constructs – is a more important focus than psychological theories of morality or moral reasoning because it is through self-regulation that a person manages their social and emotional behaviour in learning and in life generally. Behaviour measured against personal standards and situational circumstances is likely to be longer-lasting and more stable than that which is produced as a result of external stimuli (e.g. rewards and punishments). There is no doubt that *some* punishment and *some* rewards will change behaviour, but it will be a very transitory and short-term change unless something more radical has happened to the young person's thinking, beliefs, memories, perceptions and feelings. In social and moral conduct, the self-regulatory standards are more stable. As a person grows, their appreciation of moral standards grows more sophisticated, and possibly beliefs grow stronger or gradually change through experience. Often in the literature the impression is given that young people who are vulnerable and challenging have no moral standards or self-regulatory belief system. It is our contention that this is not so, but that the systems they do have are very much 'out of sync' with those that are expected, most particularly at school, where regulation is tougher than in society generally. Perhaps with the exception of a few psychotic individuals, most young people do have a code of conduct that has been developed through their lives and which they may or may not be able to articulate effectively. Young people, even young people who are apparently without moral direction or the capacity for evaluative self-reactions, are capable of developing the cognitive pathways that will enable them to self-regulate and develop effective relationships through greater self-awareness, pro-social activity and aspirations to succeed in social and emotional terms.

In the face of situational pressures to behave inhumanely, people can choose to behave otherwise by exerting counteracting self-influence. If the self-influence is not strong enough, then the person will become swayed by what is going around them and be unable to sustain pro-social behaviour in the face of pressure to misbehave or be antisocial. On the positive side, it is not uncommon for individuals to invest their self-worth so strongly in certain convictions that they will submit to harsh and punitive treatment rather than cede to what they regard as unjust or immoral. It is our contention that some young people must have some very deep-seated convictions, attached to their feelings of self-worth, to put up with the punitive treatments and social exclusions that they experience on the road to being excluded from school, and often on the road to being in further trouble later in life. What are these deep-seated convictions and how do we deal with them? In Chapter 1, some of the reasons for young people getting into such difficulty through being vulnerable and so challenging to teachers and other authority figures or challenging and aggressive towards others, more vulnerable than themselves, were explored at length. In this chapter it is now reasonable to move on to the mechanisms by which well-meaning professionals might seek to support and develop the ability of a young person to think for themselves and develop their own moral, social and emotional agency.

It is quite possible, and is often seen to be the case, for a person to engage in inhuman or antisocial conduct and then to justify and rationalise it so that it is seen to be serving socially acceptable or worthy purposes. For example, here are some different scenarios all illustrating a different view. Question: 'Why did you hit him?'

1   ''Cos he hit me first, Miss' (it wasn't my fault – displacement of responsibility).

2   'I didn't hurt him, Miss' (minimising the effect of the action – diffusing).
3   ''Cos he's always hitting other people' (his worse behaviour exonerates me).
4   ''Cos he's a pig' (justifying my behaviour on the basis of the bestial or
    subhuman nature of the other).
5   'Well, it wasn't hard, I only touched him, Miss!' (sanitising the behaviour
    with euphemism).
6   'He deserved it because he's a bastard to my friend' (not my fault, he brought
    it on himself).

It is quite possible for a person to have some moral principles and beliefs about
how people should act but in particular circumstances 'disengage' themselves
from what they know to be wrong. This kind of 'moral disengagement' is not
limited to young people who are challenging, but applies to all people, as we
saw in Chapter 2. It is at this point that the professional working with a young
person recognises a weakness in moral and social judgement, an inability to
remain engaged with their own recognition of right and wrong in given situations. This explains why some young people who get into terrible trouble at
school become completely different on leaving and develop into worthy citizens.
It is usually because certain social and educational situations or contexts
challenge a young person's personal resources so severely that they revert to
behaviour that is unregulated, or 'reflex activity' or feedback loops involved in
learning (see Figure 4.2).

Many young people who have themselves experienced difficult and traumatic
childhood events, or simply not experienced the expectations of school, will
have diminished resources for coping with the academic, social and emotional
demands of school. Others may be disengaged from or disaffected with the
education system to such an extent that they deliberately develop self-regulatory
mechanisms and a set of constructs and beliefs that put them into conflict
with schools, professionals and authority. Whether this is some deep-seated
malaise and internalised permanent 'anger' or whether it is simply a form of self-
expression (as in 'behavioural graffiti') is debatable. It is not always necessary
to pursue an emotional excavation into a young person's personality or to
'control' them through fear, drugs or radical personality change. Therapeutic
education in terms of this book implies engaging in a holistic process of
providing a safe and secure environment in which a young person can develop
their own self-regulatory mechanisms and develop a relationship with the social
environment, with others in their vicinity and with the learning materials
available.

Central to these intentions is the notion of 'self-belief'. The mechanisms of
personal agency are dependent on and integral to a young person's beliefs in
their capability to exercise some measure of control over their own functioning
and over environmental events (Bandura, 1997). The self-belief that exists in a
person is the foundation of their ability to take positive action. Many young
people have given up trying to influence events in their lives by positive means,

and some have given up trying to have any influence on anything. Others maintain some sense of self-belief by having a negative influence on events and people around them. Often these actions set up further conflicts within a young person, who may resent themselves for their own actions but be unable to regulate themselves. These beliefs influence whether a young person will think gloomily and cynically or confidently and hopefully and in ways that are self-enhancing or self-hindering. Self-belief and associated beliefs in one's own efficacy play a central role in reducing vulnerability to aggravation, stress or depression in taxing situations, and strengthen resiliency to adversity. Therapeutic education focuses on relationships and the social influences operating in selected environments to continue to promote certain competencies, values and interests long after the young person has made a decision to change the way they behave or about their own personal set of values. A central tenet of this approach is that a young person must have some means of choosing and shaping the environments they experience, and can therefore have a hand in what they become in the future.

Discrimination and identity: self-worth and self-development

The rapid pace of informational, social and technological change is placing a premium on personal efficacy for self-development throughout the course of a young person's life. In the past, a young person's educational development was largely determined by the schools to which they were assigned, and their social development was largely influenced by their immediate family. Nowadays, the Internet provides vast opportunities for students to control their own learning, and the range of media output encourages young people to develop attitudes and beliefs that are completely different from those of their elders in the family or even from those of their peers. In the Western world, young people now have encyclopedias, libraries, museums, laboratories and instructors at their fingertips, unrestricted by time and place. Good self-regulators expand their knowledge and cognitive competencies; poor self-regulators fall behind (Zimmerman, 1990). Great emphasis is placed in this book on self-regulation as a key factor in both educational and occupational life. The case study of a school that occupies much of the subsequent chapters has self-regulation as a key factor in the aims of behavioural approaches, as well as dealing with the thinking (cognitive and perceptual), social and emotional aspects of a young person's life. Young people in modern Western society have to be able to cope with rapid transformations; they have to be adaptable and be able to tune in to the demands of a fast pace of occupational, social and environmental change.

A young person's health is heavily influenced by lifestyle habits and environmental conditions. Many young people who have a reduced ability to self-regulate will experience poor health and in some cases develop drug habits simply because they were led into drug taking. The ability to self-regulate through self-management of health habits will reduce major health risks and enable people to live healthier and more productive lives (Bandura, 1997).

Nevertheless, it is possible to develop or destroy a young person's belief in their own capability by placing them in an environment in which they cannot cope. A good example of this is given by Bannister (2002: 21) in describing how physical abuse of a young child in the home can completely undermine self-belief and lead to problems of identity:

> Problems with attachments may also lead to difficulties with identity. . . . Children form their identity in relation to that of their parents or carers. If such carers are abusive or neglectful the child will form a scenario in which he or she is necessarily 'bad' because the carers cannot be other than 'good', since they provide whatever nurture or shelter is given. This self view is frequently reinforced by abusive parents.

While discrimination is generally thought of as excluding a person from opportunity and labelling an individual according to the characteristics of a (usually derided) group, there is a reverse discrimination that deliberately places a person in an environment or a circumstance in which they will fail miserably, with consequent damage to their self-belief. Furthermore, modern schooling (and current trends in modern society) does not really develop self-regulation; it seems to favour more imposed regulation to make better, more social human beings and a more equitable society. Schooling in the state sector is based not around an ideal of self-development but rather around an ideal of regulated learning along narrow curricular lines to make the young person 'fit in' to a social template that has already been forged. This template is full of assumed social norms and expectations that may well be undetectable by those who have grown up without them and who are unaware of alternatives. The kinds of norms, expectations and aspirations that are imposed on young people in their education may only become apparent once exposure to alternatives has occurred. Only then is it likely that young people experiencing negative reflections of their identity through academic failure or boredom at school, or through a massive discrepancy between their family experience and upbringing and social expectations in school, will acquire the confidence to challenge them in an appropriate and successful manner. Measures to tackle social exclusion may in fact be measures to coerce conformity, strengthening the dominance of already dominant priorities (Witcher, 2003). In other words, is it a prerequisite of inclusion in educational opportunity that a young person behaves in the way that a particular school designates as appropriate or social? In the authors' region, there is a trend of young people opting out of state-run secondary schools and into further education colleges well before their statutory school leaving age of 16 years. A significant proportion of these young people find it much easier to learn in the more relaxed and adult environment of college than they did at their secondary school.

The persistent exclusion of people with particular personal characteristics can lead to the birth of movements based on those personal characteristics, such as the women's, black or disability movements. In the case of vulnerable and challenging young people, it can lead to movements and subcultures, some of which are rather counter-productive and many of which are on the Internet. Young people who are excluded from school (or who feel like outsiders at school) may be impelled to develop oppositional counter-cultures. In some cases, exclusion from one community can automatically bring inclusion into another. Even those whom society purposefully excludes through imprisonment may be part of a community, with a hierarchy, behavioural norms and status symbols (Witcher, 2003). Witcher goes further, to express the idea of exclusion as discrimination due to a misconstrual of a person's identity. Identity is multidimensional and results from a range of influences from early family life through to value judgements about a person's 'worth' to society or community. Young people in trouble are often considered worthless renegades by the gutter press and by those who have no time for rehabilitative philosophies. Schools may easily come to regard a young person as 'worthless' (to the school) because their behaviour is affecting both other students and the school's success statistics. A parent may come to regard their offspring as 'worthless' because they are generating negative responses from friends, neighbours, school and perhaps authority figures. A young person may come to consider themselves as 'worthless' because either they are unsuccessful in academic or social terms, or school has become psychologically difficult for them and they can no longer sustain their place in the group or maintain a focus on educational goals.

There has long been debate about the mechanisms of exclusion in the relationship between an individual's disposition and behaviour at school, as opposed to the failure of school and society to provide an organised, encouraging, safe and secure learning-oriented environment. Recent times (i.e. since the late 1980s) have seen an increase in concern about young people's behaviour and particularly that of those in the teenage years but also of the general disaffection with education and the rise in the exclusion of young people from mainstream schooling. For some young people, exclusion from school is directly a matter of identity. The impact of being excluded from school along with the persistent exclusion from education of young people with shared characteristics can engender factions or counter-cultures. Young people who are having difficulty with education struggle to reprioritise or reframe social transactions in order to achieve recognition of their own personal human currency (Witcher, 2003). They attempt to redefine their social standing in such a way as to be within their grasp, hence also 'teen' subcultures. They may also be encouraged into disaffected attitudes generated by external events, or by institutions at different societal levels by over-regulation and authoritarian approaches. Within subcultures (such as teenage subcultures) the social standing and the image a young person projects also serve as indicators of identity. Objectives and norms based on current assumptions about social identity and acceptability also impact on how identity is construed, or misconstrued, in the transactional processes of education – or 'knowledge transfer', as it is currently labelled. Marion Bennathan points out that 'until schools are confidently in control of most of their pupils it is almost impossible to tell a child with real emotional and behavioural difficulties from a child who could behave well if s/he chose' (1998: 2). This and other literature going back a long way (e.g. Phillips and Jones, 1983) epitomise the different perceptions of the exclusionary process and the way that young people who are at risk are treated. One thing is pretty certain, though: whatever the outcomes and whatever the experience of the young person at home or at school, it will have an impact on that person's identity, and in turn this will affect their self-belief, their feelings of agency and their will or need to self-regulate, and so on.

Vulnerability and resilience, key factors in personal growth and learning

It is now time to challenge the notion that early childhood stressful and traumatic experiences always lead to vulnerable and unfavourable life courses and that a young person growing up in economic and social disadvantage is necessarily condemned to remain locked into an ill-fated destiny. The positive approaches and intentions outlined in this book are based as much on the ideas encapsulated in 'positive psychology' (Seligman and Csikszentmihalyi, 2000) as on the deficit models of current empirically based treatments, clinical psychology and medical practices that impact on education. There has been a questioning of empirically based evidence, which is usually focused on the negative aspects of health and deficit models of disability over the past twenty years. These stem from a turning-point study by Werner and Smith in 1982 (cited in Chess and Thomas, 1992: 79) in which a large group of Hawaiian children exposed to poverty, family instability and biological risks were studied. It was noticed that while many developed learning and behaviour difficulties, others who experienced the same environment developed into competent, happy and autonomous adults. While this was probably no surprise to most people who have a balanced view of life and accept the idiosyncratic nature of individuals, it raised many difficult questions for scientists and practitioners immersed in negative empirical models of illness and treatment. This positive view or psychology may also account in part for the success of many alternative and 'psycho' therapies that look beyond the victim, the underdog and the remedial (Seligman, 2001). Martin Seligman further suggests that the time is finally right to recognize that positive psychology is not a new idea. It has many distinguished ancestors who somehow failed to attract a cumulative and empirical body of research to ground their ideas, which challenge the authenticity of a purely negative perception. The research of Chess and Thomas (1992) and others forms part of the original evidence base of some of the guidance offered by the DfEE (2001), which later in the book is adapted and developed in Table 9.2.

Working with young people who are vulnerable and challenging requires a significant degree of optimism not only based on a humanitarian attitude but also supported by recognising change. It is also important to maintain the belief that there is always the possibility of an individual changing and developing more useful and effective capabilities and personal characteristics. This is not in the context of any normative or empirically measurable agenda; it is simply that individuals, albeit in sometimes quite extreme difficulty, will grow and learn in order to find a place for themselves in the world. The resilience factor shows quite clearly that simplistic and mechanical approaches to understanding and working with vulnerable and challenging young people fly in the face of both common sense and the evidence of idiosyncratic and individualistic response to all life circumstances. It is an optimistic and humanistic pursuit which requires a significant degree of flexibility and adaptability, as well as very good interpersonal and social skills. In Chapter 1 we were concerned with 'the human face' of this area of work, so it should also be said that a great deal of patience and persistence is required and that sometimes professionals who work in this area do become frustrated and would often like to revert to more simplistic, less effective and often more brutal forms of interaction with young people who challenge them daily. It is not a soft option and requires considerable resilience in the adults who are trying to support and teach young people immersed in their own difficulties.

Training and in-service education for teachers in the United Kingdom and the provision of education for excluded and 'at risk' youngsters are in a lamentable, fragmented state, where diversity, instead of providing a creative web of interesting ideas, is producing very variable practices and provision. In the United States there is a wide range of provision (from bare minimum to extremely comprehensive), too. This variability is largely due to socio-economic factors, where the ability to pay and where you live have a great impact on provision available (Salzman, 2005).

All children, in some sense, are at risk of developing mental health problems, but certain groups have been identified as being more at risk than others. Any development of the 'at risk' ideology must be discussed with a heavy health warning about the balance of 'resilience' factors, the acknowledgement that genetic determinants do not override environmental considerations and limit potential (Rutter, 1992), and that even when these factors are present, with support to develop self-efficacy and self-reflection, change is always possible.

The question remains as to how the conceptualisation of 'resilience', 'self-efficacy', 'positive behaviour management' and a 'holistic approach' within therapeutic environments will be of practical help in working with young people who are challenging and vulnerable. Can a set of evidence bases be brought together to provide at least a foundation for appropriate and successful approaches to the difficulties that some young people face in getting an education? It is quite clear that past, and many lingering current, approaches to behaviour and attendance at school have been problematic and have not produced the results that are being sought, as is clearly outlined in the preceding chapters. In this chapter the dichotomies of educational responses to young people have been aired, as well as the fact that social and educational policy and practices in schools also contribute to the slowly increasing numbers of young people excluded and to the general concern over disaffection and disruption in schools. For those who have been excluded or are at risk there is the challenge of developing more evidence-based practice, rather than knee-jerk or politically expedient reactions. Probably this new practice will be based on the kind of work that professionals in this field have been doing for many years but which has had little recognition within education particularly, despite being based on far sounder evidence than much of the practice currently found in schools.

This chapter has set out to raise questions about discrimination and identity in order to make the social context of educating vulnerable and challenging young people a viable factor in work with such young people, with all the implications of multi-agency collaboration, which is still very problematic in practice, if not in theory. The conceptualisation of positive psychology and positive therapy, and the challenging notions of 'resilience' in contrast to vulnerability, are extremely important as a sound basis for humanistic practices. The concept of human agency applies as much to adults and professionals working in a subculture defined by society's exclusive practices as it does to young people. Individuals need to feel that what they do and what they are have some importance for, and impact on, the social and educational context in which they are situated. So, the theories of self-efficacy and human agency, including social, moral and emotional agency, are developed as a sound evidence base for practices that go well beyond simplistic behaviour modification but stop far short of brain manipulation (through drugs, or conditioning through fear). In short, the aim has been to cultivate an ethical and principled base for working with young people who are vulnerable and challenging at the same time. In subsequent chapters our intentions are to further construct practices that revolve around this ethical and principled base, and put more detail on practical considerations and on the practice itself, from a variety of viewpoints.

Chapter 5

A curriculum for life?

Throughout this chapter readers' attention is drawn to the appendices, which reflect the practical tools that have been developed in the education setting to be described in Chapter 6. This chapter questions the need to look for 'alternatives' in education when these very alternatives should be an integral part of the educational experience available to all in schools or as part of pupils' educational experience. It is an exclusive philosophy that is prepared to accept mainstream school as it is and recommend that 'alternative' or 'hidden' curricula remain hidden or in the privacy of the family. Modern society demands a range of interpersonal skills and self-regulation that far exceeds that expected in less complex technical societies. One has only to look at the plight of many senior citizens trying to deal with complex technology or busy road systems. The quality of life has also changed, and occupations generally have become more emotionally and intellectually demanding. Schools cannot ignore these developments and remain locked into a traditionalist and retrogressive view of the school curriculum. It is bad enough that the current subject base of education harks back to the second half of the previous millennium and is not at all current in our modern (postmodern) society. There are no 'alternatives' to life itself, and the problems of young people in education have to be met head on – not demeaned or diminished by pathogenic assessments, socially inept policy making or uncreative and restricted teaching approaches.

Regulations imposed on teachers and school cultures often end up producing discriminatory practices in regular and alternative teaching and learning situations. Lifelong learning is a phrase bandied around but not necessarily incorporated or enacted in many secondary schools, whose ethics revolve mainly around surviving the next OfSTED inspection and maintaining a place on the national school league tables. Education continues to be part of a limited and competitive industrial and economic treadmill where young people are too often treated as commodities in the system, providing a substrate for teaching practices and statistics for the government. Working with social, emotional and behavioural development in a curriculum that includes personal growth, learning to learn and life skills is an interactive or integrated curriculum, not a set of bolt-on additives instead of a curriculum. In this chapter we propose not an alternative curriculum but an enhanced curriculum on the basis of the evidence mounted in previous chapters and the case study proffered in subsequent chapters.

The book is not primarily intended to be a handbook of practice. Nevertheless, the appendices contain a 'toolbox' for teachers and managers who work with troubled and troublesome young people. For example, the table in Appendix 1 derives from the McGuiness (1993) model in Chapter 2. It is intended as an examination of the links between theory, principles and examining practice in special education for challenging and vulnerable young people. It does this through the 'lens' of a case study which exemplifies a particular set of practices and has generated the practical 'toolbox' in Appendices 1–11. We intend that this will, at the very least, provide a model that can be scrutinised, used and questioned by others.

Therapeutic education and behavioural, emotional and social development (BESD)

'Therapeutic' derives from the term 'therapeutics', a branch of medicine concerned with the treatment of disease and the action of remedial agents. Its two literal meanings are as follows:

> of, for, or contributing to the cure of disease

and

> contributing to general, especially mental well-being.
> (*Oxford English Dictionary*, 1996)

The second of these definitions is certainly the more appropriate for the purpose of the case study around which this book revolves but also provides but a small clue as to the nature or extent of the term as it applies to education. Tierney (2001) explains that whereas education exists to resource the spiritual, social, emotional, physical and academic potential of each child, therapeutic education focuses specifically on significant unresolved social and emotional needs. The function of any provision to support these needs is therefore to resource emotional growth and social learning. The difficulty in pinpointing how therapeutic education operates may explain something about its nature. Perhaps it can only be defined in its broadest sense, because any attempt to be more specific would inappropriately limit the sheer range and scope of its application. Put simply, if therapeutic education is child centred and child led, then it follows that individual need dictates the response, and not the specific application of generic strategies.

Cornwall also commented on the importance of the teacher–learner relationship as the starting point for therapeutic education: 'Therapeutic Education is essentially about the teacher–learner relationship and the various ways it can be enhanced to improve engagement, motivation and learning for children who are experiencing emotional and behavioural difficulties' (2004: 5). This approach stems from the authors' belief that the teacher must also be prepared to change their behaviour and remain flexible in their approach before the learner will change theirs (see Appendix 2).

Consequently, a learning environment that is inspirational, motivating, enjoyable and inclusive could be deemed therapeutic. Bull (1995), like us, regards a positive learning environment as being of great importance but would not necessarily judge such an environment to be therapeutic, simply a reflection of good teaching. Indeed, most teachers are likely to recognise the fundamental ingredients that make a good lesson but would probably question how far this extends towards a therapeutic environment or relationship. Laslett (1977) refers to the beliefs and practice of people who supported 'maladjusted children' in a 'therapeutic' setting (before the Education Act 1981 redefined the user terms) and identifies a number of key approaches that underpinned the treatment of such children. These include:

- the primacy of fostering sound affective relationships with children;
- placing little reliance upon punishment;
- understanding the value of reparation and restitution;
- children's participation in school organisation and management;
- cooperation with other professionals;
- staff's intuitive approach and particular means of communication;
- provision of appropriate learning opportunities.

These points certainly provide greater insight as to the possible ingredients of a therapeutic approach in a school and have been echoed in more recent literature. A closer look also reveals them to be very topical and not out of place in current thinking (e.g. *Every Child Matters*). If one considers that they are based upon sound theoretical principles and remain prevalent in special schools, then this cause is unlikely to have been helped by an ever-tightening inflexibility in the education system itself. Tierney (2001: 37) comments on the plight of young people as a result of a narrowing of educational perspectives over a number of years: 'Therapeutic Education for children with severe emotional difficulties has collapsed and there is confusion in special schools for children with less intensive emotional and behavioural difficulties.' In an educational climate that is heavily driven by pupil performance and academic attainment, one might be sympathetic to the special school that has redirected attention from less tangible or measurable aspects of its work to focus greater attention on the more easily recognised 'content' curriculum. Since its conception, the main thrust of OfSTED has been to ensure every school's ability to deliver the National Curriculum. Given the intensity in which most inspections are executed and the strict criteria upon which they have measured performance, it is naturally going to be difficult to explore, understand and assess aspects of school provision that are effectively outside their remit (e.g. some areas shown in Appendix 1). So in this case, not only do the therapeutic approaches described in this book need to be upheld (and potential consequences avoided), but there must also be sufficient credence given to aspects of the established content curriculum. Ironically, it appears that the right balance of ingredients in these special schools is as important to their success as a balance of focuses is to the inspectors who hold judgement over them.

From this standpoint two further tasks emerge. The first is to examine in more detail what these ingredients might consist of, and the second is to clearly identify the appropriate balance of those ingredients. Cornwall (2004) explored the potential of a suitable link for this by focusing on the humanistic perspective to education as opposed to the hard-edge 'boot camp', disciplinarian approach to teaching. He identified some more specific ingredients of therapeutic education that begin to expose a different dimension to the traditional teacher–pupil relationship. The focus is very clearly on the pupil through valuing their views and giving them responsibility for their own learning, and recognises that effective teaching starts from 'where the learner is'. It deals with the curriculum by integrating and complementing content and makes explicit what skills are needed in order to grow and learn. Assertive strategies and skilled teaching are used to avert any undue conflict and stress, thus allowing teacher and pupil to engage successfully and with confidence. On an organisational level the proactive and pro-social management of the school depends upon a whole school or team approach. This is exemplified by strategies developed and illustrated in Appendix 3, 'Proactive and pro-social management of behaviour'.

Developing therapeutic relationships in learning and teaching

The emphasis is on the work being child centred and child led, thus allowing for individual expression and attention, then using this output to work with and shape. It is an approach that is essentially intent on healing or making space for self-expression, and gives time for understanding the problem as far as possible to achieve solutions. In the case-study school, it is a fully 'hands on' process by the staff, offered on an individual basis or within small groups. The work is sometimes 'objectified' with targets (e.g. art therapy or music therapy) and challenges existing conditions, habits, responses or circumstances (this is exemplified in Appendix 4, 'The points system'). The singular notion of 'therapy', therefore, may expose a side of education that few contemporary or purist practitioners would want to reveal, much less explore. One significant reason for this may lie in 'therapy' being almost devoid of 'performance' or 'outcomes' in the quantitative sense. The client is guided towards a resolution through interaction with the therapist. A resolution might be arrived at in terms of physical or mental healing or achieving different perspectives on an issue or situation. For a teacher whose job is built around structures, timetables and other external constraints, the inevitable conflict looms threateningly on the horizon of timetabling and performance measurement.

It therefore follows that to ensure effective interaction and develop an appropriate therapeutic relationship necessarily requires the further empowerment of the child, and the teacher's further relinquishment of 'control' in the traditional sense. 'A therapeutic relationship between a carer and troubled individual is an alliance based upon equality and mutual respect. It is also based upon unconditional positive regard for the individual' (Zarkowska and Clements, 1996: 13).

It would seem, then, that some elements of therapy and education are entwined. Other aspects may require an adjustment in teaching approach and style and a broadened view about how behaviour can be managed. At the heart of therapeutic education there seems to be situated an intuitive recognition of individual needs and a balance of priorities. This is best summarised in Goddard's (1996) 'Interlinked curriculum' model (Figure 5.1), which successfully abuts the key areas of individual development that therapeutic education is based upon. We have adapted this curriculum model proposed by Del Goddard (1996) in the context of 'lifelong learning'. It is composed of four 'interlinked' aspects:

1   *Personal growth curriculum*, including such things as self-esteem and confidence building;
2   *Life skills curriculum*, including creative problem solving and self-management;
3   *Learning-to-learn curriculum*, so learning can be motivating and fun-filled, e.g. organisation skills, study skills;
4   *Content and National Curriculum*, generally with integrated themes or themes within subjects and built upon previous levels.

This model seems to have distinct parallels with Dilt's (O'Connor and Seymour, 1990: 89) 'unified field theory', which demonstrates that emotions and feelings

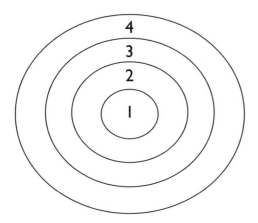

Figure 5.1 Goddard's 'interlinked four-part curriculum' model. (Source: Goddard, 1996.)

are inextricably tied to the process of learning. It also illustrates the power of dealing with cognitive (thinking) and affective (feeling) aspects of learning rather than just the external behavioural outcomes – the power that a young person will have to change themselves and engage with their own personal growth rather than be passive recipients of managed and limited specific behavioural changes. This is reflected in the overview of the 'interactive curriculum' model at Westwood School (Figure 5.2).

The interlinked curriculum explains that teaching is a multidimensional activity of which the National Curriculum (NC) is an integral (not an isolated) component. Areas of personal growth remain at the core of the model, surrounded by concentric areas of life skills, learning to learn, and finally the content curriculum (NC). This model acknowledges that effective teaching and learning comes about through the planned focus on the 'inner' dimensions of the model before any substantial or sustained progress can be made on the outer 'content'. This is still a notion contested by those who cling to the National Curriculum as a traditional framework for learning or as an entitlement and a measure of social currency. By identifying and working on specific areas of focus through therapeutic intervention, it is more likely that the young people will be able to access and engage in subject-specific aspects successfully. Conversely, it is contended that the more effective the formal subject teaching, the more intrinsic impact this will have on the 'inner' areas such as self-esteem, healthy relationships and positive attitudes to learning.

Inherent in the arguments is the implication that strategies and interventions that seek to make a difference to the quality of educational experience for troubled and troublesome children within a special school environment can be regarded as therapeutic. The interventions to support learning discussed in this

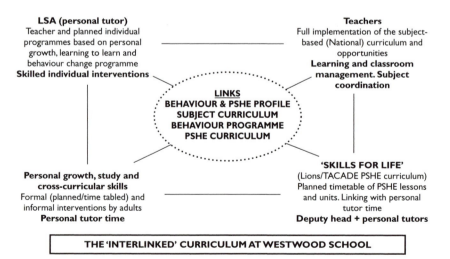

Figure 5.2 The interactive curriculum model at Westwood School.

context also encompass four known theoretical perspectives (Ayers *et al.*, 1995). Therapeutic education is an eclectic and ecumenical activity. Because it centres on the young person and their progress, it is of necessity adaptable and inclusive of a wide range of useful theoretical underpinnings and evidence bases. The behaviourist models focus on overt, observable and measurable behaviours and their reinforcement, being principally based on the work of Pavlov (classical conditioning theory) and Skinner (operant conditioning theory). Cognitive models focus on personal perceptions, attitudes, images, attributions, expectations and beliefs that account for behaviour. Ecosystemic models are based on 'systems theory' (Bertalanffy, 1950, 1969) and focus on positive and negative interactions between different internal and external systems. Lastly, psychodynamic models tend to focus on emotional aspects and perceptions of the person which may be unconscious in origin, explained through the psychoanalytical work of Freud (ego defences and transference or counter-transference), Klein (unconscious fantasy) and Bowlby (effects of attachment and loss).

Previous chapters have explored the related work of Bandura, who has developed a social learning perspective to explain the idea that behavioural, cognitive and ecosystemic theories are interlinked and influence each other. They call this 'reciprocal determinism'. This conceptual grouping is supported by Zarkowska and Clements (1996), who explain that psychological perspectives that were once thought to be incompatible and mutually exclusive are now being considered in more holistic terms on the basis that human behaviour is far too complex to be viewed in any singular way. 'Each perspective – the conscious mind, subjective experience, unconscious processes, environmental influence and the quality of relationships has something to offer in relation to our understanding of people who experience coping difficulties' (Zarkowska and Clements, 1996: 7). This is an appropriate standpoint for the purposes of explaining how therapeutic education can be an umbrella term encompassing whatever works, and it is further reinforced by the practical reality of the school case-study research that follows. The strategies and interventions explored in this section are not necessarily limited or confined to one perspective alone.

Are we making a difference? The nature and scope of BESD provision

Every school boasts its own special characteristics, expertise and operational tools for supporting children with different abilities and needs. A child who experiences severe learning difficulties is likely to need a more specialist setting, and hence the 'special' characteristics and features of that school will be more extensive and diverse in nature so as to have a sustained impact on the child's education. 'The aim is to offer a structured and logical framework within which emotional and behavioural difficulties can be understood and assessed; a framework from which appropriate therapeutic interventions can be systematically planned and implemented' (Zarkowska and Clements, 1996: 8).

Tierney (2001: 37) offers further insight into the conditions in which therapeutic education can exist and the nature of the provision: 'The conditions which
enable such development include protection, control, consistency, acceptance,
guidance and insight within the context of long term relationships with adults'.
He suggests that in a practical context, schools would need to create a flexible
approach to the curriculum, with class groups based upon dynamics rather
than age, and allowing sufficient time with key staff to permit good relations
to develop. The restriction on pupil roll would ensure that children could be
managed without the need to resort to punitive sanctions or behaviourist systems
of control. However, Tierney qualifies these comments by suggesting that schools
that are structured to resource the full range of the academic curriculum would
be unable to sustain the type of conditions advocated above. Clearly, to make an
impact on the education of troubled and troublesome children, environmental
factors, operational conditions and organisational structures all affect the possibility of being able to offer differentiated and individualised support. Indeed, it
may be that the very concept of differentiation is at the heart of a school's ability
to offer therapeutic provision. Over recent times there has been an abundance
of professional literature and debate over the subject and its application within
both mainstream schools and special schools. The National Curriculum Council
(1990; quoted in Weston, 1992) in a previous incarnation defines differentiation
as 'a set of judgements and procedures whose purpose is to accommodate
differences in children's abilities, aptitudes and needs'.

Although the approach is generally accepted as effective in ensuring equal
access to the content curriculum, given a child's individual level of understanding
and ability, it is by no means the only viewpoint. Some would argue that differentiation is a negative process that implicitly devalues the child and perpetuates
inequalities (Lindsay & Thompson, 1997). On these grounds the very notion of
'special education' is controversial. Consequently, this subject will be pursued in
the belief that difference is a positive means of recognising what is relevant to
an individual's learning and development needs (Norwich, 1994, cited in Lindsay
and Thompson, 1997). Differentiation demands considerable effort from the
school both on a curriculum planning level and in terms of preparation within
theclassroom. Stratling and Saunders (1991; cited in Weston, 1992) make distinct
the idea of 'differentiation between groups' as opposed to 'differentiation between
individuals'. On an organisational level a school will establish methods of
grouping pupils to ensure that optimum learning takes place. At an operational
level a teacher will need to determine what concepts, skills or knowledge to
introduce and how best to introduce them so they are most easily understood
by all members of the group. In practice this might require a variation in teaching
style, setting alternative learning objectives, gearing tasks and exercises according
to need, using extra resources or supplying additional help and support. There
may also need to be a greater awareness of how each individual pupil interprets
processes and expectations (self or otherwise), and uses this information to
achieve an end result.

Every pupil presents unique personal qualities and potential for learning. Since the teacher will develop individual relationships and respond differently to each pupil, then it follows that it would be very difficult not to see differentiation occurring at some level, either consciously or unconsciously. However, it is clear that without an awareness of how this impacts on the individual pupil or group there is no way of ascertaining its effectiveness. Falconer-Hall (1992) explains the importance of knowing the pupils for effective differentiation to take place and goes on to identify some key considerations. These include the knowledge, skills and abilities pupils bring to the task, their hearing, sight and possible physical impairments, the language understood by pupils and, perhaps most significantly, pupils' feelings, motivation and emotional needs. These considerations, while being wholly appropriate, may also offer some insight into a more extensive use of differentiation techniques. Pupils in special schools are more likely to experience the benefits of curriculum differentiation because of the nature of the provision, the teaching arrangements and the expertise of the staff. Group sizes that are considerably smaller than in the average mainstream class, coupled with increased staffing levels, are conducive to a more individual approach to the curriculum and school life in general. Yet for all the effort that has been placed upon differentiating the curriculum to match a child's learning needs, the idea of using the differentiation model as a basis for managing a child's emotional, behavioural and social difficulties is less clear or accepted. However, there are obvious comparisons; for example, one might argue that an adjustment in teaching style or approach in the classroom could apply to helping a child understand a concept better, but it could also be used to focus a child's attention. Equally, one could conclude that the following definitions of differentiation, taken from National Curriculum Council (1989) as quoted in Weston, 1992, could apply to a whole range of interventions geared to supporting individual needs:

> A positive approach to enhancing children's learning by adapting the total learning experience to the needs of the child.

and

> The process of identifying, with each learner, the most effective strategies for achieving targets.

In this way, differentiation could be seen as a vehicle through which a special school environment is adjusted and shaped. This applies not only to the curriculum but also to the physical environment, organisation, culture, people (attitudes, values and beliefs), behaviour programmes and interventions. It may also serve to highlight an essential difference between mainstream and special provision. In order to 'shape' an environment in this context, a school must adopt the notion of 'positive behaviour support' (OMRDD, 1998). The rationale upon which this type of support is based includes:

- a non-aversive approach to behaviour management and behaviour change;
- minimal use of negative consequences and punishments;
- a focus on teaching functional skills to eliminate the need for negative behaviour;
- a multi-element approach involving several interventions implemented simultaneously.

Behaviour management and therapeutic strategies that stem from this approach will bear some common features such as being proactive in nature, being defined by the needs of the individual, including activities that will enhance the individual's quality of life, enabling the individual to experience success and generally bringing about significant lifestyle changes. Such strategies can be very difficult for staff who rely on the security and comfort of clear boundaries, rules, expectations and consequences in order to engage the pupils with any degree of confidence. Zarkowska and Clements (1996) identify some interesting components of a therapeutic package that acknowledge the features described above. For example, a way to encourage the absence of inappropriate behaviour and promote appropriate behaviours is the use of a simple reward system, which can be surprisingly effective if implemented in a suitably differentiated way. Praise, public acknowledgement, tokens, gifts and privileges are all commonplace in many schools. However, unless the school recognises individual preferences and needs, a reward system may not actually offer any incentive to the children at all.

Comprehensive assessment of behaviours and events that identify 'setting conditions' (physical, social and occupational climate), 'triggers' (stimuli that set off actions), 'actions' (observable behaviours) and 'results' (events that follow) is a proven and proactive means of support. The 'STAR' approach as advocated by Zarkowska and Clements (1996) is a form of 'functional analysis' that focuses on specific problems presented, factors involved and planning for appropriate responses and interventions to manage the behaviour. Entwined within this model is the idea of reshaping the environment in order to reduce generalised anxiety or stress. This can be done in a number of ways, including changes to the physical or social environment, providing more personal space, or adjusting structures, routines and schedules. It can also be achieved by exploring attitudes, values and beliefs among the staff team to ensure that there is consistency in approach to positive behaviour support, and that therapeutic relationships are being cultivated. Sound therapeutic relationships between staff and pupils are complex yet critical in enabling the pupil to come to terms with and take responsibility for their behaviour. The relationship requires *respect* (for the individual and their preferences and opinions), *warmth* (a genuine interest in the child's feelings and thoughts) and *unconditional positive regard* (acceptance of the individual whatever they may do, say or feel).

It should be reiterated here that unconditional positive regard does not mean allowing a young person to behave as they please, to take advantage of others or to abuse others in any way. All too often, professionals' and even researchers' thinking is unnecessarily and uncritically polarised on this subject. It is crucial that professionals understand that it is possible to have unconditional positive regard, while at the same time drawing clear boundaries about behaviour and expecting a young person to take the consequences of their actions, both positive and negative. However, the difference lies in working through those consequences *with* the young person, not just relying on the consequences alone to do the job. This is the basis upon which children can be encouraged to set goals for themselves, monitor their own actions, take control of triggers that set off inappropriate behaviour, use strategies to reduce arousal and generally increase control over their own environment. OMRDD (1998) refers to this as a 'locus of control' that shifts between adult, carer or teacher and child. A number of behaviour programmes use 'life-space interviews' (see Appendix 5, section 2) as a structured means of problem solving on a one-to-one basis, re-establishing the 'locus of control' with the child and reaffirming the therapeutic relationship. The young person also begins to understand the value of 'reparation' and 'restitution' (Laslett, 1977), and to develop the social and interpersonal skills involved.

Teaching alternative skills to replace problematic behaviour, thus allowing the pupil to achieve the same needs, requires patience as well as thoughtful and sensitive planning by staff. Material on this subject is extensive and relates to two broad areas of intervention: those that are implemented in a precise and structured way, and those that are more natural and incidental (Zarkowska and Clements, 1996). Regarding the latter, Long and Fogell (1999: 92, 93) summarise the basic categories of some of these techniques, which include:

- modelling (relating to others' appropriate behaviour);
- social skills training (rehearsing social and conversational skills);
- relaxation (breathing, calming exercises);
- self-cueing (conditions that trigger a more appropriate response);
- self-reinforcement (providing positive outcomes for appropriate behaviour).

More formal interventions include 'anger management group work' (Sharp, 2001: 56), 'solution-focused brief therapy' (Rhodes and Ajmal, 1995, cited in Long and Fogell, 1999) and specialist counselling.

Nevertheless, an interactive approach to the curriculum does not undervalue the important part that many aspects of the formal or content curriculum also play in this area. Over recent years, schools that have focused their efforts on children's behavioural, emotional and social development have been limited to what has been fondly described as 'the hidden curriculum'. However, there is now considerable flexibility and scope in the timetable to explore more person-centred development. Vocational studies, work experience and careers education have all grown in profile and popularity. A steady increase of generic personal, social and health education (PSHE) materials are available to offer consistency and progression to what has traditionally been seen as an appendage to the National Curriculum. All subjects have the innate capacity to develop appropriate social skills and coping skills, and also to engender self-confidence, self-esteem, personal satisfaction and a sense of achievement. Nonetheless, without focus or overt planning, any growth in these areas becomes reliant on luck rather than judgement.

Finally, removing or altering results achieved by inappropriate behaviour through the use of 'pro-active, active and re-active interventions' (OMRDD, 1998) remains essential and central to the operational practice of staff working alongside troubled and troublesome children.

- Proactive interventions are those that address children's needs and problems before they arise (through analysis, planning, etc.).
- Active interventions are used when there are signs of stress, anger, etc. (calming techniques).
- Reactive interventions are used when a behaviour has occurred (reprimands, sanctions, physical interventions).

Specific behaviour programmes aimed at meeting the needs of troubled and troublesome young people operate in a whole range of establishments and sectors, including health authorities, residential units and special schools. Some of these packages appear to offer a therapeutic approach to behaviour management. TCI (Therapeutic Crisis Intervention), TEAM TEACH (Techniques that are Effective with Aggression Management utilising Therapeutic, Educational Awareness, Communication, Handling strategies) and SCIP (Strategies for Crisis Intervention and Prevention) programmes are used widely and advocate some common features of a therapeutic approach. These include a safe and secure environment, good adult role models, relationships based upon trust and respect, an understanding and acceptance of limits, rewards and sanctions, and the opportunity for clients to talk and be listened to without being judged. These programmes also describe restrictive physical intervention techniques that claim to be used as part of a positive and therapeutic process (sometimes referred to as 'crisis as opportunity'). Certainly the principles listed above equate closely with those conditions and approaches described earlier. However, the use of restrictive physical intervention (RPI) techniques is a very contentious issue. By its very nature (controlling, use of force, power, etc.) it arguably constitutes a reactionary and hostile regime. Advocates of these strategies state that RPI is used only as a last resort, and this is mirrored in the DfES guidance (2002b). The contention is not always a black and white (should we use these techniques or not?), but also revolves around adults who are only partially trained in de-escalation and who precipitate conflict because they are unable to take preventive steps prior to conflict, and even use physical restraint as a disciplinary tool.

In addition, individual teachers who have not been sufficiently trained in the skills of avoiding 'precipitation' into a challenging response could well escalate situations unnecessarily (Cornwall, 2001). It takes many months or years of training and practice to effectively and safely use control and restraint techniques, and such lengthy training is neither desirable for teachers nor available to them. So, it is a half-measure in every respect, and its place in schools, and particularly mainstream schools, should be seriously questioned. In any event, this is an area that lacks proper evidential bases to support its application throughout the education system, and some of the above approaches have no research base or provenance that could qualify them as 'therapeutic'. 'The carer's ability to influence change is through credibility not formal power or physical strength. Carers may utilise a range of skills including listening, empathising, problem solving, information giving and skill teaching' (Zarkowska and Clements, 1996: 13). The BILD *Code of Practice* (2001) refers to the principle of using 'the least restrictive intervention and minimum use of force', but one suspects that this type of approach is seen by many to overshadow those more positive and proactive elements within the therapeutic toolkit.

How do we measure the quality of teaching and learning, quality of relationships and quality of life?

Now that we have identified the nature of therapeutic education, the nature of troubled and troublesome children, and some of the ways that a school might 'make a difference', this section draws these discussions together by exploring how one can measure the effectiveness and quality of this type of provision. The term 'Best Value' seems to be part of the common business language applied to the education system and the schools of today. As a government initiative launched in 2000 it aimed to ensure that local services were responsive to the needs of citizens and were efficient and of high quality, and that policy making was joined up, strategic and forward-thinking. Guidance for school inspections (DfES and OFSTED, 2002) qualified this further by identifying four principles of 'Best Value': it challenges existing practice; it compares a school's performance with that of other schools; it consults stakeholders; and it engages in competition with similar providers. All these elements should be woven into the school's management routines to secure continuous improvement. Lindsay and Thompson (1997) explain a similar measure of quality termed 'value added' and explain that this is a formula based upon the improvement made differentially by the school given the ability of the pupils on entry. Both terms are ways in which inspectors may report on school achievement.

'Best Value' and 'value added' can be measured in a number of ways, and therefore it is important to be clear as to how a therapeutic approach to education can contribute.

As a starting point, Stanley (1994) refers to the OfSTED criteria for measuring the quality of education through 'progress' (in knowledge, understanding and skills), 'learning' (including observation and information skills, deeper under-standing, communicating ideas, posing questions and solving problems, applying and evaluating what has been learned) and 'attitudes' (motivation, interest, and the ability to concentrate, cooperate and work productively). OfSTED criteria also refer to personal development and behaviour, covering 'spiritual development' (personal beliefs, reflection on experience and to search for meaning), 'moral development' (knowing right from wrong, respect for persons, truth and property, making reasoned and responsible judgements, etc.) and 'social development' (quality of relationships, exercising responsibility, and cooperative and productive participation in work).

All these areas of focus are key to the development of any school and therefore key to any monitoring and assessment process. The quality of teaching and learning, the quality of relationships and to some degree the quality of life for school children should all be reported on through formal monitoring and inspection mechanisms. However, Stanley also puts this in the context of a therapeutic arena:

> In supporting a child to make the greatest progress possible, to gain access to a broad, balanced curriculum we need to be able to do so keeping in mind the plan for each child. That plan needs to include an assessment of individual educational and emotional need that links to the ethos and sense of purpose found in the aims and objectives of the school.
>
> (1994: 39)

This idea was encapsulated and succinctly documented in the (now super-seded) Kent Education Authority Special Needs Audit. The audit was an ingenious method of assessing the nature and extent of a child's special educational needs in order to identify and resource appropriate provision across the mainstream–special school continuum. It was also able to measure and evaluate the effectiveness of such provision on an annual basis. The concept was 'ground-breaking' in the sense that up to the early 1990s, special educational needs (SEN) funding for UK schools had been largely determined by the economic demographics of the surrounding community (the number of pupils eligible for free school meals was used as an indicator of special educational needs!). The new system ensured that devolved funding to schools was more accurately targeted to make the greatest impact on the children who most needed it. The audit was effective in matching the type of school most likely to suit the child's needs (i.e. mainstream or special) and it went some way to determining the nature, scope and intensity of provision that might be needed within that particular setting. However, it was evident that the more specialised the setting, the less the audit was able to identify the precise operational char-acteristics of the school that would ultimately determine the success of the placement. This was particularly true of schools that specialised in dealing with children with behavioural, emotional and social difficulties. Moreover, the scales relating to the audit failed to detect the somewhat conflicting characteristics of a child who intellectually was quite bright, but displayed severely challenging behaviour. This left teachers in some confusion about the final audit level given to the child (he or she could be level 1 academically but level 5 behaviourally!). Ultimately, the audit procedure was abandoned, not least on ethical grounds, since it was seen by some to encourage schools to label pupils negatively in order to achieve greater funding. In fairness, the SEN audit, although not perfect, actually went a good way to fulfilling what it set out to achieve. In particular, it provided a neat link between the child's level of need and the DfES 'Code of Practice' statementing procedure that at the time was based upon a similar hierarchy of intervention.

There may have been a presumption that if the audit had been too prescriptive in its detail of the nature of provision, this might, in turn, have inhibited the school from developing its own unique characteristics and features. However, the characteristics and features that shape a special school are not so obscure that they are impossible to document or measure. Cole and Visser (1998) argue that effectiveness measures used in mainstream school inspections are applicable to special schools but with additional criteria added regarding the content curriculum, coupled with a greater emphasis on spiritual, moral, social and cultural dimensions. This seems a sound basis upon which to measure the quality of teaching and learning, quality of relationships and overall quality of life for troubled and troublesome children. The following quantifies these areas in order to identify the evidence needed to demonstrate effectiveness and the school's capacity to make a difference. In terms of the content curriculum, Bull (1994) makes it abundantly clear that the rigorous implementation of the National Curriculum is required in schools catering for troubled and troublesome children regardless of any therapeutic dimension the school also offers. She makes a strong case for

> accessing pupils with emotional and behavioural difficulties and disturbance to a curriculum which raises their standards of achievement; encourages a willingness in them to participate fully in the educational process, and provides opportunities for them to gain cumulative accreditation for their work in a way which will enhance their life chances.

We would temper this view somewhat by suggesting that the broad National Curriculum needs to be adjusted to be meaningful and relevant to pupils who are socially immature or have differing abilities. 'Access' in this context is a loaded word, full of assumptions and not clearly defined in the context of pupils with social, emotional and behavioural difficulties. We would also point out that a key element of the work with disaffected young people is actually getting them to 'buy in' to the personal currency that the National Curriculum is supposed to represent. For some young people, the National Curriculum is not seen as a passport to anything at all, or as desirable social currency. In short, Bull is making all kinds of assumptions that the National Curriculum, in its entirety, is both an achievable and a desirable goal for everyone.

Lund (1991) identifies some key lesson ingredients of particular importance when dealing with troubled and troublesome children that include using achievable tasks through stimulating material, a variety of learning experience, offering practical 'hands-on' experience, and understanding and accepting individual differences and levels of attainment. Mongon *et al.* (1989) reveal that manageable units of work delivered within a small group situation with plenty of visual aids are also key factors. They go on to assert that if the teacher offers lots of encouragement and pupils are given the opportunity to discuss their work with others, this too makes a significant difference to the quality of lessons. Interestingly, most of these points could be measured through established lesson/teacher observation systems or via formal inspections and visits. Contextual information based on academic performance outcomes would also be of value here.

With regard to personal development and behaviour, it is now generally accepted that effective schools are those that operate a whole-school behaviour management system that regularly uses praise and reward set in a secure and encouraging physical environment. Charlton and David (1993) draw together further factors conducive to effective behaviour management, including good leadership, a high level of pedagogical skills, proactive and non-punitive classroom management, and meaningful and humanely enforced behavioural expectations. Clearly, a detailed behaviour policy coupled with further evidence from classroom observations should provide an overview that could then be compared to contextual data on pupil attendance, exclusions, interventions and more. Margerison and Rayner (1999: 88) also point out that for behaviour management to be effective, a structured evidence-based behavioural assessment framework should be in place in the school: 'It is an approach which will reflect the new culture of target setting but in such a way that individual needs and EBD [emotional and behavioural difficulties] are met as part of the teaching and learning taking place in the school curriculum.'

Individual education plans (IEPs), behaviour management plans (BMPs) and other evidence of identifying and setting learning targets would demonstrate this feature of school organisation. Furthermore, this information should describe the particular interventions and strategies used in order to achieve particular targets and elaborate on new skills to teach, environmental adjustments to be made and specific cognitive- or behaviourist-based approaches or techniques to use. By way of the social climate within a school, Charlton and David (1993) identify a number of other crucial factors that measure effectiveness, including a supportive, professional relationship between all adults and children, involvement of pupils in school organisation, and a sound system of pastoral care. Staff attitudes, values and beliefs surveyed and matched against pupil perceptions and views would provide information pertaining to the quality of relationships within a school. This could be evidenced through the school's self-evaluation system (surveys, discussions, etc.) and identifying any specific references made or targets set within school improvement plans. References to this area will undoubtedly be made in external monitoring visits or inspections. Socially constructive relationships with young people recognise and acknowledge the individual's potential for operating with increasing autonomy and initiative. This can lead to greater interaction in the classroom, with teachers allowing pupil responses to drive lessons and shift instructional content. Classroom observations would certainly reveal something about the interactions between staff and pupils that encouraged this approach.

Cole and Visser (1998) explore an ecosystemic view of special school effectiveness and consider that judgements made during inspections should have a greater focus on the physical environment, staff and other agencies that offer support to the children. The physical environment would include the buildings, furnishings, operational procedures and daily routines, with particular attention given to the timetable, length of lessons, space and activity areas, breaks, and allowance for individual attention and support through the effective use of quiet areas. Interestingly, Polsky (1965) believed that residential schools and treatment centres must be fused architecturally and psychologically. Evidence to support good practice in this area would derive from a physical survey of grounds and buildings. Further evidence would be contained in inspection reports, policy documents relating to ethos and environment, and sections within school improvement plans if work of this nature has been undertaken.

The second area of focus that Cole and Visser (1998) also consider to be of particular importance when evaluating effectiveness is the perspective of professionals who operate beyond the sphere of the school but nevertheless have a legitimate interest in the education and welfare of troubled and troublesome children. Those working in the field of care, social services, justice and health will view the efforts of the school in the light of their own needs and expectations. Such professionals as therapists, child and adolescent mental health services (CAMHS) workers, social workers, care workers and LEA officers, all working in partnership with the school, would offer a valuable source of information pertaining to school effectiveness. Many schools have built a component into their self-evaluation system in order to survey such views.

Having explored a number of ways that:

- one can measure the quality of teaching and learning; and
- one can demonstrate the quality of relationships in a special school,

this section concludes by exploring how one can make an accurate assessment of the school's impact on the children's overall quality of life. 'Quality of life' in a generic context is defined as

> the degree of enjoyment and satisfaction experienced in everyday life as opposed to financial or material well-being.
>
> (*Encarta World English Dictionary*, 2000)

This is a concept that reaches well beyond the gates of school, and external factors, influences and events will inevitably play a significant part in determining a child's quality of life. Of course, these will effectively be beyond the school's control to a large extent, although the government Green Paper *Every Child Matters* (Treasury, 2003) makes specific reference to the central role that schools play in securing the overall welfare of the child. The school will undoubtedly have an impact on the child's values around family, relationships, health, love and home (OMRDD, 1998) and help to shape them through sound relationships, working together, problem solving and creating a vision for the future. Clearly, the child's quality of life will be, in part, dictated by any improvement in quality of teaching and learning, and the quality of relationships within the school. Consequently, all evidence that pertains to school effectiveness will reflect on the child's quality of life. Beyond this, a number of other sources could be usefully drawn on to ascertain 'best value' for the child. For example, information regarding a particular individual that refers to their background, previous educational experience and current difficulties before entering a school could then be compared to reports, profile statements and assessments during the period attending school and possibly beyond. Such case studies could reveal much about the progress made and the overall impact the school had on the child during that period. Other contextual evidence such as noted improvements in attendance, reduction in exclusions, reduction in the need for restrictive physical interventions, and progress in academic areas are all contributory measures that would further indicate an improved quality of life. On a general level there is much to be said for a child who has a relatively stable and comfortable school life when this clearly has not been the case previously. The school's regular and positive contact with parents, carers and professional agencies is also reflective of the child's general stability and happiness. Lastly, information regarding the pupil's ability to progress and achieve formal qualifications before leaving the school, coupled with evidence of further education, training or employment destinations, on the whole mirrors a successful and prosperous association.

This chapter has explored the many aspects of a potentially therapeutic approach but within the confines of current frameworks and expectations for entitlement to a content or national curriculum. It asks the question of schools 'Are young people getting a curriculum that will really prepare them for life and for success in life or at the very least for being able to manage and control their own lives successfully?' It has examined how theories and concepts of therapeutic education interlink themselves around what is currently thought of as good practice in education generally and in specials schools where behavioural, emotional and social development (BESD) is a priority. There are some intangible and practical issues around the possibilities of developing therapeutic relationships in learning and teaching, particularly in the context of the rather limited and constraining practices of school inspection. Conversely, some of the notions of 'best value' could well be used to good advantage when applied with a child-centred perspective. The chapter has been chiefly concerned with whether or not a range of models and approaches in the nature of therapeutic education will make a difference both to young people experiencing BESD and also to the nature and scope of BESD provision. To achieve some kind of measure of the quality of teaching and learning, quality of relationships and quality of life for young people is at least a start in ascertaining the effectiveness of holistic and therapeutic approaches in the educational context.

Chapter 6

The case study and grounded research

This chapter takes the reader into the workings of a five-year research programme undertaken by the authors, whose process has generated a wide range of questions and thoughts and partially informed the content of this book. We use the term 'grounded' because the research is centred within the case-study school and is longitudinal, rather than research generated outside the school and looking in. It has also been informed by both authors' joint experience over many years in this area of research, teaching and school management. Some international perspectives have also contributed to this book through one of the authors' experiences in working and researching provision in the United States and in France. The other author is principal of the case-study school for young people who have been excluded. He has undertaken the role of participant researcher for the past five years. The basis for the international comparisons throughout stems from one author's experience teaching teachers and from research in the United States and from a large-scale European (Interregs II and III) research project in which he has taken part over the past three years and will continue to do so for the next three years. The former involved teachers working with disabled and disadvantaged young people in the United States and the latter focused on pupils and students who were socially and educationally marginalised and excluded in the Pas de Calais, France, and the Isle of Thanet, Kent, England.

This chapter is a description and analysis of an ongoing school development process that has led to practical changes and the development of 'therapeutic education' in a living school context. The results described here are not an end in themselves but part of ongoing school development (as all school development inevitably is!). We would like to make it very clear that this research and the book are meant not necessarily as expert opinion but as an open process of development that will allow readers to pick out for themselves meaningful and useful concepts and practices for school and practice development elsewhere.

Introducing the school-based research programme

The case study in question takes place within a non-maintained special school in Kent and is concerned with the process of therapeutic education in the context of whole school development. The school supports a population of up to thirty secondary-aged boys and girls with behavioural, emotional and social difficulties (BESD) and is governed through the auspices of NCH (Action for Children), the country's largest children's charity. By the very nature and philosophy of the organisation, it was inevitable that the school would create and foster a 'child-centred' approach to education. Inevitably, across the years, one comes across numerous 'off-the-shelf' generic programmes, schemes and systems that purport to have achieved success in managing challenging behaviour. Each and every school houses a unique combination of staff, pupils and a whole host of operational conditions that create a small but complex social system. This delicately balanced environment is as easily disturbed by minor internal developments as by major national initiatives. A range of factors, influences and circumstances dictate the school's ability to provide a high-quality service. It is only when these elements are properly measured and analysed that effective operational constructs can be formulated. Clearly, some of these factors will almost certainly fall outside the remit and influence of both the school and its parent organisation (national economic and political factors, for example). It is the ability to respond appropriately to such variables that will ensure the school's longevity and success.

The school's approach to education is examined in this case study using the working hypothesis and central question: Does a therapeutic approach to education make a difference for troubled and troublesome children? Preceding chapters have developed a theoretical and principled basis for the developing practice and for the research itself. They have been concerned with defining the basic parameters of therapeutic education and have focused on the needs of vulnerable and challenging young people who may be troubled and troublesome children in school but who all too frequently become troubled and troublesome adults. This is followed by the exploration of key issues covering the effect of a therapeutic approach within a BESD special school and the difference this particular approach makes to the quality of children's lives ('best value' or 'value added'). This chapter will focus on how therapeutic education might apply to a special (BESD) school, the nature and needs of a 'troubled and troublesome child', and how we should measure the quality of teaching and learning, the quality of relationships and the quality of life for these young people. In previous chapters we have engaged in a review of professional opinion and research relating to the application and effectiveness of therapeutic education in the context of a special school. All aspects of school life are examined in detail, including its culture, code of conduct, content curriculum, pastoral work, operational practice, incidents and interventions. This is achieved through the identification and analysis of a number of pertinent data sets which are outlined in Appendix 6, 'Case study data and analysis'.

The school is committed to pursuing a therapeutic culture and developing an encouraging learning environment in the belief that it will make the most difference to the quality of life for the children and young people it supports, and, in so doing, secure the school's central aims and objectives. The school's approach is characterised by its use of what is described as 'The interactive curriculum' (adapted from Goddard, 1996; see Figure 5.2). The interactive curriculum is the prime vehicle by which the school is able to coordinate its operational systems and features, and perpetuates the therapeutic basis of the work.

It makes sense to draw from a wide evidence base in measuring 'quality' within school and making accurate judgements regarding a school's effectiveness. For this particular study it was felt to be appropriate to limit the investigation to this one school to generate relevant evidence to demonstrate progress and development over a period of time as a profile. In order to achieve this, the study focused on performance indicators that would measure the following:

- quality of teaching;
- quality of learning;
- quality of relationships among and between pupils and staff;
- quality of life for the children and young people.

Numerical data have also been gathered over a four-year span and then used for analysis and comparison. These data were expected to give a clear indication of the extent to which strategies and interventions have made a difference to the quality of teaching and learning within the school. Contextual data have been collected covering the following areas, among others:

- restrictive physical intervention statistics;
- behavioural incidents;
- academic records;
- attendance/exclusion statistics;
- school roll;
- leaver destinations.

Supporting information was also gathered from descriptive examples that serve to provide illuminative evidence regarding particular aspects of the school. This includes reports and commentaries from several sources. In this way, a far more accurate picture can emerge that better reflects the quality of relationships and overall quality of life for the children and young people. Similarly, this more flexible stance can equally be applied to two further recognised research disciplines and their relative merits and use in this context. Although empirical data were gathered through established administrative systems within the school, other evidence was sought through 'chalk-face' observations as well as both internal and external monitoring and review systems. In this respect the following evidence was gathered:

- advisory reports;
- teacher observation reports;

- inspection reports;
- annual review documents;
- ongoing school statistics;
- business plans.

In order to appreciate and accurately judge the effectiveness of a school, one must become suitably absorbed in its environment. On these grounds one might assume that *action research* is a key approach to use for this study, as defined by Kemmis (1988: 44):

> a form of self-reflective enquiry undertaken by participants in social/ educational situations in order to improve the rationality and justice of a) their own social or educational practices, b) their understanding of these practices, and c) the situations in which the practices are carried out.

This process was intended as a working, living research process aimed at engendering positive change. The design links the research process closely to its context and consequently has a very practical base that was likely to bring about such change. The school incorporates much of the above in its own monitoring and evaluation system. The research was essentially a case study of the school aimed at profiling features of an operational and strategic nature that might have a positive impact on its pupils. The study highlights how a range of proactive strategies and interventions can be effectively combined and refined to match children's needs. The internal systems, management and organisation of the school provide a very convenient means by which contextual information, professional opinion and other relevant data could be accessed and analysed. These are presented as a preliminary analysis in Appendix 6.

The study also utilised other individual pupil case studies on a smaller scale to provide comparative information. Descriptive research relies on a range of data-gathering techniques in order to seek accurate descriptions of activities, objects, processes and persons. 'Survey research in education involves the collection of information from members of a group of students, teachers, or other persons associated with the educational process, and the analysis of this information to illuminate important educational issues' (Rosier, 1988: 108).

The use of surveys was particularly helpful in this context as it ensured that information was drawn from both within the establishment and across a wide band of external agencies working with vulnerable children and young people, and not necessarily with a direct educational perspective. For example, professionals operating from the local child and adolescent mental health centre were able to provide unique insight into effecting and developing a therapeutic environment. Consideration was given to the construction of questionnaires distributed to the groups identified through probability-stratified sampling (sampling within groups of the population). This inevitably produced a prime and rich source of information. The main questionnaire, distributed to staff who work directly with children and young people in the school, was specific to the central question and it was felt that further opportunity to elaborate on these responses through formal interviews was not necessary. A further, more general questionnaire targeting a carefully selected group, using non-probability purposive sampling (hand-picking typical or interesting cases) across a number of professional areas, was suitably representative of others who work with, or on behalf of, troubled and troublesome children. This was expected to provide further evidence pertaining to the nature, extent and needs of children in the context of challenging behaviour and people's perceptions as to the most effective approaches to dealing with them.

Additionally, the research has made use of comments and views of the children themselves. Again their views were obtained through an appropriately constructed questionnaire and a number of group and individual interviews, using the same sampling methods. However, further qualitative and quantitative information was expected to derive from the use of observations and written feedback from intervention strategies. Teacher (i.e. classroom) observation, an integral part of the school's self-monitoring and evaluation procedure, was seen as a useful means of collecting further evidence regarding specific approaches to effective learning and teaching in the classroom. This was organised on the basis of non-probability event sampling (using a system already in place). Furthermore, data collection through a range of school-based administration and monitoring systems provided a host of statistical information spanning a four-year period. Significantly, this was through a time of immense change in terms of the school's operational procedures, intervention strategies and underlying philosophy. There are no fewer than ten distinct data sets upon which the research draws, each casting a unique flavour and insight into aspects of the school. It was hoped that this information would raise some interesting points and lead to some illuminative responses to the working question.

Data sets, synthesis and analysis of data

The data used for the purposes of this ongoing action research were gathered from a number of sources that relate directly to operational features of the school covering a time frame of five years from 1999 to 2004. These data reveal much about the work of the school, the nature of special needs catered for, the quality of provision offered and its overall impact on the lives of the children. It enabled the school and the headteacher to draw tentative conclusions about the therapeutic education approaches being developed in the school and to plan for further developments on the basis of the beneficial impact for the young people of specific strategies. Although confined to one small special school, these data yield some interesting and illuminative information that not only supports the theme of this study but may have some value for professionals in the field of care and education. This is largely attributable to the innovative developmental work that has consumed the school over roughly the same period. Consequently, the study was a means by which the work could be examined and progressed. Needless to say, this had, and will continue to have, a profound impact on the school's overall philosophy and practice, to say nothing of its long-term success. Appendix 6, sections 1–11 is a presentation of the range and form of the data that were gathered. The following provides an analysis or summary analysis of the areas identified above and, where appropriate, makes explicit any correlation between the issues raised and related literature. It is not within the remit of this book to present the whole of the data gathered, although they are held in a data archive, should any readers be interested in further investigation.

These data are, to a large extent, reflective of the general growth of the school across a significant time of change. The school came under fresh ownership from late 1997 and with it an extensive recruitment programme that spawned a new management structure and a significant change in the staffing establishment. This marked something of a renaissance period for the school. There are limitations in using such a small sample group to ascertain quantitative trends and patterns. However, it does serve to illuminate some trends over time. The following analyses derive from the preliminary analyses and data in Appendix 6, and their related sections are shown here:

Secondary analysis of pastoral contextual data from Appendix 6, section 2

- Poor attendance rates shown (66%–83%), primarily due to unauthorised absences where pupils would abscond from school. Although there has been a downward trend in sessions lost by exclusions, the number of pupils who have been excluded one or more times over the period has remained relatively constant. Most recent figures (2005) show an increase in attendance to within OfSTED-acceptable levels (90%).
- Similarly, the number of pupils requiring physical interventions has remained relatively constant despite the actual number of restraints falling slightly over the period.
- The downward trend in exclusions is a healthy sign that the proactive and active measures being developed in the school are having an impact.
- The level of injuries seems reasonably low, given that the figure also includes minor medical attention. Staff are more able to ensure their own safety and the safety of pupils they support by raising their level of self-awareness. This can be achieved by a system of formal training, good communication among staff and gaining greater knowledge of the pupils.

Secondary analysis of pupil case studies from Appendix 6, section 3

This section compares six children who, as of July 2003, were all on roll at the school. The children were chosen at random in order to show a cross-section of referrals, their background circumstances and particular difficulties.

- Young people referred to the school have complex developmental, social, emotional and learning needs.
- All young people referred arrive with multi-agency involvement that includes psychological services, health and clinical services, the social services department or child and family services.
- The range of needs is broad, from those with ASDs (autistic spectrum disorders) or ADHDs (attention deficit hyperactivity disorders) through to abuse and trauma at home; all have been permanently excluded.
- Some children have had other school placements break down before arriving; others have been out of school for considerable periods of time.
- The demand on referral is for a supportive educational environment with access to small group work and individual programmes of study while setting clear and consistent boundaries for behaviour (usually nothing about therapy or pastoral care).
- The biggest challenge facing the school is to deal with deep-seated and well-entrenched problems that have developed over a number of years.
- Academic delay is often in the areas of literacy, despite average intelligence measures, but the main problem the children seem to face is the inability to form any kind of relationship.
- Small class size and the ability to develop good relations and provide support in the classroom are crucial.

Secondary analysis of academic contextual data from Appendix 6, section 4

A variety of basic contextual data are collected about the school each year covering the period from 1999 to 2003 and show attendance rates, Standard Attainment Test (SATS) results, formal examinations achieved and pupil destinations.

- The school is populated by a predominance of boys; a small group of girls provide an academic equal opportunity challenge.
- Disaffection and general unwillingness to engage in school life hampers progress.

- The quality and success of the children's previous education experience will heavily dictate their effective engagement in any formal academic courses.
- Attainment is low by mainstream standards; it is probably more realistic to judge achievement on the basis of progress.
- The majority of leavers have shown a preference to take up college courses upon leaving the school or take up apprenticeships. A small minority leave without any identified progress in routes, and these are referred to Connexions for follow-up.

Restrictive physical intervention (RPI) analysis from Appendix 6, section 5

Appendix 6, section 5 is a summary of the analysis of restrictive physical interventions at the school reported over the period 1999–2004. The statistics give an important indication as to the effectiveness of the school even though they report on but one aspect of the work of the school and are reflective only of a small selection of the interventions used on a day-to-day basis.

- Restrictive physical interventions (RPIs) are used only as a last resort in the case of challenging behaviour when all other strategies have been exhausted and any other course of action is likely to result in personal injury or damage to property.
- The overall purpose of RPIs is to stabilise a crisis situation and allow the young person to regain self-control as soon as possible.
- The most significant statistics show a fall in the number of physical interventions used over the period by some 40%. This could be attributable to the school's capacity to offer an increasing range of proactive and therapeutic strategies, although a number of other factors and variables are bound to impact on this figure.
- Another common feature of these statistics is the lower number of RPIs used across the 14- to 16-year-old age group (Key Stage 4) when compared to the 11- to 13-year-olds (Key Stage 3). These figures accurately reflect a different approach to supporting the older pupils by developing (in Key Stage 3) and allowing a greater capacity to self-advocate in times of crisis.
- The statistics have revealed that learning support assistants (LSAs) have a significantly higher involvement in RPIs than any other group of staff, consistent over three years and not at all surprising since their role has evolved into pastoral and welfare matters. In an everyday classroom situation this would leave the teacher free to maintain continuity with the other pupils.
- The time of day when RPIs most often occur appears to be shortly after arrival at school and shortly after the lunch break. The less intense and

demanding these times can be made, the less likely it is that aggressive outbursts will ensue.

- The data reveal that a higher percentage of interventions occur shortly into each term, with a gradual reduction as the term progresses, suggesting that as children become accustomed to the environment, staff, regime, rules, and so on, then there is less reason for them to respond aversively, and with each new term this pattern will recur.

Inspection reports analysis from Appendix 6, section 6

The reports derive from various sources and are useful in highlighting key milestones in the development of the school from year to year. Over the five years covered in this study, there was at least one inspection or external monitoring visit per year.

- February 1999 identifies a number of serious weaknesses across the school, including curriculum, staffing, accommodation, resourcing and behaviour. The Advisers' Report (Position Paper, July 1999) explains the school's desire to shift what was a very rigid and confrontational regime to a more proactive and systematic approach to managing behavioural difficulties.
- At this stage, planning, content and delivery methods were not well refined or consistent, and this resulted in some children disengaging from the lessons.
- The Her Majesty's Inspector's (HMI) visit in November 1999 recognised that planning for an appropriately broad, balanced and relevant content curriculum was well under way and it was noted that a sound behaviour policy had been installed and was taking effect.
- The HMI visit in June 2000 indicated that lessons were all deemed to be at least satisfactory and behaviour management was acknowledged, including the incentive schemes, the use of withdrawal in avoiding crisis situations and the techniques and methods used in restrictive physical interventions (RPI). Areas for development were consistency in the quality of teaching and learning, improving attendance levels, and providing more focused support for literacy difficulties.
- October 2000:
  - The curriculum provides opportunities for the development of self-esteem through promoting self-advocacy, decision-making skills, risk awareness and communication skills.
  - Relationships are characterised by openness, respect and the promotion of dignity.
  - There are clear and appropriate policies for behaviour management and bullying.

- Children's rights are fully respected and embedded in practice.
- Children have a nominated adult for support and guidance.
- The school actively promotes independence skills and manages the transition to the next phase of education/adult life.
- January 2002:
  - Some children's acute anxiety and stress are spilling over into the classroom.
  - The younger pupils still have some way to go to establish good attitudes and behaviour patterns. They have all made steady and in some cases marked improvements since joining the school.
  - Staff work hard to establish and maintain good relationships with the pupils and to foster a secure and caring learning environment.
  - The parents surveyed mostly expressed positive views about the work of the school in promoting the personal and social development of the children.

The reports identify a steady improvement in terms of the quality of teaching and learning. However, of particular interest here are the comments that were made regarding the quality of therapeutic care offered. Given the emphasis and significance placed on the management of children's emotional, social and behavioural difficulties, it was odd but not entirely surprising that inspectors should make only passing or general comments such as 'good behaviour patterns' and 'good relationships with pupils'. Little or no reference was made to the interactive curriculum, intervention strategies or PSHE profiles that had been devised and developed within the same time frame. The most significant observations came from the LEA advisers, who seemed to have a better understanding of, and interest in, these matters, and realised their significance and central role in a school like this one. Only the LEA advisers made much reference to the social and emotional needs of the pupils and how these were met through the additional and therapeutic approaches adopted in the school. Perhaps the conclusion to draw from this is that both OfSTED and HMI are not really very interested in the social and emotional welfare of young people specifically sent to provision like this (and only interested in academic outcomes!). Maybe they are constrained by a framework that really is not in tune with the kind of specialist provision that is needed by young people who have been excluded from mainstream school and provide a challenge to the education system. Or perhaps they are less confident about the role of education in securing access, participation and engagement through relationships and holistic, therapeutic approaches. This is much in line with the views of the critics cited in previous chapters, who are uncomfortable dealing with emotions or simply do not recognise them as being important in learning. There is much work to be done in the English and Welsh education system to acknowledge that learning for everyone is more than just delivery of curriculum, knowledge or skill. It is far more than managing behaviour, but there is still a marked reluctance to deal with what is important rather than what is easily quantifiable or simplistically recognisable.

Summary and analysis of annual review and business plans from Appendix 6, section 7

The annual review and business plans (also called school development plans) serve as useful reference points as they further track the development of the school over the period 1999–2004. There are three documents used, each reviewing the previous year and planning for the forthcoming year. The information contained within each document was the result of a systematic and detailed survey of staff opinion followed by whole staff discussion. As 'working documents', all the material within the business plans can be used to provide further insight as to how effective staff have been in progressively applying and managing new therapeutic strategies within a rapidly changing culture and environment as they are all measures of the quality of service that the school offers. The targets are outlined in section 8 of Appendix 6 and give an indication of the way that evaluation has guided development of organisational targeting.

Summary and analysis of staff questionnaire from Appendix 6, section 8

The survey was administered during June and July 2002 and distributed to all staff working directly with children at the school. It was divided into five segments (see Appendix 6). The questionnaire yielded a 92 per cent return. A number of overarching themes were embodied in the five sections of the questionnaire and a number of conclusions drawn:

- Staff appear generally confident in explaining why the school is here, the service it offers and the value of that service and feel that, on the whole, other professionals, parents and carers are aware of the nature of the school's provision but are less confident that the pupils themselves fully understand what the school provides for them.
- Common phrases were evident when describing the underlying philosophy of the school such as 'caring', 'therapeutic', 'safe', 'secure', 'nurturing' and 'sensitive'.
- 'Special features' of the school included a strong, experienced and qualified team and a positive, caring and proactive ethos with a family-oriented approach to school life.
- Operational features included the high staff : pupil ratio and the high level of support available, the size of each class and the size of the school generally.

- Good, clear structures, procedures and policies were also felt to be important, in particular an effective behaviour policy.
- It was felt that the school was able to offer a relevant curriculum and one that was enjoyable yet challenging for the pupils.
- The school had developed strong links with parents and carers and shared common goals.
- Being part of NCH, the United Kingdom's largest childcare charity, was a clear strength.
- Pupil difficulties or characteristics that were of greatest concern to staff on a personal level included aggression and violence, poor social skills, disaffection, disrespect and destructiveness.
- Another significant concern is the degree of home support that the school can expect, which cannot easily be determined until the placement is well under way.
- An interesting contrast between staff perceptions and HMI and statistical results indicates a mismatch in perceptions about priorities (staff: aggression, violence, poor social skills, immaturity and low self-esteem; HMI: attendance). Staff felt that attendance, criminal activity and destructiveness were not really an issue, whereas the school takes criminal damage very seriously.
- The responses to the effective staff team question indicates the following:
    - Characteristics that appeared to be most important in the team were resourcefulness, flexibility and the ability to be a good team player.
    - Their own personal theoretical perspective in each of the four commonly known models: behaviourist, cognitive, ecosystemic and psychodynamic (listed in descending order).
    - A work style that was consistent, supportive, caring, empathic and assertive would be most effective.
    - The least effective was considered to be controlling, authoritative and dominant.
- Responses to the feasibility and effectiveness of 'therapeutic approaches':
    - There is a view that the essence of therapeutic education is contained in the school's 'content' curriculum and 'hidden' curriculum, implying a restricted view of the process and its potential for extended and enhanced intervention programmes.
    - The use of physical intervention techniques was generally considered to be therapeutic, yet some staff suggested that removing the use of physical intervention techniques would result in the loss of a power base – indicating conflicting principles.
    - There were high levels of response (over 50%) to the following descriptors:
        a. Maintains and raises self-esteem and self-awareness.
        b. Values pupils' views and gives them responsibility – helps them to manage themselves.

    c.   Gives staff and pupils the confidence to engage with one another and the curriculum.

    d.   Challenges existing conditions, habits, responses or circumstances.

- Practical examples of how the staff see therapeutic education operating in their particular field of work:
  - The use of time on something like a 'personal challenge' – giving them personal attention, building rapport and enabling them to understand that with help they can achieve.
  - Enabling the young person to develop strategies and tools for them to become an individual with their own thoughts, feelings and emotions.
  - I brought a hand puppet into school – a small cat. The pupil has a cat at home called Honey. I introduced the puppet in a non-threatening way and the pupil immediately put it on and 'became' Honey. Honey could then write out spellings, dance to French tunes and do maths and enjoy school – without James losing face. After a while, Honey was just left on the pupil's desk but is used in times of stress to 'do the pupil's work'
  - Use of the PSHE profile and hence target setting in order to modify and put into place strategies is often a useful tool. This method of negotiation with the pupils in order for them to arrive at solutions can prove to be effective.
  - Making tasks and environment clear and defined, so as not to allow the child to become upset or dwell upon problems, not allowing the opportunity for adverse behaviour.
  - A pupil was having trouble with being able to resist the peer pressure to abscond (mainly first thing in the morning). Plants were bought for the classroom and the pupil was given the opportunity to take responsibility for the care and watering of the plants. This took place first thing in the morning. The pupil knocked on the door every morning voluntarily, to come into the school. He enjoyed the one-to-one attention and his absconding was not such an issue, even after the activity stopped.
  - Verbalising the students' feelings for them; confirming that it's OK to be angry and setting out ways of dealing with feelings appropriately. Then repeating this process as necessary.
  - Maintaining and raising self-esteem and self-awareness – with one particular child who was also trying to go against authoritative ruling. He is now able to self-talk and give explanations about behaviour.
  - Students now show an enthusiasm for personal/imaginative writing. Previously, poor spelling skills and lack of confidence to attempt work prohibited this. Word banks created on the whiteboard by brainstorming ideas – fluency and self-esteem gradually improved.

- After restraining a child I always talk to them when they are calm, explaining why the restraint was necessary and what we can do to stop the situation escalating that far again.

On the whole, these examples are useful and informative illustrations of how the school operates in a diverse and creative way while remaining within the context and scope of therapeutic education as it has been defined in this study.

- Responses to questions about the nature of an 'alternative curriculum' and its place in their work:
  - It was a critical feature of a BESD environment and not a 'cop-out' for not tackling the content curriculum effectively.
  - It sits alongside the National Curriculum and is fully embodied in the pastoral time and PSHE lessons (suggesting no development of further creative, therapeutic approaches?).
  - Asked to define the 'alternative curriculum', over 50 per cent of staff favoured descriptors such as 'individual', 'child-focused', 'relevant', 'interactive' and 'positive'. The 'interactive curriculum' was sited as the best model for implementing an 'alternative curriculum', as it:
    a. incorporates all aspects of personal development;
    b. is a live tool, monitoring performance and establishing patterns of behaviour;
    c. is a means of feeding key reporting documents in the school;
    d. utilises an assessment system that identifies specific behaviours and targets.
  - Eighty per cent were confident about the direction the school was taking with regard to supporting pupils with emotional, behavioural and social difficulties.

These responses indicated the need for further staff discussion about the nature of the curriculum and ways in which therapeutic approaches in addition to the curriculum might be integrated further into the school day.

Analysis of pupil questionnaire and interviews from Appendix 6, section 9

The analysis of the pupil questionnaire and interviews was essentially feedback from a questionnaire designed for the purposes of the school's annual review procedure and was launched in January 2004.

- Most pupils felt valued, listened to and welcomed in the school and they thought staff showed care and consideration for all pupils.

- They felt that some people did not treat others with respect and were equally concerned that rules and punishments were not always effective in curbing the behaviour of some children.
- They expressed a clear sense of what to do to behave well at the school and felt that their efforts to improve behaviour were recognised.
- They felt strongly that they knew where to get help when needed and that staff would help to sort out problems fairly.
- They were less content with the school's efforts to involve all parties in school development and were not satisfied that the organisation as a whole worked in partnership with all parties to help the pupils.
- They liked the teachers and appreciated the incentive systems in the school.
- They felt that overall the regime was fair, but one pupil commented on disliking the security around the building and felt that greater access to places where they could cool off would be beneficial.

There are some interesting points here, but overall the analysis gives an indication that pupils do have a sense of ownership and feel they have an ability to have some control over the school environment in an organised and positive way, through their opinions.

Analysis of agency questionnaire from Appendix 6, section 10

The agency questionnaire was distributed in January 2004 to all partnership authorities, external services and other professionals that work on behalf of the children in the school within health, social services or education sectors. This survey was the first of its kind and formed part of the school self-evaluation and monitoring procedure.

- Excellent rate of return with a number of positive points.
- Felt that the school made them feel welcomed and valued.
- People treat each other with respect and staff show care and consideration for all pupils.
- A strong feeling that agencies should have greater opportunity to be involved in school life and in making decisions about the school and its development.
- A positive response regarding the level of service received from the school.

Analysis of the school behaviour policy from Appendix 6, section 11

The analysis of the school behaviour policy has particular relevance to this study for a number of reasons. First, it is a document that has grown with the school's development and has been adjusted and updated regularly not only as part of the school's formal annual review process but as and when it was considered appropriate, in full consultation with the staff. Second, it is a document that incorporates an extensive array of information pertaining to many aspects of school life from theoretical perspectives to practical interventions, strategies and procedures for managing children who present severely challenging behaviour. Third, as a 'live' working document it says much about the standards that the school has set in terms of the quality of support that is offered to the children and young people.

The 'aims and objectives' section of the policy succinctly describes how the school sets about its purpose of supporting children in a proactive way, and this is a thread that runs throughout the whole document. Proactive support is exemplified in a number of ways, including the use of a flexible incentive system, the use of teaching skills on a routine basis, and recovering from a crisis situation. The 'life-space interview' technique is used in a variety of situations to offer active support to a child who may show signs of distress or anger. That this and other active techniques are so prevalent is a mark of the good rapport and trust that staff and pupils are able to develop in the school environment. The policy also describes the routine of the day and the additional mechanisms that have been installed to shape the environment around the needs of the children. The policy describes the 'interactive curriculum' and further indicates the school's commitment to planning the management of challenging behaviour on an individual level through the use of individual education plans (IEPs), STAR analysis and the formulation of behaviour management plans (BMPs).

Brief summing up

Further evidence related to each of the above and the way that this has had a positive impact on and made a positive contribution to the quality of relationships and overall provision can be seen in the reporting systems used within the school. These include incident sheets, pupils' records, individualised pupil documents, pastoral notes, staff meeting minutes, supervision notes and performance management documents. There is much to be pleased with in the general analysis of the data gathered over a significant period of time but it would not be right to ignore the developmental issues that have arisen. The distillation of these is a key feature of a self-evaluating school that has self-awareness as a key theme in the promotion of a therapeutic approach for the young people at the school. Earlier in the book it was suggested that learning and teaching are about more than just a transfer of knowledge; they are about more than trying to delve into a young person's difficulties. The process is about setting up an environment in which the young person can not only have some effect in a positive way, but also see 'models' (human and systems) all around that show a skilled way of conducting oneself to achieve the things that are wanted and needed in life.

The school itself is a social model for young people, and if this isn't beginning to get it right in terms of an environment and atmosphere that are conducive to good and positive learning and social relationships, then what hope has a young person of turning a corner in their own life?

Chapter 7

Measuring the effectiveness of holistic and ecosystemic interventions

In the previous chapter the analysis and examination of the inner workings of a school laid bare some of the encouraging and hopeful aspects of introducing a therapeutic approach into the process of learning and teaching. It was, and is, both a curriculum development and a whole-school development process in which all the staff, pupils, parents and a number of outside agencies are involved. Interestingly, the outside agencies, particularly the foster care agencies, expressed a wish to have more contact, and more influence over school planning. This chapter continues the 'positive psychology' theme and does not shy away from more subjective, more complicated issues and the problems of meaningful enumeration. Devaluing or reducing the rich complexities of real events and situations by trying to quantify them has become a commonplace activity. Reductionist empirical research, over-concerned with notions of objectivity, often leads to contestable statistical conclusions brandished by politicians as if they are the arbiters of truth. In analysing organisational activity, objectivity is desirable but it is at its most dangerous when governments use empirical research to simplify complex processes and then justify and 'enforce' the simplistic notions arising from the generalisation. OfSTED Frameworks contain many complex and subjective statements that can be interpreted in a whole host of interesting and creative ways. In that sense the constructions can become comprehensive and, to a great extent, match reality. The problem often lies in the way that inspectors are required to 'enforce' simplistic interpretations of these complex and creative processes.

We, the authors, pursue a positive psychology path because this seems to be most hopeful and most applicable to the enterprise that this book is mainly concerned with.

> The field of Positive Psychology at the subjective level is about positive subjective experience: well being and satisfaction (past), and flow, joy, the sensual pleasures, and happiness (present), and constructive cognitions about the future – optimism, hope, and faith. At the individual level it is about positive individual traits – the capacity for love and vocation, courage, interpersonal skill, aesthetic sensibility, perseverance, forgiveness, originality,

future-mindedness, high talent, and wisdom. At the group level it is about the civic virtues and the institutions that move individuals toward better citizenship: responsibility, nurturance, altruism, civility, moderation, tolerance, and work ethic.

(Seligman and Csikszentmihalyi, 2000; Gillham and Seligman, 1999)

This seems to be a suitable and useful theoretical basis and one that has underpinned much of what is being developed in this book in terms of a practical model of therapeutic education. However, it does come back to the problem of integrating these positive, hopeful but subjective constructs with a system of education that requires measurement and is obsessed with easily measurable outcomes. To do this, we have spent time researching and attempting to deconstruct the process, most clearly epitomised in the summary of the research in the previous chapter. Often, holistic and ecosystemic interventions are difficult to measure in the short term and even more difficult to evaluate in terms of long-term benefits. It is not easy to quantify the benefits of whole-school cultural and social approaches within a school curriculum for pupils who have been excluded from school. The frameworks for gathering data for the project in this book were fairly simple, but supported sensible and sensitive evaluation of benefits, changes and guidance for further development. This project is not a discrete 'in with the research method, gather data and then out with the results and finish' affair. It is an ongoing, living project that is developing all the time. One of the difficulties we have had is simply the decisions that have to be made to evaluate an organic system in constant flux which produces an enormous amount of complex data. Hence, the reader will see that many decisions about what is important and what areas, functions and perceptions are important have been made. The result is a whole school approach where therapeutic education is the central plank but which also recognises the need to 'render unto Caesar what is Caesar's' – or in this case, render unto the education system the accountability that is required but without sacrificing the central elements of provision and practice that the practitioners themselves feel is crucial.

Demonstrating that therapeutic approaches are effective in a school context

The school has embarked on a journey founded upon the notion that a therapeutic approach to education is appropriate for this particular clientele and one that will offer 'best value' to its users. Note that the concept of 'best value' here is applied to the principal stakeholders, who are the users of the service, not the local authorities, the government or even the parents and carers (they are secondary stakeholders). Discussion suggests that there are few established 'norms' or standards that relate to this approach. The implementation of new initiatives is likely to stem primarily from internal review and development shared by staff. External demands or constraints have to be 'internalised' in order to take root. In this respect the procedures used for reviewing school policy and practice are entirely appropriate. They allow staff to focus on key organisational and environmental factors, and make adjustments that 'best fit' the needs of the clientele. However, aspects of the annual review data coupled with some of the staff questionnaire responses around sanctions, control and consistency illustrate the need for appropriate guidance and advisement when discussing new proposals and initiatives. This would ensure that they are founded upon good practice and not simply knee-jerk reactions to issues and problems that arise. As part of a national children's charity, the school is clearly in a strong position in terms of appropriate external support to pursue a child-centred philosophy.

How far should or could one progress with the notion of a therapeutic approach to education in this particular school and is there a point at which it is deemed to become ineffective? Conversely, is there a point at which reliance upon a highly structured regime with the use of punitive measures and sanctions becomes counter-productive? These measures still exist, as the behaviour policy clearly states, but what effect do they actually have on the 'quality of life' for the pupil? 'Good order and discipline' is a term not only used in the behaviour policy but also seen in many other documents that are referred to. There is clearly a need for good order in any school, but reference to disciplinary procedures seems to lay an unnecessary emphasis on a negative and controlling environment as opposed to a proactive one. The data from staff questionnaire responses reveal some confusion and more than a little trepidation regarding the definition and application of what therapeutic education actually means in practice. The responses give an overall feeling of uncertainty to committing to the notion, possibly due to staff lack of knowledge or expertise coupled with the worry of straying too far from educational 'safe ground' to unfamiliar 'therapeutic' territory.

In order for the school to demonstrate that it makes a difference to the lives of children, it must first show that the current school experience is an improvement on previous experiences. Second, the school must be able to show 'Best Value' or 'value added', in that the quality of school experience makes a significant difference to the quality of life for the children and young people. One could argue that the school is not achieving all the 'Best Value' criteria because the data sets reveal significant failings from key performance indicators. These failings, in 'system' terms, include:

- not achieving minimum attendance requirements;
- showing no improvement in school academic targets;
- showing no significant improvement in exclusion figures;
- showing no significant improvement in restrictive physical intervention (RPI) figures.

However, in contrast, the 'value added' measure is more positive, with the pupil case studies indicating that they have all made some progress in the school despite significant disruption to their previous schooling, in some cases coupled with early childhood trauma. Relatively settled periods at the current school and progress being made in a number of academic and personal growth areas were reported. This is confirmed in the evidence from the OfSTED inspection report, as discussed earlier. The individual responses to the staff questionnaires indicate a general acknowledgement of the importance of positive behaviour support within a therapeutic setting. However, in a number of returns staff showed some uncertainty in understanding the basic concepts involved. One conclusion here is that staff genuinely wish to cling to traditional school values within a stiff inspection regime. If this is the case, then its development will be undoubtedly slow and ultimately fruitless. A more likely interpretation of these responses, given the school's development so far, is that staff, albeit a little hesitant about the notion of therapeutic education, have a genuine interest in seeing the school develop in this way. However, this is a process that takes time because it involves a significant change of attitudes, values and beliefs. Staff may need further and continued support and guidance in order to help realise and fulfil the school's potential in shifting not only its approach to education but its whole culture.

Of all the school targets that have been set over the past five years, the most significant (and possibly the most difficult to achieve) have been:

- to raise attendance levels;
- to reduce exclusions;
- to reduce the need for physical interventions.

These targets offer very clear and tangible indicators as to the effectiveness of the school. Raising attendance levels demonstrates that we have a healthy and thriving population of pupils, and reducing exclusions reveals the extent to which we are managing challenging behaviour without resorting to punitive measures. A reduction in physical interventions suggests that the school is effective in employing preventive techniques of dealing with potential crisis issues. An inspection at any level will almost always focus on these areas as a guide to assessing this essential dimension of school life in terms of behavioural, emotional and social difficulties (BESD) provision. The targets have particular relevance because the school has engaged in an evolutionary process of creating a therapeutic learning environment. These targets are by no means the only indicators we might use, and demonstrate only some aspects of a therapeutic provision, but they are a reasonably accurate, quantitative starting point.

Applying the basic features of human agency and self-efficacy

The core features of personal agency and self-efficacy address the issue of what it means to be human. This should be the first requirement of a 'humanistic' and holistic approach to young people in trouble. Key factors in 'humanising' the approach to learning and teaching young people who are challenging, and key themes in this book, are:

- To turn away from an apologetic stance where all these young people are the victims of society, poor upbringing or trauma in their lives which shackles the professionals and adults who work with them. The only way they can be 'made whole' is by experts, medical or quasi-medical 'treatments'. The other alternative is that poverty, their family or the media have made them this way. Both these positions disable teachers and other professionals, in the context of education, who would try a variety of creative approaches to change the situation.
- To turn away from simplistic and often too hard-hitting, discriminatory and yet indiscriminate practices that focus on:
  - *either* systematising punishment and reward, regardless of the individual contexts and individual struggles to overcome difficulties;
  - *or* relying entirely on performance and outcomes as measures of personal growth, learning to learn or the range of skills, coupled with awareness needed to survive in life, without due regard being given to the importance of the processes and 'how' these are achieved.

Or, in the words of Seligman (2001: 6), discussing a negative psychological perspective (and one that we feel has driven so much practice in education for too long), a humanistic approach should reflect all sides of the human character: 'We saw human beings as passive foci: stimuli came on and elicited responses (what an extraordinarily passive word). External reinforcements weakened or strengthened responses, or drives, tissue needs, or instincts. Conflicts from childhood pushed each of us around.'

The following is a digest of the main characteristics of self-efficacy (Bandura, 2001), which we feel provides a cornerstone on which to develop further, more detailed school development, recording and monitoring perspectives related to therapeutic approaches to learning and teaching.

Self-reflectiveness

Young people are not only agents of action but self-examiners of their own actions and their own modes of functioning. To be able to reflect upon oneself and the adequacy of one's thoughts and actions is another distinctly human core feature of agency. Through self-conscious thoughts, young people evaluate their motivation and values, and the meaning of their life and the pursuits they choose to follow. It is a high level of self-reflection that enables young people to make choices between the conflicting obligations and compulsions in their lives, and then act on them. Having made decisions of this kind, young people can then judge the effectiveness of their predictions and plans of action against the outcomes of their actions. In an educative setting they can be encouraged to take account of the effects that other people's actions will have and what others believe (about them or their actions), and to make some deductions from established knowledge and the consequences of that knowledge. The school curriculum can be adapted to focus on personal and social aspects of life (for example, an introduction to the history of the First World War could also focus on the way in which arguments are resolved). Given the time and skills of teachers or other adults who use multilevel teaching, and given the right context, thinking skills can develop through the curriculum. Another important activity that can take place in school is creative writing, which involves much self-reflection if handled in the right way. It probably also accounts for the way that many young people 'in trouble' turn to poetry and writing as a means of self-reflection.

Intentionality

To describe an act as being done 'intentionally' implies that the young person can choose to behave in a challenging or antisocial manner or, through the exercise of self-influence, to behave otherwise.

> An intention is a representation of a future course of action to be performed. It is not simply an expectation or prediction of future actions but a proactive commitment to bringing them about. Intentions and actions are different aspects of a functional relation separated in time. It is, therefore, meaningful to speak of intentions grounded in self-motivators affecting the likelihood of actions at a future point in time.
>
> (Bandura, 2001: 5)

Unfortunately for many young people, their plans do not always have the effect they desire. Instead of focusing on low self-esteem and the behaviour it is said to generate (this is something of a tautological connection), we could instead focus on what the intentions are in any given plan of action. It is not uncommon for young people to play a part in their own misfortunes through intentional acts of non-compliance or through their wholly inaccurate perception of the consequences for themselves or for others. The power to originate actions is a central part of human agency, and young people in trouble usually do act in some way or other. In fact, it is their actions that often bring them into disrepute, rather than their lack of action. Instead of attributing these actions to things that we would find it harder to determine, why not simply act on their 'planning' abilities and ability to perceive what the consequences of this planning is likely to be? Many problem-solving approaches use this technique to develop good problem-solving skills in young people and it is not hard to see how this fits with the concept of 'intentionality' and how it could avert disaster. It is a learning process but one that has a therapeutic outcome. By structuring the planning or problem-solving process, the teacher, assistant or other professional enables the young person to self-regulate and change course (or develop the ability to change course when necessary).

Self-regulation is also a first step towards 'shared intentionality', in which a young person begins to plan with another person or with another person in mind. Such planning can herald the beginning of the development of the sociability and empathy that are markedly absent in many troubled and troublesome young people. Interestingly, self-regulation fits neatly into the area of goal setting with a young person, and this has become a feature of working with young people. However, it needs to be approached with caution, and research flies in the face of much current practice where goals (or targets) are thought of purely in terms of simple (or easily measurable) outcomes or 'performance'.

> Modern theories on goals include the claim that a person's behaviour is not solely determined by the motivational variables of feasibility and desirability. The ways people frame goals and how their goal pursuits are self-regulated are said to make an additional contribution.
>
> (Oettingen *et al.*, 2000: 728)

Oettingen *et al.* go on to add that setting learning goals is more beneficial than setting performance goals when it comes to task enjoyment and coping with failure, and that instigating learning goals seems to demand that positive fantasies about improving one's standing are contrasted with aspects of reality that hinder effective learning. Effectively, the young person needs to be encouraged to fantasise (because this is the origin of any ability to set goals) and that the 'fantasy' can then be shaped and developed in the light of reality. Having taught young people for many years, we are only too aware of these factors in planning. It is a worthwhile and salient process to go through in helping the young person become more aware of their intentions generally, but, more important, to develop the ability to match those fantasies up with reality. Incidentally, this is a key process in reducing low self-esteem but a practical everyday activity that teachers and others can engage with.

Forethought

Many people try to motivate (or coerce) young people by allusion to future events. 'If you do that, this will happen', and so on. Yet future events cannot be causes of current motivation and action because they have no actual existence. It is only if the young person is able to 'represent' the future event in their mind's eye (cognitively) that the future event will have some kind of reality. Again there is a problem for many young people who get into trouble. It is the problem of not being able to represent future events effectively or even to see themselves as part of any future events that might take place. This anticipatory function was developed by George Kelly (1955) in his theory of personal constructs. He then used personal construct psychology and repertory grids in his work with troubled and troublesome young people. It worked well. Why? He worked in the cognitive domain and developed a system whereby a young person could examine their own plans, anticipations and thoughts in an objective way. They were able to look into the future through examining the ways in which they made decisions. One of the authors is now developing this very technique again to use with young people, and he is not the only one. However, in any school situation the learning points are clear. The process of planning and goal setting requires the ability to project one's thinking forward, and this is where a young person will need to learn the cognitive skills of building a picture of current conditions that they are experiencing or living in and then examining their own personal standards, their perception of positive outcomes, and so on. When they have an appreciation of the current situation and what are thought of as positive outcomes, then a young person can develop what Bandura (2001: 8) calls 'foresightful behaviour'.

> However, by being represented cognitively in the present, foreseeable future events are converted into current motivators and regulators of behavior. In this form of anticipatory self-guidance, behavior is motivated and directed by projected goals and anticipated outcomes rather than being pulled by an unrealized future state.

Self-reactiveness

As well as planning and forethought, which are skills to be developed through problem solving, for example, a young person also has to motivate themselves to take some form of action in line with the planning. This involves a significant degree of self-regulation. In other words, it is easier to plan than to stick to the plan, as most of us know too well! Once more, this is a process that many young people in trouble are completely unfamiliar with. More often than not, they do not realise why they have got into such difficulties, or they attribute blame always to external sources, rather than to how they have planned things. Work in this area can be very useful in getting a young person to take responsibility. If the person has explicitly planned a course of action in a transparent way with someone else, it is very hard then to shift the blame for its undesirable outcome on to someone else.

How do we monitor our own actions during this process? Goleman (1998) sees this as a feature of emotional intelligence: 'using our deepest preferences to move and guide us towards our goals, to help us take initiative and strive to improve and to persevere in the face of setbacks and frustrations'. Frustration is usually against the way that the plans are taking shape and the results that occur. The remedy then requires what could be called self-guidance via personal standards and engaging in corrective self-reactions. These are skills that can be developed once the process has become explicit and shared.

The management of 'fortuity'

People's lives are never completely planned. Fortuitous events make a great impact on our lives and can change our circumstances and a whole range of things at one fell swoop (for example, marriages coming about as a result of a fortuitous encounter, and so on). Of course, not all fortuitous events have such a profound effect on a life, but a whole host of smaller fortuitous events do occur every day in our lives. It was Louis Pasteur who said, 'Chance favours the prepared mind', and Albert Bandura has developed this thought into the concept of 'fortuitousness'. However, it is in the controllability of the effects of such fortuitous events that a young person will need to engage in self-development. The management of unplanned events and influences in one's life may seem like an unlikely thing to teach, but it lends itself very well to the classroom, where all kinds of scenarios can be developed in a safe and secure environment.

> On the self-development side, the efforts center on cultivating personal resources that enable individuals to exploit promising fortuities. On the safeguarding side, individuals are helped to expand their self-regulative capabilities that enable them to resist fortuitous social traps leading down detrimental paths, and to extricate themselves from such predicaments should they become enmeshed in them.
>
> (Bandura, 2001: 11)

It is one of the basic tenets of education and training that scenarios, simulations and constructed situations are the basis of important learning for young people, and particularly in dealing with social situations. This is why drama, media events, television documentaries, and films, art and literature are so powerful in providing the 'what if' situations in education and training. The emphasis has been driven back on to the teaching of literacy, numeracy and basic skills in such a mechanical fashion that any attempt at creativity and foresight has been thrown right out of the window. The challenge for teachers and professionals working with young people is to develop techniques for making future possibilities 'live' in the present.

The approach of the 'Second Step' curriculum in the United States is to develop skills in empathy, impulse control and anger management. Multiple lessons are presented to students, which teach these skills in a developmental sequence, incorporating affective, cognitive and behavioural teaching modalities. A review of existing programmes for children which focus on one or more of these skill areas shows that these directions in prevention and intervention show effectiveness and promise (Grossman et al., 1997). Many of the cognitive process outlined earlier, such as self-reflection, intentionality, self-regulation and planning, are all the educative or learning elements of what are regarded as 'therapeutic' (for example, some anger management techniques can revolve around identifying 'triggers' – in self-efficacy terms this involves problem solving and planning based on self-awareness or self-reflection). The researchers at the Harborview Injury and Prevention Research Center in Seattle, Washington State, came to a number of conclusions in evaluating the 'Second Step' curriculum and in doing so illuminated some interesting features of the ways in which these approaches changed pro-social and aggressive behaviour. They compared children on the programme with those who did not pursue it and found that:

- Aggression decreased from autumn to spring among children on the programme and increased among students in the control classes.
- Six months later, students in the Second Step classes continued to show lower levels of physical aggression.
- Hostile and aggressive comments also decreased over the school year in the Second Step classrooms, and increased in the control classrooms.
- Friendly behaviour, including pro-social and neutral interactions, increased from autumn to spring in the Second Step classes, but did not change in the control classes.
- The Second Step curriculum led to moderate decreases in aggression and increases in neutral and pro-social behaviour in school.
- Where there was no focus on empathy, impulse control and anger management, behaviour worsened, becoming more physically and verbally aggressive over the school year.

These were classroom-based therapeutic interventions and there is clear evidence that it is possible to integrate these interventions with normal classroom routines if it is planned carefully. It therefore should not be strange to see therapeutic approaches as perfectly at home in the classroom, and anyone who denies the social dynamics of a classroom, or feels that they are unimportant, has clearly not done much teaching. The dynamics of interpersonal, social and emotional exchanges are, and always have been, a permanent feature of teaching in schools, simply because of the group dynamics and make-up of the groups involved. We would like to see more professional approaches developed by the professionals who know about them and will use them given the status they deserve. This used to be called 'grass-roots' development but has been largely quashed over the past twenty-five years. Government agencies tend to promote specific approaches to learning at the expense of other methods and then enforce them, on the basis that they are said to be improving contestable standards. This is a crucial theme running throughout this book, and the fact that the numbers of pupils excluded from school has not decreased, nor has the problem of antisocial behaviour in society, nor the rate of violent crimes, has made it important. It is not within the remit of this book to delve into the links and pathways from school and social exclusion through to prison populations, but we simply reflect the perceptions of professionals we work with in this field, who plainly see the links as young people follow a downward spiral.

Social and emotional skills: learning to behave, behaving to learn and learning for life

There is nothing new in the idea that social and emotional skills are important for learning, and there are lots of examples of social and emotional skill learning, expressed mainly as performance outcomes in the QCA end-of-Key Stage statements for personal, social and health education (PSHE). For example, at the end of Key Stage 3:

> Pupils can reflect on their achievements and strengths in all areas of their lives, and recognise their own worth. They show respect for differences between people. They can recognise and identify positive ways of managing strong emotions (for example talking with a friend or teacher about their feelings on divorce or falling in love).
>
> (QCA, 2005)

Or:

> Citizenship:
> Children describe, discuss and debate topical issues they have researched with others (for example articles on a national news website). They explain why rules are important for living and working together and know consequences of breaking these for individuals and communities. They know that rules can be changed and how individuals and groups work to try to achieve fairness. They know that in the UK laws are created through parliament and enforced (for example knowing that laws relating to crime are enforced by the police and the courts).
>
> (QCA, 2005)

According to Goleman (1998), social skills are about handling emotions in relationships well, accurately reading social situations and networks, interacting smoothly and using these skills to persuade and lead, negotiate and settle disputes, for cooperation and teamwork. Young people who are in trouble are often limited not only because of their inability to be sociable but also because of their negative experiences in life. Social skills deficits or problems can be viewed as errors in learning or they can simply be regarded as part of learning to learn and then as learning for life itself. It is not necessary to adopt a 'deficit' viewpoint about social or emotional skills. These Key Stage outcomes are so often taken for granted when they should really be expanded and given the emphasis they deserve. The statements quoted in the previous paragraph are aimed at mainstream school provision, but when one is working with young people in trouble, the appropriate skills may need to be taught directly and actively. Often social skills are taught and thought of separately from 'emotional skills' (if there are such things), and also separated from behaviour management plans and activities. Emotional intelligence is the labelling and part-conceptualisation of the way that a person is aware of and able to process and assimilate emotional constructs related to events and actions in their life. The notion was popularised by Daniel Goleman, who wrote about it in the work or organisational context. However, the role of emotion in learning and in behaviour has been long researched and explored. Emotion has been defined by many people. Goertzel (2004) asserts that a mental state arises spontaneously in an individual rather than through conscious effort, and is often accompanied by physiological changes.

George Kelly (1955) defined emotions as non-verbal constructs or as the events that occur when a person's construct system (that by which they anticipate events in life – immediate or otherwise) cannot cope with the circumstances or becomes overloaded. This is rather negative, and the physiological changes incurred by emotions can of course be pleasurable where existing constructs are reaffirmed and reinforced by pleasant experiences and the neurochemical changes that accompany them. Research indicates the involvement of the limbic system in the brain and the release of neurochemicals and hormones around the body. They can be paradoxical, and it is our experience that a young person can experience pleasure when, for example, being 'told off', if that event is one which they have become accustomed to. It can induce a sense of coherence and famil-iarity in some, whereas in most people it would induce discomfort. Also, paradoxically, a young person who has become used to being abused and insulted may feel extreme psychological discomfort in a nice school where everyone is 'nice' and polite to each other. So, emotions are complicated and interesting but are tied up in everything we do from basic movements to interpreting the sounds of an orchestra playing a symphony. They are inextricably tied up with learning and performing, as any performer will testify. They are very powerful and yet can be very subtle to the point where a person may not be aware of the emotions that are driving their reactions and behaviour. So, emotions are not easy to define, extremely difficult to quantify effectively and yet they are all-pervading and, some would say, make life worth living.

Theories of 'emotional intelligence' (EI) have recently become favoured in education both in the United Kingdom and in the United States, and have become subjects of scientific inquiry (Ciarrochi et al., 2001) contributing to a broadening of the perspective in the pursuit of engaging young people in their education. This chapter seeks to develop the argument that a narrow and predominantly intellectual (or purely academic) view of education has ceased to be productive in our modern society. It must now be supplemented by a strong concern with social and emotional skills and an equally strong concern with providing a positively encouraging, caring and sometimes therapeutic learning environment. To continue to ignore what science and psychology in particular have taught us about brain function, human learning and memory, and to pursue a narrow view of 'discipline', is once more to ignore the writing on the wall.

'A primary principle of EI is that caring relationships form the foundation of all genuine and enduring learning.'[1] A moment's reflection on one's own educational experiences will reveal the fundamental truth of this point of view. We have all learned under adverse conditions, but it is not the best way to produce regular and lasting learning and we need to bring our educational systems into alignment with this reality.

(Elias, *et al.*, 2001: 133)

Emotional intelligence describes abilities distinct from, but complementary to, academic or other forms of intelligence. The work of both Mayer and Salovey (1993, 1997) and Gardner and Hatch (1989) is breaking down our rather outmoded and ineffective or specialist concepts of 'intelligence' – that is, in a useful, day-to-day and meaningful way. It is being rescued from the reputedly objective and yet disputed tool of measurement and turned into working and meaningful concepts that are more helpful to teachers in their quest to encourage and develop successful learning. Research on brain function also plays an important part in our new understanding of intelligence related to our emotions. We tend to assume that intelligence is situated in the neo-cortex, which is the more evolved layers at the top of the brain. The emotional centres of the brain lie further down in the more ancient sub-cortex and in the limbic system. Goleman's (1998: 317) adaptation of previous work on emotional intelligence includes five basic social and emotional competencies:

- *Self-awareness*: Knowing what we are feeling at the moment and using those feelings to guide and support our decision making. Having a realistic sense of our own abilities and a well-grounded sense of self-confidence.
- *Self-regulation*: Handling our emotions so that they facilitate rather than interfere with the task in hand.
- *Motivation*: Using our deepest preferences to move and guide us towards our goals, to help us take initiatives and strive to improve and to persevere in the face of setbacks and frustrations.
- *Empathy*: Sensing what people are feeling and being able to take their perspective. Cultivating rapport and attunement with a broad diversity of people.
- *Social skills*: Handling emotions in relationships well and reading social situations and networks accurately; interacting smoothly; using these skills to persuade and lead, negotiate and settle disputes, for cooperation and teamwork.

In the case of young people in trouble, there are some who see emotional literacy and conceptions of emotional intelligence as *the* answer to all the problems. We reject this notion. Uncritical claims about emotional intelligence and emotional literacy should be approached with caution. We accept that the phenomenon cannot be ignored, and working with emotional development is both complex and, to some extent, still experimental. Adults who work with challenging young people often use their own intuition (it could be called emotional awareness) and intuitive skills to very good effect. There have been many problems with the scientific and academic establishment acknowledging the role of emotion. For some reason, over the years, it has become equated with woolly thinking and lack of objectivity and cleverness, the female element, and so on. All this has impeded a proper understanding of the role of emotion in daily life in a more academic or scientific manner. 'Connecting to our feelings is neither a soft, nor an easy option. Disconnecting from our feelings is not clever' (Antidote, 2001).

The study of emotion is still in its infancy in many ways as regards learning and social interchange, and we should be wary of the pendulum swinging the other way. There is no doubt that children's emotions can have a huge impact on their school life and that emotions can carry over from home to school and vice versa. Children are sensitive to anger and yet most do not have the skills of adults in handling emotional drives and influences. Emotional literacy has been described as the ability to recognise emotional triggers and conditions, understand them, and handle and appropriately express emotions. Well! There probably isn't anyone in the world who can recognise all emotional conditions, and as emotions are non-verbal constructs in the main, some emanating from early childhood, it is hard to see how we can ever fully understand emotions, or 'consciousness' for that matter. As for appropriately expressing them, well this is also very dangerous ground. Who knows what 'appropriate' means in this context? Much of what is written under the heading of emotional literacy has already been considered and really is nothing new. It is just another name for something that already exists in people's consciousness. What we do know is that some forms of behaviour that are a result of emotional tensions and outbursts are uncomfortable, sometimes very challenging and difficult and sometimes downright dangerous, and therefore must be handled. But there can be no overall 'appropriate' way to express emotions or else we would not have the diversity of expression we have. It smacks little of 'gulag' thinking and yet another way of getting young people to 'conform' – so we would refer readers back to the 'behavioural graffiti' of Chapter 2 and leave it at that.

Emotional development and awareness, social skills and self-efficacy are all highly interrelated and should be conceived as such in a school situation. Behaviour management plans are also plans for developing social skills, interpersonal skills, self-efficacy and emotional awareness. Teaching social and emotional skills is not much use if there are no contexts and planned opportunities to practise them. Learning about emotions is not an academic or intellectual activity at all and relies on context and modelling by adults. In a therapeutic education mileu these things must all be interactive and intertwined. The adults must be comfortable with working in a multi-approach, multilevel manner (and therefore more coherent, more complex) and therefore more realistic planned environment.

Keeping it all together: it is experience that counts in the end

This chapter has attempted to bring together and pick out the salient issues and features of social skill development and air some current issues to do with a young person's emotional development and its impact on learning. It has also explored more of the constituent parts of the conceptual base of Albert Bandura in his life's work on self-efficacy. We feel that this is a very positive way of encapsulating the kinds of theoretical base that can underpin work with challenging and vulnerable young people. It contrasts with the way that self-esteem enhancement, emotional literacy and behaviour modification or management are currently wafting around in education, almost as separate entities. This is partly because there are a whole range of agencies and organisations all jostling around to catch the attention of schools and teachers. What is important from the point of view of young people is that these areas of knowledge and new research should be seen as a coherent whole and not as separate 'answers' to a range of different problems. The young person's experience is not fragmented, but the solutions still seem to be.

In Chapter 4 an adaptation of Kolb's experiential learning cycle was used to illuminate the discussion on the way in which a young person learns, and the chapter criticised passive exposure to either behavioural manipulation or intellectualised (academicised) curricula relating to social and emotional matters. Subsequent chapters have developed the notion of neurological change also being associated with experience of social and cognitive events. We have also proposed that neurological change, the interplay between the social cognitions of a young person and their actions are all tied in together. The thrust of the arguments through this book is that a young person who is in serious trouble, serious enough to be excluded from school, is not going to react positively to 'more of the same', whether that be behavioural regulation or a curriculum in which they can find little meaning or motivation. Radical change is needed in order to make their learning more experiential and to make it a more real and satisfying experience. Working in social, emotional and self-efficacy domains can help with motivation, engagement, participation and access to the formal school curriculum. It must, though, receive proper priority in order for a young person to engage with the social cognitive changes that are necessary in order to give that young person the best chance of success at school and later in society. The latest catchphrase, 'emotional literacy', lacks properly articulated evidence bases (as opposed to social and psychological theories of emotional development and emotion). Just as shaky are unsupported notions that disaffected and vulnerable young people can learn just as well solely through the National Curriculum and 'discipline'. The first is still in the experimental tray along with emotional intelligence and the latter is in the anachronistic or dinosaur tray with academic supremacists and social elites. Proper evidential bases for this kind of work are developing and we feel that the heart of these are in social learning, emotional development, vulnerability and resilience and established social cognition theories.

Chapter 8

A real alternative to an 'alternative curriculum'?

The 'holistic' approach described and researched in this book so far has involved a 'whole school' approach within a regular school curriculum (i.e. in England and Wales, National Curriculum subjects). However, it is much more than simplistic 'behaviour management' strategies bolted on to the side, or the application of emotional sticking plasters to individuals or small groups of children identified as being emotionally underdeveloped or even emotionally unwholesome. Young people in difficulties are challenging and troublesome to the adults who are working with them, but they are not stupid. It does not take very long for a young person to recognise that they are being regarded (once more) as 'lacking' or 'unwholesome' or 'deviant' and to reject (in their minds, if not their behaviour) the attempts to 'remediate' their emotional shortcomings.

Therapeutic education, as with education generally, is about creating an environment that will energise, sustain and recognise personal growth, learning to learn and crucial life skills. These elements are vital in developing relationships generally and, in particular, developing 'learning' relationships. In this way, young people can become engaged with, participate in and gain access to a wider academic curriculum. We have also been resolute in our focus on self-regulation, self-awareness and self-efficacy. Related concepts such as emotional intelligence, self-esteem and self-worth are also worthy psychological constructs, but it has been argued that they tend to become more bolt-on remedial approaches rather than being integral to the learning processes found in schools and in the curricula we teach. We have emphasised the importance of developing a 'therapeutic environment' in the school and have begun to build an outline of practices resting on theoretical bases and principles emerging from research and practice.

Previous chapters have shed further light on the internal workings of the school case study. Throughout the book we have referred to 'young people', as this epitomises the age group of 11 to 16 years. However, in this chapter readers will notice the interchangeability with the term 'student' or 'student' in the school setting. We aim to clarify how the headteacher, staff, students, parents and associated agencies began to work together to make radical changes in their practice to match the needs of young people with social, emotional and behavioural difficulties. This chapter utilises the principles and models emerging and translates them into policy and practice.

The interactive curriculum and young people's behaviour in the school context

The school has worked on developing an 'interlinked' model to the subject-based curriculum and the personal, social and health education (PSHE) curriculum. This includes the key components of 'personal growth', 'learning to learn' and 'skills for life' (Goddard, 1996). The model is intended to ensure a proactive and educational approach to the academic and personal development needs of students with emotional and behavioural difficulties. It extends beyond mere 'behaviour management', which is often contingent and hence reactive, and it will, in the longer term, enable students to regulate and take responsibility for their own behaviour. It also provides for active and involved roles and responsibilities for *all staff* at the school. The management and learning support staff have cultivated the role of 'personal tutor' in order to offer cohesive learning support in and beyond the classroom. This enables the teaching staff to take full responsibility for subject coordination and teaching the curriculum effectively. The deputy headteacher has overall responsibility for an integrated approach to PSHE throughout the school, but it also enshrines an active role for learning support assistants. They have responsibility for individual and small group work on specific areas of the interactive curriculum, and, with the deputy headteacher, for aspects of the PSHE curriculum, as appropriate. The central planks (and assessment of needs linking with other assessment tools) are the 'behaviour and PSHE profile' (see Appendix 8) and subject-based curriculum assessments. The PSHE programme itself also provides assessment information to feed into the 'behaviour and PSHE profile'. Figure 8.1 illustrates how the 'interactive curriculum' operates within the school. Specifically, it shows the links between key intervention strategies, curriculum delivery and individual assessment and recording systems.

Importance of a school's 'statement of purpose' (policy statements)

The following sections of this chapter are taken directly from the school policy for managing a caring and encouraging learning environment for young people who are vulnerable and challenging. Accordingly, the reader will notice the change of tone from a series of discussions and interpretations into prose that is more intended to clarify the intentions of the school, the staff and the young people in it. The way policies are written is somewhat directive in an attempt to make clear what the shared values of the staff and young people amount to. It should be emphasised that a first stage in making these workable and worthwhile is to engage in a process of development and discussion with all involved.

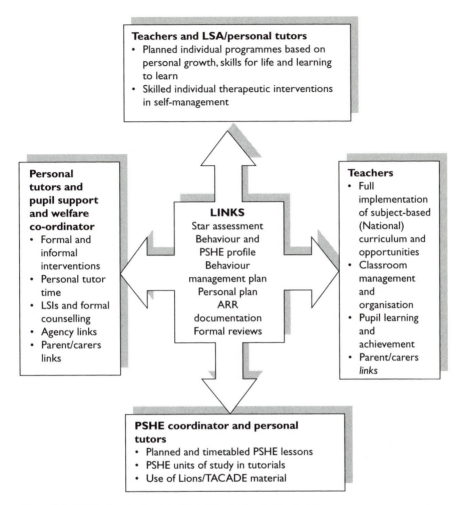

Figure 8.1 Operational aspects of the 'interactive curriculum'.

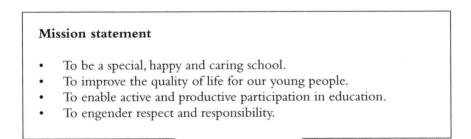

Mission statement

- To be a special, happy and caring school.
- To improve the quality of life for our young people.
- To enable active and productive participation in education.
- To engender respect and responsibility.

- To raise standards of teaching and learning.
- To celebrate achievement and success whenever and wherever we can.
- To prepare our young people for the future.

The school policy has taken nearly three years to formulate properly and it is an ongoing process involving continued staff and student discussion, broadening now to other professionals and the agencies involved with the young people at the school. This is an important development, and there appear to be clear differences between schools that are 'open' and that genuinely work with other professionals and agencies, and those that largely remain closed to outside influences (except perhaps OfSTED!). The policy statements contained in this chapter are an emphatic statement of the values, principles and strategies that are used in the school and also form the basis of staff development. They are also intended to support a coherent and consistent approach to managing relationships in the school.

School aims

The school:

- will support 'statemented' children identified as having emotional and behavioural difficulties and recognise individual needs;
- will foster a safe and caring environment for all, and actively seek to forge strong links with home and the community;
- will offer the National Curriculum to all its pupils between the ages of 11 and 16, and meet all statutory obligations;
- will offer a range of subjects most appropriate to the needs of its pupils through effective planning, assessment, recording and reporting;
- will offer both academic and vocational options at Key Stage 4;
- will regularly review all aspects of teaching and learning, and strive to raise pupil standards;
- maintain staffing levels which should always be sufficient to maintain an excellent staff : pupil ratio of approximately 1 : 3;
- will follow recommendations from advisory visits and inspections in order to make further improvements.

Staff will:

- be trained and qualified to carry out their duties to the highest possible standard;
- be trained and qualified wherever necessary to ensure the safety and well-being of all members of the school community.

The achievements and success of all members of the school community will be celebrated.

Without an orderly atmosphere, effective teaching and learning cannot take place. If children are permitted to misbehave at school, or to absent themselves from it, they prejudice their own educational potential. Worse, they disrupt the education of children around them. Good behaviour and discipline in school and classroom are an essential prerequisite to successful teaching and learning.

Classroom rules

We:

- walk quietly into the classroom and sit down ready for work;
- listen to staff carefully and follow instructions;
- put up our hand if we want help, without calling out or shouting;
- treat and speak to others with respect and never use put-downs or swear words;
- always try our best and work hard and never prevent others from working;
- look after our work and respect other pupils' work;
- look after our classroom and keep our desks tidy and clean;
- ask permission before leaving the room and always knock before entering another classroom.

The ethos of the school should reflect a clear vision of the values that matter within the school and the community surrounding it. These values should include respect for others and property, honesty, trust and fairness, and the virtues of self-respect and self-discipline. Young people should be taught that as they grow up they take on responsibilities and duties in the community that go hand in hand with their rights as citizens. An effective behaviour policy is central to enabling all pupils to access a broad, balanced and relevant curriculum regardless of their social, emotional and behavioural problems. One of the primary aims of any behaviour management strategy is to equip pupils with the skills and knowledge to be able to control their behaviour in a range of social situations. All behaviour management needs to be on a personal level, and communication of rules and regulations is important within all school situations.

We expect pupils to:

- treat everyone in the school with respect;
- treat the school and property with respect;
- wear the appropriate school uniform;
- be polite and only use acceptable language;
- use litter bins in and around the school;
- eat only during breaks and only in appointed areas;
- wear seatbelts in school vehicles

. . . and not to:

- smoke;
- bully others.

Systems that aim to encourage discipline through self-control cannot be divorced from systems of management and systems of care. Each pupil placement within the school must have clearly defined objectives that are understood by the staff. Similarly, all children and young people must understand the reason for their placement.

Relationships between the staff and young people need to be based on honesty, mutual respect and recognised good professional practice which is regularly aired and discussed among the professionals involved. Some young people need to experience care which compensates for the loss of the attention and security they would otherwise receive through the direct care of their parents.

It is futile to engage in arguments, lacking authority, about whether an educational context is the place for social and emotional strategies when faced with young people who clearly need them. A well-structured environment is unlikely to be achieved unless there is an established framework of general routines, and individual boundaries of behaviour are well defined. Children and young people need to be aware of what is expected of them and how the arrangements for their care actually work. Schools are obliged to provide proper provision for the social, physical, emotional and intellectual needs of children and young people. It is important that there should be a structure to the young people's day and that the correct balance should be achieved between free and structured time. Over- or understimulated children and young people will tend to resort to previously learned, habitual and often inappropriate behaviour. Young people provided with an appropriate balance of stimuli are in a better state of mind with which to learn new and more positive behaviours and strategies.

A range of appropriate leisure-time activities fulfil many learning purposes, but they are also an excellent way of relieving tension, increasing flow and reducing stress in the young person's life, and there should be ample opportunity for young people to participate in these. Such opportunity to participate will aid the maintenance of a purposeful and well-managed environment. Problems will occur where expectations of behaviour are unrealistic or inconsistent, or insensitive methods of control are used. Good professional practice would recognise that misbehaviour by young people often stems from a failure by adults to be sufficiently receptive to the needs and problems of the young people rather than from a wilful defiance of authority. The need to avoid labelling young people as disruptive or seeking to resolve misbehaviour by moving them on to new placements without the original behaviour being properly addressed must be recognised. Moving young people on when they get too difficult to manage should be contrasted clearly with a proper referral approach where a more suitable environment is identified by all concerned. One of the principal purposes of managing behaviour and encouraging discipline is to enable a young person to develop inner controls so that in time they learn self-control, establish feelings of worth and self-respect, and are motivated towards improved behaviour and enabled to live in harmony within a group. They should also be encouraged to develop a proper awareness of their rights and responsibilities and those of others as part of the process of self-regulation.

It is essential that children and young people should be consulted and their wishes and feelings ascertained in matters concerning them. Good order is much more likely to be achieved when children and young people are routinely involved in decision making about their care. They should be encouraged to accept responsibility for their own care, appropriate to their age and understanding. It is essential that staff should be aware of their importance as role models for the young people cared for by them. Staff should set high standards by their own behaviour.

The physical environment offered to children and young people sends out clear messages to them, which will contribute either positively or negatively to the maintenance of good order. It is important that the physical environment sends out the correct messages. It should be well maintained and cared for, any damage being rapidly repaired. Communal areas should be tidy but not clinically so; they should be places to which both young people and staff are proud to welcome visitors. The décor and choice of pictures and posters in communal areas should reflect the positive images and tastes of people from the full spectrum of our multicultural society.

Without clear messages about what the school aims to achieve, no policy would have any meaning or relevance. The following statements illustrate some typical messages a school might wish to relay to its service providers and service users:

> We aim to provide:
>
> - a clean and pleasant school;
> - a secure and calm environment;
> - the freedom to learn;
> - the opportunity to talk and listen;
> - appropriate attention and support;
> - the best education possible.

For any policy of this kind to have an impact on the lives of our pupils, the involvement of parents or carers and other support agencies is crucial. Parents or carers need to recognise that the work that is done at the school on a daily basis will often need to be pursued beyond school hours at home in order to maintain the consistency needed to reinforce acceptable behaviour. The school's behaviour policy is a core policy that all parties should fully understand, contribute to and feel ownership of. To this end, the school maintains a high level of communication with the home. Much of this work is done through our pastoral tutors, who are each assigned a number of pupils. Parents/carers are also able to consult regularly with staff in order to deal with current issues and problems arising both at home and at school. Each year, the school's management team invite parents and carers into the school to discuss the behaviour policy. The policy is also distributed to the local social services department (SSD), local education authority (LEA) and the local police constabulary.

Theoretical and legislative precursors to creating a therapeutic environment

A school with the aim of creating a more holistic approach to the education and care of the children must first construct a behaviour policy, and this should be guided both by the legislative framework with which it must comply and by the nature, philosophy and operational conditions of the school itself. The school policies should be the result of meetings among all those who work for, or in partnership with, the school, resulting in the combination of thoughts, feelings and opinions of the teaching staff, non-teaching staff, pupils, carers, parents and managers of the school. Any good policy acknowledges and is guided by a number of key legislative and guidance documents to ensure that practice is appropriate to the needs of the clientele. In this case the policy must be formulated within the framework of permitted disciplinary measures as identified in the Children Act 1989. It must also give due regard to the following:

- DfES Circulars 8/94, *Pupil Behaviour and Discipline*
- DfES Circular 9/94, *The Education of Children with Emotional and Behavioural Difficulties*
- DfES Circular 10/94, *Exclusions from School*
- DfES 1997, *Excellence for All Children*
- Section 550A of the Education Act 1996 and subsequent DfES Circular 10/98, *The Use of Force to Control or Restrain Pupils*
- DoH/DfES draft guidance 2001, *Promoting Positive Handling Strategies for Pupils with Severe Behavioural Difficulties*
- BILD Guidance 1996, *Physical Intervention: A Policy Framework*
- DfES 2003, *Every Child Matters*

The Elton Report (1989) gave sound guidance on good practice for behaviour management in schools, stating that the behaviour policy should ensure that a whole range of important school processes are consistent with one another. In particular, the following recommendations made by the committee are closely adhered to in the case-study school. Elton recommends that:

- Schools should ensure their rules are derived from the principles underlying their behaviour policies and are consistent with them.
- Schools should strike a healthy balance between rewards and sanctions, and both should be clearly specified.
- Pupils should learn from experience to expect fair and consistently applied sanctions for bad behaviour, sanctions that make the distinction between serious and minor offences apparent.
- The headteacher and teachers should ensure that rules are applied consistently by all members of staff, but there is flexibility in the use of sanctions to take account of individual circumstances.
- The headteacher and staff should avoid the sanctioning of whole groups.
- Staff should avoid sanctions that humiliate pupils.
- Staff should be alert to signs of bullying and racial harassment and deal firmly with all such behaviour by taking action based on clear rules that are backed by appropriate sanctions and systems to protect and support victims. Pupils should be encouraged to inform staff about serious cases of bullying and racial harassment of which they are aware.

Permitted disciplinary measures are encapsulated in Regulation 8, which requires that, except as otherwise stated by the Secretary of State under Section 53 (2) of the Children and Young Persons Act 1933 or Section 22 (7) of the Children Act 1989, only such disciplinary measures as are approved by the Department shall be used in the schools. It is recognised that some form of sanction will be necessary where there are instances of behaviour that in any family-group environment would reasonably be regarded as unacceptable. Staff should be trained to be proactive in dealing with potential problems or unacceptable behaviour using non-confrontational gestures, expressions and tone of voice, and maintaining verbal interaction. Staff will often pre-empt a pupil's unacceptable behaviour by recognising and responding to trigger factors and antecedents, thus being able to diffuse a problem before having to resort to more formal measures of discipline. The imposition of formal disciplinary measures should be used sparingly and in most cases only after repeated use of informal measures has proved ineffective.

There should be a system of rewards (for example, commendations, or extension of privileges) as well as sanctions. Under normal circumstances, children and young people should be encouraged to behave well by the frequent expression of approval by staff and by the appropriate use of rewards rather than by the extensive imposition of disciplinary measures. Where sanctions are felt to be necessary, good professional practice indicates that these should be contemporaneous, relevant and, above all, just. The following sanctions are not permitted in school:

- corporal punishment;
- deprivation of food and drink;
- withholding of medication or treatment;
- restriction of visits or communication;
- being required to wear distinctive or inappropriate clothes;
- deprivation of sleep;
- imposition of fines, apart from contributing to damage;
- intimate physical searches;
- use of physical accommodation to restrict liberty.

Implementation and management of the behaviour policy

Schools can and do make a difference. They have the capacity to lead, support and encourage pupils in developing good behaviour and in learning to play a responsible role both within school and in the wider world. All staff will have key roles in achieving such a capacity. The most important task of the school is to educate young people. The more effectively the school carries out this task, the better motivated will its pupils be.

An effective curriculum appropriately differentiated to stimulate and engage the pupil is a key factor in maintaining an orderly learning environment. It is also very important that teachers should have high expectations of all their pupils, in terms of both achievement and behaviour. Discipline is most effective when teachers can be constructive and positive, and when they are specific about what behaviour is expected of a pupil and what is unacceptable. Pupils are likely to behave and learn better when they feel responsible for their learning and capable of success. Pupils should be encouraged, under the guidance of the teacher, to set and organise learning goals for themselves, reflect on their own progress and work cooperatively with their peers.

Beyond that, good teachers pay attention to the features of teaching and classroom management that are conducive to maintaining good discipline and effective learning in the classroom. Effective classroom managers:

- have clearly understood procedures regarding pupil discussion, participation in lessons, movement in class, the way in which work is handed in, and what pupils should do when tasks are completed;
- give clear presentations and explanations;
- have clear work requirements of pupils, and monitor progress carefully;
- give clear instructions so that activities run smoothly.

Misbehaviour is handled quickly and calmly so that the pace of a lesson is not lost and further disruption is minimised.

In detail, these principles of effective management of the classroom involve attention to basic good practice through:

- ensuring that the work is appropriate to pupils' abilities;
- setting clear goals for each work activity and making sure all pupils understand them before an activity begins;
- starting and ending lessons on time;
- ensuring as far as possible that a classroom is suited to a particular activity;
- taking care over seating arrangements – these will often be dictated by the activity, but particular attention should be paid to the location of the more troublesome pupils and those easily distracted;
- minimising external interruptions wherever possible – such interruptions can distract even the most attentive pupils and can trigger unsettled or disruptive behaviour;
- ensuring the availability of necessary materials for a given activity.

The quality of leadership provided by the headteacher and the school's management team is crucial to the school's success in promoting acceptable behaviour. It is the duty of senior staff, by example, actively to promote the conditions for pupil success in the school. This involves determining measures for the formulation of rules and the provision for enforcing them. Also, it means ensuring a proper regard for authority, respect for others, a high standard of acceptable behaviour and the general regulation of the conduct of all pupils. The headteacher is responsible for developing the school rules and code of conduct, which influence the overall behaviour policy. This must take into account any guidance given by the DfES and the local education authority (LEA). The elected governing body has a duty to monitor how the headteacher discharges his or her statutory, contractual and locally agreed responsibilities.

The system of behaviour management is contextualised within the framework of PSHE, the school curriculum and the general school ethos and environment. The model that we have adopted for this purpose is termed 'the interactive curriculum' and it features the following key areas:

- personal growth;
- life skills;
- learning to learn;
- the National Curriculum.

In this way we are best able to identify short- and medium-term individual behaviour targets to supplement the child's personal planning. Each target is matched to an appropriate strategy for dealing with the problem area at one of three levels:

- *individual* – i.e. praise, points system;
- *group* – i.e. units of work, discrete PSHE, class rules;
- *general* – i.e. school code of behaviour, ethos, environment, values.

The school's PSHE programme is central to our approach in dealing with challenging behaviour. Among the key topics that are covered in these lessons, the issue of 'bullying' is dealt with at some length as it is recognised as a likely occurrence in a school containing pupils with emotional and behavioural difficulties. It is also given high priority through the pastoral system within the school. It is our aim to create a caring, cooperative ethos in which teachers are expected to assume the role of teaching social skills and emotional awareness in a conscious and systematic way.

Operational procedures and methods of promoting good behaviour

The following narrative details the level of support and intervention strategies currently offered to students on a routine daily basis in order to deal with their emotional and behavioural difficulties. This section contains what we consider to be key points or activities in maintaining a therapeutic environment within the school. On arrival every morning, each pupil is greeted individually and settled in their place. The teacher or personal tutor will sit and talk with a pupil during tutor time, discuss the theme of the week or offer to play a game to gather the class together and prepare them for the day. They are each given their point sheet for the day, which identifies general rules and work in each session. Forty per cent of the day's points are available through individual behaviour goals that are identified from their PSHE profile. These targets are reviewed every half-term.

During lesson time, pupils are often given one-to-one teacher or personal tutor support. As they settle to their work, they are praised and encouraged to complete the task and participate fully in the lesson. Appendix 7, 'A schedule for observing and assessing a therapeutic approach to learning and teaching', represents a detailed itemisation of strategies and actions in the classroom developed from analysis of practice. The PSHE curriculum will articulate some of these, but purely as outcomes for young people. The interactive curriculum, though, requires that teachers operate on a multilevel teaching basis (as most effective teachers do).

Within the checklist (Appendix 7) are a number of important factors. First, the teacher's (or adult's) behaviour is also a key factor in teaching and modelling skilled social behaviour. The adults concerned need also to model good skills in managing conflict. Non-aversive techniques will enable the young person to see working models of the kind of skilled social interchange and emotional awareness in action. This is very important and should be an integral part of all teaching. Within this checklist are embedded techniques that will empower young people who are vulnerable and yet provide firm boundaries for the challenging behaviour that they exhibit regularly. This is all part of the daily round of teaching and managing the therapeutic learning environment. Due attention should be paid to the need for advanced skills and understanding (as suggested in Appendix 7) and for consistent and shared attitudes and values (as expressed in Appendix 2, 'Therapeutic education assessment for shared values'). It is important to understand that without this firm base for relationships in the classroom, very few other (and often more remote) strategies will have any significant impact.

If the student is unable to settle, they are then offered the opportunity to work either in the classroom in a quiet area or out of class by themselves or with tutor support. A student may wish to take a five-minute break if they feel uptight and unable to concentrate. If a pupil leaves the class, they are 'shadowed' by a member of staff until they return. If the student remains reluctant to return to class or is involved in a serious incident of some sort, they may sometimes ask to speak to a particular member of staff to talk over issues/problems. This discussion would form the basis of a life-space interview (LSI) that is aimed at analysing, and effecting a short-term resolution to, the issue. The welfare coordinator (who is a counsellor) or teacher may carry this out.

Incidents may occur that result in physical intervention. This intervention may entail no more than a simple single passive escort to guide a young person to a particular destination. In extreme circumstances where the situation demands a significant degree of intervention, physical restraint techniques could be used. After any major incident the young person is given an LSI conducted by a member of staff. In so doing, there will be an explanation of why the young person had to be restrained and how future incidents leading to a full restraint could be avoided. The interview also gives the young person a good open forum in which to talk about internal or external events that may be posing a problem for them.

Table 8.1 Stages to the 'life-space interview' in the event of a serious incident or problem

I	Isolate the young person	There must be privacy and space for discussion to take place
E	Explore things from the child's point of view	The child's view of reality must be heard without criticism
S	Share	Providing a reality from the staff's point of view
C	Connect	Making links with similar situations that identify how feelings affect behaviour
A	Alternatives	Ideas from the child as to how they might handle things better next time
P	Plan	Identify the best course of action for next time, allowing the child to feel fully involved in the decision-making process
E	Enter	Summarise what has been agreed and start the reintegration process

On occasion, a young person is placed on a 'personal challenge' when it is clear that they are unable to self-manage in the classroom or another designated working area of the school and that no learning is taking place by conventional means. 'Personal challenges' are a new and innovative dimension to the school curriculum. They offer an alternative cross-curricular approach to education with a practical outdoor emphasis. Teaching and non-teaching staff guide young persons through a series of common tasks and goals, encouraging open dialogue, trust, respect and healthy relationships. The challenges include orienteering exercises, surveys, countryside walks, etc., all linked to specific skills within the National Curriculum.

In the classroom, the students will follow the National Curriculum, differentiated to suit their individual needs. Their work may include (if year-appropriate) a vocational programme that is geared to the Key Skills programme. When a task is completed, free choice is available until the next lesson. The student can choose from a range of games, computer activities, drawing or reading. In the afternoon they can sometimes choose to play extra football. After break and lunch, some of the students are often given time to calm and compose themselves with a member of staff before they are ready to resume lessons. Sometimes a student may settle to work in isolation because it is often better for them to attempt work without distractions. The young person is reintegrated into class as soon as they are able to cope. On some afternoons, class groups are taken out to visit sites of interest or take part in activities in the locality linked to areas of study. Choice of these can be limited by the students' inability to understand appropriate language or behaviour when with members of the public. Students may require very close support and supervision on these occasions to minimise risk of inappropriate behaviour and to avoid negative interaction with their peers.

Students can gain a range of incentives and rewards during the course of the school day. They can gain points for achieving individual daily targets and conforming to a basic code of conduct. The points are saved and can be 'cashed in' at the end of the week for a variety of merchandise. For each full day of attendance every young person receives a raffle ticket that is entered in a Friday draw with the prize of a free-choice lesson and the opportunity to play games on a computer. Students have shown a great deal of enthusiasm for this system and we have seen a marked difference in attendance rates as a result.

Each week the students are able to participate in a range of PE activities as well as art, DT (design and technology) and food technology. Each activity needs to be risk-assessed because of the varying degrees of self-management exhibited by the students. The students will often require direct and continuous support when working with tools or sharp objects, as they may be a risk to themselves and others. Requiring such a comprehensive system of young person support inevitably has a marked impact on the school's overall staffing structure. The extent of some intervention strategies is substantial and is only typical for those children who are at the very extreme end of our range of need. In order to have any impact on educational attainment and level of behaviour, a high level of staffing is essential. This staffing allows us to provide more consistency of support for the unusual and sustained demands on our time and expertise.

Handling conflict and potentially violent situations

Staff are aware of the need for positive approaches that are applied consistently throughout the school. In the majority of cases, potentially violent situations can be de-escalated by assessing the aggressor's emotional state, identifying trigger factors, maintaining communication and offering problem-solving strategies. However, there are times when specified techniques in escorting and restraining are necessary when dealing with severely challenging behaviour. These techniques are used when all other options have been exhausted and only if there is a risk of a young person committing a criminal offence, harming themselves or others, causing significant damage to property (or engaging in any behaviour prejudicial to maintaining good order and discipline – section 55A of the Education Act 1996 10/98). The last of these should be regarded with extreme caution as it could give carte blanche for over-rigorous disciplinarians to justify physical force.

The following statements describe the physical intervention techniques used as part of a gradient response to challenging behaviour. Investigation and research have led to identification of the most appropriate range of interventions to match the nature and needs of the students in the school. They have been formulated and refined over years of practical application and continue to be subject to review and updating in response to new demands, needs and expectations. The application of such techniques is made in full knowledge of the personal circumstances of each young person and with reference to his or her statement of special needs, individual behaviour plan and behaviour management plan (BMP). When escorting or restraining, staff will work in pairs or a team as soon as possible to ensure that the procedure is effective and safe for all concerned. The lead staff member will be in constant communication with other staff and regularly assess and reassess a situation and plan of action in response to individual needs and other environmental and operational factors. The school recognises that using reactive and restrictive techniques remains at the centre of much professional debate and controversy, especially the use of supine restraint at floor level. While the application of this technique is limited to relatively few students (as identified on their BMP), the school believes that it remains an appropriate, effective and safe means of dealing with extreme challenging behaviour that poses a direct threat or risk to people or property. All such events are carefully logged and monitored both internally and by the parent organisation. Statistical evidence gathered over the past three years demonstrates an excellent health and safety record for all physical interventions used in the school. It must be emphasised at this point that the following brief descriptions are for information purposes only, and should never be applied in practice without first undertaking the appropriate 'BILD'-approved training, and only then as part of a planned organisational response to challenging behaviour.

Escorting a young person

Passive escorts offer security and confidence without 'overpowering' the young person. Staff may use a gentle hold to the lower forearm and one flat palm resting on the young person's shoulder (*Touch Support*). A more secure technique for a single member of staff requires one hand on the forearm with the other arm extending around the young person's back and holding the other forearm (*1 Person Escort*). The same position is used with two staff members mirroring both sides but adopting an underarm hold with the member of staff's nearest hand (*2 Person Escort*).

During escort the young person will be informed of staff intentions. There will be constant reassurance for the young person, explaining what is happening and why. Staff will also be able to apply or disapply the techniques according to the demands of the situation. Peaceful de-escalation is used when a young person is actively distressed and out of control rather than overtly violent, where reassurance is more important than restraint and where a degree of privacy is possible. This may be done by lowering the young person to a sitting position and creating personal space around them.

Seated restraint

Two members of staff will lower the young person into a wide seating area from a two-person escort (as described above). They will retain the appropriate holds and sit down simultaneously. This position benefits from being quick and easy to effect, and it is very safe and comfortable for all concerned. This position can be easily relaxed into a natural setting for a life-space interview (LSI). During restraint, the young person will be informed of staff intentions. Once again, there will be constant reassurance for the young person, explaining what is happening and why. Staff will also be able to apply or disapply the technique according to the demands of the situation.

The recovery phase and life-space interview (LSI)

During restraint, there will be regular dialogue with the young person in order to calm and comfort. When the young person has regained control to the extent that all staff agree to release the hold, they then proceed by gently releasing and moving away one by one. A transition from supine to a supported seated position is also a common form of recovery. With the young person 'under (self) control' from the recovery process and accepting directions from staff, a 'life–space interview' (see Table 8.1) should follow.

This discussion takes place after a short pause given to the young person to have a drink, straighten their clothing and gather their thoughts. Although 'distance' should be maintained, staff will continue to communicate acceptance and warmth as the discussion begins. The basic aims of the 'life–space interview' are:

- to continue the calming process with the young person and regain self-control;
- to explore with the young person his or her responsibility for what has happened;
- to identify alternative strategies for the young person to use in future;
- to plan for the young person's reintegration into school or class.

All staff should complete an entry in the physical interventions and sanctions file and incident book within twelve hours of the event.

This chapter has described and traced the operational procedures and rationale that link the theoretical principles and models expounded earlier in the book with the practical realities of running a school and constructing a therapeutic learning environment. It started with the interactive curriculum that has been developed, and explained the ways in which this 'interacts' with young people's behaviour in the school context, thus providing an integrated experience of education and learning. The importance of a school's 'statement of purpose' (policy statements) is emphasised as a means of communicating purpose and intention within the school among staff and students, but also outside the school to parents, carers and outside agencies. Theoretical and legislative precursors to creating a therapeutic environment cannot be ignored, and this section has attempted to make links between, on the one hand, the current legislative and statutory context and, on the other, the theories developed and how these can manifest themselves in school organisation.

The implementation and management of the behaviour policy in the school is the key activity that will determine whether or not the school is able to generate and then sustain a therapeutic learning environment. Consideration of operational procedures and methods of promoting good behaviour reflect the ways in which the staff and whole school respond to young people whose behaviour and difficulties need to be handled and minimised, not escalated by careless management. The potential for violence and escalation is there and the school has a carefully planned approach based on a series of carefully planned hierarchies of action in order to act preventively but firmly at all times. Firmness of purpose and prevention are a reflection of the skills needed by staff in managing the therapeutic learning environment.

Chapter 9

Achievement and lifelong learning

A 'principled' approach

In the previous chapters the outline of school strategies and policies and their development illustrates the practical application of social cognitive theories as well as current ideas about developing social and emotional awareness and skills. A therapeutic environment should empower and encourage a young person to learn new strategies and skills, and hence learn their way out of the difficulties generated by their behaviour towards others. We do not discount many other ready-made packages for working with young people in terms of their cognitive, social and emotional development. There are some on the market that are very effective in their way and there are some that are not so effective and some that are questionable. There are packages around and publications that make claims for their work that are not supported by evidence and for whose authors the commercial imperative has outweighed the need for accuracy. There are authors writing guidance for teachers who do not give due recognition to the sources of their knowledge and pretend that they have come up with a new idea, an idea that is all too readily accepted by uncritical audiences. Teachers are bound by necessity to look out for new ideas and are regularly assimilating new practices but tend to reject some of the more obscurely academic outpourings even though these have better provenance. There comes a point when professional practice in education needs to be better supported by proven evidence bases, and professionals should have ready access to these in a straightforward way. A principled approach to educating troubled and troublesome young people depends not only on the honesty and integrity of those who are promoting strategies and practices, but also on the willingness for scrutiny of the theoretical and evidence bases of the work.

Therapeutic education: arguing for new solutions to old problems

This book is not about individual therapeutic practices, as we have tried to make clear throughout. It is about therapeutic education. This is concerned with developing a whole school environment that combines a therapeutic approach with teaching a curriculum. It happens that in England and Wales there is a

National Curriculum, and this has to be recognised as important for teachers and schools. How important it is in the long run to young people remains to be seen. What is important is that they leave school with the ability to make their way in the world, and the *first* prerequisite for this is to be able to form relationships, rather than to be able to read and write to a particular standard. However, the one does not preclude the other. In a school or centre for young people, there must be a multi-element approach to learning and teaching. In Chapters 6–8, and the associated appendices, the components of a whole school or whole centre approach was elaborated and evaluated, and our intention is to proffer a potential toolbox for colleagues to use or develop in their own ways.

The case-study example continues to provide a basis for some further discussion around examples of distilling the theories expounded in previous chapters and turning them into useful resources for schools. These will embrace monitoring events and conditions within and outside the school, with the implication that outside agencies and parents or carers should be involved at all times. It also takes forward the idea of sometimes dissociated behavioural checklists and develops them into a single assessment and recording tool that is related to an interactive curriculum model. The 'behaviour and PSHE profile' (in Appendix 8) is a structured and comprehensive assessment and recording system, and moreover offers a vehicle by which the theoretical perspectives discussed in previous chapters can be applied using proactive and solution-focused techniques and procedures. This system provided a most comprehensive and effective tool, and one that has proven to be successful over the past five years in the case study examined in this book. Each student is assessed using this profile, which directly reflects the areas of the 'interactive curriculum' that underpin 'access' to, 'participation' in and 'engagement' with the content curriculum, whatever that may be (e.g. academic, national or vocational). This gives an immediate picture of where the learner is and also clearly demonstrates that key word 'progress'. Current inspections frameworks are built on the assumption that academic progress (e.g. in literacy, numeracy and so on) is enough and reflects progress within the individual. This is not enough. There needs to be better understanding of what it means to a young person to recognise their progress with their own personal growth and study abilities. Only after that is it possible to use the incentive (or the 'judgement') of progress on academic targets. In this respect, current inspection regimes are failing the teachers and schools that they purport to be improving.

Previous chapters have emphasised the need for a holistic and strategic approach to young people experiencing difficulties in their behavioural, social or emotional development. They also accept that some of these difficulties may lie in events and circumstances outside school and those that have developed over a significant period of time. Some critics of non-academic approaches to education tend to be very reserved about dealing with the emotional and social side of learning because they see it as 'blaming' the young person and trying to change an individual to suit the social whims of the time.

The importance that Government policy makers attach to solving problems . . . is driven by the conviction that some of the key problems facing people are rooted in a private sphere that characteristically fosters emotional havoc and which produces emotionally illiterate individuals who are unable to sustain thriving relationships. . . . Parenting classes, sex education, bullying initiatives, help lines, drop in centres, counselling are attempts to find professional-led solutions to problems that are essentially to do with difficulties encountered in everyday encounters and relationships. This is an area, where public policy can do little good and is likely to do a lot of harm.

(Furedi, 2003)

There are clearly important arguments and discussions to be had. These should clarify some very hazy and woolly ideas banded together around the current favourites of, for example, emotional literacy, emotional intelligence, multiple intelligences and brain learning. However, many young people in difficulty in school are not experiencing the 'difficulties encountered in everyday encounters and relationships'. They have experienced very serious and often extremely damaging encounters. It is clear that Furedi is not considering this significant minority of young people.

We also accept that therapeutic education is not the only way of conceptualising a 'humanistic' approach to education. Nevertheless, the development of what some would call 'soft' approaches to educating young people may simply be a counterpoint to the very hard and relatively 'inhuman' approaches that have been promoted over the past thirty years. An education system that is driven by results, by statistics, negative and sensationalist imagery and by punitive cultures such as OfSTED partnered with local and national newspapers does not, in effect, put the learner at the centre of the process. We are extremely wary about medicalising educational practice and about individualising blame by only expecting the young person to change, when it is clear that some of the problems lie in the systemic 'pathogens' (McGuiness, 1993; and see Chapter 2) of school and of society. We do not in any way say that it is the individual who should change, no matter what the circumstance. Quite the contrary: a holistic approach means being aware of the social, political and environmental factors involved in the difficulties experienced by a young person who is either excluded or at risk of being excluded. This book is not about making young people outcasts by labelling them with medical syndromes (e.g. ODD, ADD, ADHD) or about pacifying with treatments and drugs, but about energising, motivating, and engaging with the disaffection that many young people feel in school and afterwards. Critics who say that young people in great difficulty can be supported without recourse to any considerations of social and emotional or individual ('psychogenic' – McGuiness, 1993) aspects have clearly never worked consistently with young people who are both challenging (troublesome) and vulnerable (troubled) or in trouble.

So how do therapeutic approaches to education fit in? They encapsulate the best aspects of humanistic approach to education, in direct contrast to the hard-edged 'boot camp', disciplinarian approach to teaching. That is not to say that a teacher must not be firm, assertive, employ a skilled approach to group management and dynamics, and have a clear idea of what they are trying to achieve. It simply means that coercion is not the best way of achieving cooperation and appropriate or active compliance. Working with children and young people experiencing social or emotional difficulty or disaffection is often unpredictable, and each young person will be different with their own set of experiences, beliefs and capabilities. Each 'case' will be unique and will require new solutions. Applying the same old solutions to new problems, even when using a systematic approach, is doomed to failure if it does not have some creative component that depends upon the individual case in hand. It is hard to be consistent, particularly when the only thing you can be sure of is the inconsistency of the situations you find yourself in. To make it worse, a young person's behaviour does different things to different people, and young people behave differently in response to different adults. The various adults that any one child has contact with will also have differing expectations. Working with young people experiencing social, emotional and behavioural difficulties requires self-confidence and well-thought-out strategies as well as a positive approach to young people. There is little room for impatience or a judgemental attitude. Where teachers often feel they cannot cope, this feeling sometimes comes from setting unrealistic goals for themselves as well as for young people in particular circumstances. The goals are not always set by the teacher, and problems are often added to by the pressures of curriculum and performance management in a driven educational economy. It is important to be clear where one's own personal boundaries and values lie, as well as those behavioural boundaries and values that are set for the young people in question. This can be supplied through a well-thought-out structure or framework for both sharing problems and getting to a variety of solutions that suit *your* context.

Introducing empowerment concepts into the school ethos

A principled and therapeutic approach to teaching young people who are troubled and troublesome requires a set of shared values and the ability to monitor and test those values on a regular basis – for example, when a new member of staff joins the team. Remaining flexible, having positive values and being prepared to learn new skills should enable a teacher (or teaching team) to bring to bear a range of approaches to teaching and learning that come under the umbrella of 'therapeutic education'. In a suggested three-minute seminar on Neuro-Linguistic Programming, O'Connor and Seymour (1990: 27) propose outcome, acuity and flexibility as the only three things one needs in order to be successful in life, and we believe that the same applies to teaching.

[T]o be successful in life, you need only remember three things.

Firstly, know what you want; have a clear idea of your outcome in any situation.

Secondly, be alert and keep your sense open so that you know what you are getting.

Thirdly, have the flexibility to keep changing what you do until you get what you want.

In a paradoxical way these three tenets express the need for coherence and consistency alongside the need for flexibility in dealing with challenging situations. We are dealing with the role of the teacher's or other adult's behaviour in both reducing and dealing effectively with challenging events and difficult behaviour. Implicit in O'Connor and Seymour's three points is the message that if we want others to change their behaviour, then we must change our behaviour first and remain open to the possibility of change. This is crucial to a therapeutic approach to education and to creating appropriate and successful learning environments for young people who have been excluded from school or are at risk of being so. We have developed a simple tool for doing just this and 'testing' for shared values among a staff team. This assessment and development tool can be found in Appendix 2, 'Therapeutic Education Assessment for shared values'). It is simple enough and covers specific areas of understanding and professional development, and is intended as an addition to normal classroom observation of teaching:

- *knowledge and expertise* – with children, of school aims, flexibility, theoretical principles, child-centredness and proactive/reactive approaches;
- *attitudes, values and beliefs* – concern and care for children, positive outlook, preparedness to discuss and talk, share aims for young people;
- *self-awareness & self-control* – confidence, perceptiveness, assertiveness, consistency, manner and approach to young people;
- *performance/practice* – use of encouragement, sharing practice, teach skills not controlling, actively listen, non-aversive approach;
- *limiting factors* – development points as a person/a professional, deeper understanding, tendency to escalate situations, consistency.

A simple five-point scale can be used for self-assessment, professional development, staff discussions, and so on. This therapeutic context for delivering the curriculum is a working model being practised at Westwood School in Kent. It continues to be a basis for teaching the curriculum at the school and is continuing to evolve and develop. 'Therapy' does not necessarily need to define limited outcomes for constrained or the individual. It does not need to produce 'performance' from the young person, of any sort. It is simply contingent on, and developed through, the young person's own responses to the therapist's actions or words. The therapist responds to the client and then interacts and guides towards resolution as far as possible. Resolution may be in achieving new perspectives or new developments – in enabling the client to move on more successfully.

There are many who have a similar view of education – that is, 'e-ducere' (Latin) – to lead out, a view of education that means getting the best out of each young person, enabling them to achieve their inherent potential. This liberal view of education has been downplayed since the 1970s and replaced with a more hardline view of 'performance', outcomes, target setting and the curriculum merely as chunks of static knowledge. The question is whether more recent notions of what 'education' is can be seen in the same frame as constructs of 'therapy'. It is our contention that in practical teaching terms education is, and should be, therapeutic. Skilful teachers form relationships with children and young people that enhance their learning – indeed, more often than not are crucial to it. Through these positive relationships, an increase in skill, knowledge and understanding should lead to more control of the world around a child and a subsequent increase in self-esteem. There is, though, some light at the end of the tunnel in the beginnings of a broadening of government statements on inclusion and inclusive practices.

Reviewing the problems of young people in education

Chapter 1 explored the relationship between social and educational exclusion, concluding that educational exclusion often rides on the back of social exclusion and that schools, far from being the remedy for social problems and exclusion, are part of the problem. More often than not, the very challenging behaviour exhibited at school can be traced back to extreme conditions in the family or to societal influences such as those mentioned previously. Unfortunately, the fairly bankrupt policy approach and apparently knee-jerk reaction in the setting up of another national talking shop of teachers and headteachers[1] will not change the basic 'pathogens' (McGuiness, 1993) that are endemic, particularly in the secondary education system. Nor will it deal with the wider issues of conflict and tension in society. Schools are clearly a reflection of the communities around them, and this is nowhere more manifestly exemplified than in the recent research into institutional racism (Parsons *et al.*, 2004). It is time not just to react to the outcomes of conflict and tension but to examine some of their causes. It is time to go beyond the notion of education as a socio-economic or social inclusion project dependent on success within limited (albeit functional) academic terms and regard education as equally important in nurturing young lives and providing genuine opportunity for personal and social growth.

More particularly relevant to this book is the question 'Why is it that young people get into trouble when they are in school because of their challenging behaviour or are unable to take advantage of the educational opportunities on offer?' There are combinations of complex factors involved in the inability of a young person to sustain their place in a mainstream education environment. This book generally focuses on positive empowering strategies, but at the risk of being negative for the purposes of examining the problem, they may:

- not possess or have had the opportunity to develop a useful language of social interaction in which cooperation and sociability can transcend tendencies towards conflict;
- be unable to respond assertively rather than aggressively because of the social models (e.g. peer and adult behaviours) they have experienced or have observed in their lives so far;
- have developed low self-esteem and poor self-image as a result of the negative feedback received from significant adults in their lives (including teachers);
- have been directly discouraged from developing 'emotional intelligence' or sensitivity to their own feelings in a competitive and conflict-laden social context (or community);
- have experienced a series of academic failures, experience specifically identifiable learning difficulties, have poor self-belief and have successfully adapted their behaviour in order to 'avoid' failure in future, without regard to the personal cost;
- have developed a set of 'habitual' conflict-laden behaviours or adaptive behaviours to avoid being challenged or 'put down' by others, as a matter of survival in some cases;
- be in foster care or temporary family care pending decisions about foster care and may have experienced enormous emotional upheavals and attachment difficulties;
- be very vulnerable and lack 'resilience' (Tizard and Varma, 1992); despite the appearance of external toughness, challenging young people are often very fragile and lack a feeling of identity and self-worth.

Some of these effects can be traced (not always by direct causal or empirical links, as yet) to social and community conditions that impact on growth, personal development and learning in school, such as:

- low income and parental unemployment;
- homelessness;
- poor parenting;
- poor schooling;
- post-natal depression among mothers;
- low birth weight;
- substance misuse;
- community factors, such as living in a disadvantaged neighbourhood.

In addition to the demands on a young person due to their life circumstances are the demands of school. In order to include a young person in educational 'success', schooling also demands:

- the ability to defer immediate goals for longer-term achievements, which many young people see as well beyond their needs or capabilities or simply as of no interest to them;
- that young people 'buy in' to the target-based economy of education in order to achieve goals and aspirations that they may not subscribe to or understand;
- a significant degree of social ambition and self-efficacy to offset the reality of crowded classrooms, noisy environments, peer pressures and hard-pressed teachers with little time for individual problems;
- a hopeful vision of how to achieve 'equality' through academic success to overcome the inequality they often experience in their own lives;
- a greater level of conformity and cooperation than in most other social environments and often impossibly different expectations from those that they may have experienced prior to, and outside of, their school experience;
- stability in the home background in order to live up to the academic pressures, which need to be sensitively managed by teachers and schools who are also under pressure to produce 'results'.

Developing effective and empowering practices and a humanist ethos

Developing a learning environment that promotes personal responsibility, self-efficacy, self-esteem, confidence, and emotional and social skills, or compensates effectively and sensitively for learning difficulties (either specific or global), should be inextricably woven into the fabric of our lives (and into educational practice) and not reduced to isolated traits or innate deficiencies (paraphrasing Clough and Barton, 1995) or even as 'disabilities'. The interactive curriculum model proposed in Chapter 8 illustrates how a more therapeutic approach to young people, to the curriculum and to the school ethos was developed.

Figure 9.1 starts with the young person and illustrates that the processes involved are to do with personal change and growth. The question is 'How much time is really spent in schools on issues of personal change and growth?' There are no doubt many, many teachers up and down the United Kingdom who strive to pay heed to young people's personal growth and the challenges of change they encounter. Paying attention to personal growth and change is vital in enabling a young person to engage increasingly and more independently with the learning experiences on offer.

If we take the young person as a starting point and move across Figure 9.1, we propose the areas of identity, social and emotional skills and awareness, and

Figure 9.1 Troubled and troublesome children: identified needs in terms of care and support.

self-efficacy, to be of vital significance in enabling both participation (the relationship with others, including the teachers) and access (the relationship with the curriculum and learning experiences) (Powell *et al.*, 2004). Having established that it is important to confront the wider causes of a child's difficulties, it is necessary to make sure that the background knowledge and resources are available. This requires teachers to have the personal and professional resources to respond positively to difficult challenges. It also obliges schools or learning environments to be sufficiently well thought out to enable learning rather than simply attempt to enforce conformity with the threat of exclusion.

Again we argue that the process of schooling and individual learning is far more complex than the simplistic and politically motivated notions of social engineering, target setting and skill acquisition that drive significant proportions of the current education system. A more sophisticated response is necessary, most particularly for those young people who have been injured by life itself outside school and whose behaviour may be extremely challenging and difficult but who are themselves not resilient but vulnerable. However, it is also suggested that the complex social and emotional factors in the learning and teaching process itself, as a social and psychological interchange, are part of the process that needs attention in all schools, not just as a bolt-on to the education system for 'special' cases. Therapeutic approaches and techniques involve all areas of the curriculum and the social environment of the project. Engagement in education is about the relationship with oneself (Powell *et al.*, 2004) in terms of having a secure identity, having some self-belief and feeling confident. A closer look at the systemic educational priorities in England and Wales, particularly in secondary education, shows that not only has the young person's experience at school narrowed because of the rigid impositions of the National Curriculum (Kelly, 1994), but schools have become increasingly driven by the target-setting culture towards setting priorities that have little to do with personal growth and development. Please refer to Appendix 1, which is intended, by giving some examples, to trigger your thoughts about where and how you could monitor and develop some areas of working in your project, school or centre.

Monitoring and developing a learning environment that is 'therapeutic'

In the previous three chapters we presented a case-study view of a school and its strategies in encouraging self-determination, self-regulation and self-efficacy in young people. The school is not primarily a mental health facility, but its ethos, attitudes and practices will impact on the mental health of young people in the same way that any community will have such an impact. This is clearly attested to by the sad cases of suicide following bullying that have been reported in the press in the United Kingdom over the past few years. In previous chapters we have also attested to the influences on our work of positive psychology emphasised by self-efficacy (Bandura, 1997) and self-regulation (e.g. Zarkowska and Clements, 1996). A phenomenon that has grown from the study of positive psychology and one that has developed over a number of years, and is mentioned in Chapter 3, is the concept of 'resilience'. There is not the space to discuss issues of 'vulnerability' and resilience' in great depth here. However, therapeutic education aims to construct a positive environmental approach that uses 'resilience' as the key factor in developing the school ethos, a curriculum or behaviour development plan and guides individual interactions with young people in trouble. The following list takes from the conception of 'resilience' in the early years but, when modified, is just as applicable to young people in their teens. Resilient young people have the ability:

- to develop psychologically, emotionally, intellectually and spiritually;
- to initiate, develop and sustain mutually satisfying personal relationships;
- to use and enjoy solitude;
- to become aware of others and empathise with them;
- to engage in social or group leisure (play) and group learning situations;
- to develop or acknowledge a sense of right and wrong;
- to resolve (face) problems and setbacks and learn from them.

Health professionals identify emotional and behavioural problems as mental health problems, but it is arguable as to whether doing so is always useful unless there is a framework of practice that would support joint interventions in schools. *Every Child Matters* in the United Kingdom is energising some thought in this direction and there are initiatives building on the therapeutic model in developing more awareness in schools. We are involved in such initiatives in Kent and are examining alternatives to attending school for young people who have been habitually excluded or have excluded themselves. Many mental health problems will be experienced by a young person as being mild and transitory nuisances to their education, whereas others will have serious and longer-lasting effects. The following is an extract from *Promoting Children's Mental Health within Early Years and School Settings* (DfEE, 2001) and should be noted with respect to the brave new world of professional and interdisciplinary cooperation that is absolutely necessary for progress to be made:

> When a problem is particularly severe or persistent over time, or when a number of these difficulties are experienced at the same time then a young person may have mental health problems. . . .
>
> Such definitions will include many children who experience or are at risk of experiencing mental health problems; such as those who are so withdrawn and anxious that it is significantly impacting on their ability to learn, or those whose behaviour is so extreme they are not able to sit and concentrate. However, not all children with mental health problems will necessarily have special educational needs. . . .
>
> For other children however, their behavioural difficulties, which often have a significant emotional element to them, may be so intertwined with their inability to concentrate, to learn and to get on with their peers, that an approach which does not include attention to the educational alongside their emotional, social and behavioural needs will fail to provide the range of support that they need.

Certain young people and groups of young people are more at risk of developing mental health problems than others. These are situated in a number of particular areas specific to the young person, to their family, their environment and life events. Other young people, against all the odds, develop into competent, confident and caring adults, a phenomenon that is at the heart of the concept of 'resilience'. Understanding the factors that enable a young person to be resilient is of great importance in the relationships between learner and teacher but also in the management of a school or centre. There is a complex interplay between the range of risk factors in the child's life, their relationship with each other and more positive resilience factors.

> Risk factors are cumulative. If a child has only one risk factor in their life, their probability of developing mental health problems at school has been defined as being 1–2%. However, with three risk factors it is thought that the likelihood increases to around 8%; and with four or more risk factors in their life this increases to 20%. We know therefore that the greater the number of risks, and the more severe the risks, the greater the likelihood of the child developing a mental health problem.
>
> (DfEE, 2001)

When agencies or researchers or authority figures in science use the term 'we know . . .' it always begs the question 'Who is "we"? and what kind of "knowing" is involved?' However, DfEE (2001) testifies to the many positive projects going on up and down Britain, mainly focusing on early years and primary school. Early intervention is important but we are still faced with the problems of young people in their teens, and the bulk of exclusions still seems to be in Year 8 in the United Kingdom. Added to which, the above document cites a recent Office for National Statistics survey showing that 10 per cent of children aged between 5 and 15 experience clinically defined mental health problems (no reference is given, again undermining evidence-based practice). In our experience there are a great many more whose problems either have not reached the level of diagnosis in medical terms or whose difficulties are masked by their own ability to compensate for their difficulties in social and educational terms. There is an issue also of 'expertise'. This government guidance thankfully does not imply that schools and teachers have to 'wait' for medical advice before doing anything. The prevalent 'expertise' model in education is disempowering for all and should be rejected. Table 9.1 clearly illustrates the ways in which schools, centres and other provision for young people can develop and change to encourage more resilience in young people. Readers will see quite clearly that the strategies, attitudes and ethos of a school or centre quite clearly contribute to the vulnerability or resilience of the young people in their charge.

This chapter presents a developing view of therapeutic education. We see therapeutic education as encapsulating a principled approach to educating troubled and troublesome young people. Transparency in developing strategies and practices is important in order to share professional practice and evaluate it. The willingness for scrutiny of practices is intended to enable development of the theoretical and evidence bases of the work. In fostering the concepts associated with therapeutic education, we are arguing for new solutions to old problems. These new solutions should go beyond the played out bolt-on behavioural checklists and adherence to mechanical curriculum demands. They should venture into the less certain and uncharted areas of the learning relationships involved and explore the way that the school ethos itself encourages and empowers young people. There are clearly important arguments and discussions to be had, and these should clarify some very hazy and woolly ideas that are hindering teachers' own problem-solving abilities.

Implicit in this chapter is the message that if there is to be a change in the way that young people become disaffected and excluded, then there must be some more radical changes in the way education is delivered. One of these changes involves more seamless cooperation between the professionals and agencies involved. The question 'Why is it that young people get into trouble when they are in school?' has been reiterated and it leads to some final tools for monitoring and evaluating less easily measured effects of school and community on young people. It proposes the concepts of vulnerability and resilience as key to understanding how therapeutic environments can be developed in school. In the next chapter there is a final pulling together of the complex range of activities that exemplify lifelong learning, the interactive nature of the curriculum and finally a summary of what characterises therapeutic education. The evidence

Table 9.1 Summary of vulnerability and resilience factors and their impact on children and young people

	Individual children who:	School or centre	Home/family and community
Vulnerability factors	experience somatic disorders, e.g. chronic fatigue syndrome	Low morale and weak leadership in school	Socio-economic disadvantage
	experience psychotic disorders e.g. schizophrenia, manic depressive disorder, drug-induced psychosis	Single-minded focus on academic achievement to the detriment of the spread of ability in school	Homelessness
	experience hyperkinetic disorders e.g. disturbance of activity and attention	Children who are withdrawn and anxious and go unnoticed	Natural or man made disasters
	experience emotional disorders, e.g. phobias, anxiety states and depression that may be manifested in physical symptoms	Lack of attention to bullying, group dynamics, social and emotional interactions in the school. Lack of behaviour policy that is practised	Discrimination against the family or just against the individual – labelling and bullying or setting up for punitive consequences – to satisfy bystanders
	exhibit conduct disorders, e.g. stealing, defiance, fire-setting, aggression and antisocial behaviour	Lack of socialising pre-school experiences combined with family/ home problems or lack of guidance	
	experience developmental disorders, speech delay, social ability or those with pervasive development disorders; attachment disorders; habit disorders, e.g. tics, sleeping problems; soiling; post-traumatic stress syndromes	A culture within the school which pays no heed to the importance of trust, integrity, democracy, equality of opportunity and the place of the school in an inclusive society. A school with a weak (non-existent) PSHE curriculum and that ignores daily social dynamics	Loss or separation from parental affection and contact – resulting from death, parental separation, divorce, hospitalisation, etc.

continued

Table 9.1 continued

	Individual children who:	School or centre	Home/family and community
	experience loss of friendships especially in adolescence, family breakdown that results in the child having to live elsewhere	An ineffective pre-school curriculum for young children that does not pay any attention to socialisation or teach the use of pro-social resolution strategies	
	experience life changes, e.g. birth of a sibling, moving house, changing schools	Schools with a narrow curriculum strategy and that ignore non-academic opportunities	
	experience traumatic events – abuse, violence, accidents, injuries, war or natural disaster	A culture that ignores the contribution of those engaged in the care and supervision of children	
Resilience factors	are able to establish a secure attachment to their parents in the first year of life	High-morale school with positive policies for behaviour, attitudes and anti-bullying	Affection coupled with clear, firm and consistent discipline. Wider supportive network
'Resilience seems to involve several related elements ...	are able to communicate effectively	Schools with strong academic and non-academic opportunities	Supportive long-term relationship or absence of severe discord
Firstly, a sense of self-esteem and confidence ...	have a positive attitude, problem-solving approach	Promoting activities positively aimed at promoting the mental health of all children	At least one good parent–child relationship with good communication
Secondly a belief in one's own self-efficacy and ability to deal with change and adaptation; and ...	have the ability to reflect and achieve emotional 'distance' from family problems or demands	A programme of social and emotional learning with a range of activities for young people and staff	Support for education and positive involvement in child's learning
	are female		

Thirdly, a repertoire of social problem solving approaches'	An effective pre-school curriculum for young children that actively teaches the use of pro-social resolution strategies	Good role models(s) of pro-social behaviour, empathy and friendships. Stable childcare arrangements with low staff turnover
(DfEE, 2001)	Children learn to be self-critical, without shame, to set high goals while seeking objective feedback, e.g. High Scope curriculum	Range of positive sport/leisure activities that allow development outside family confines
can achieve a degree of 'self-insight' during the developmental years to master environmental demands and challenges	Skilful teaching that arouses a young person's interest and motivates	Good housing. High or at least good standard of living
are planners and have a belief in control and in being able to achieve personal targets	A culture within the school which values teachers, lunchtime supervisors, and all those engaged in care and supervision	Support outside the family – e.g. network of friends and relations
have an easy temperament when an infant	A culture within the school recognising the importance of trust, integrity, democracy, equality of opportunity and relationships	
have higher intelligence and have developed creative and physical abilities	Each child being valued regardless of their ability	
Have humour or religious faith or level of social and emotional development in the early years	A senior management team committed to equity, proactive work with parents and good relationships	

Source: Adapted and extended from a variety of sources, including DfEE (2001).

base for factors contributing to the success of a therapeutic environment is the result of five years of work exploring the case study of the school and its context. The implementation of a therapeutic learning environment and interpretation of the evidence also incorporate the many years of practical experience of both authors of the book and of the staff involved at Westwood School.

Chapter 10

Putting it all together, together

The public view of 'troubled and troublesome young people' is, on the whole, a gloomy one. Little sympathy is extended to young people who fail to live up to society's demands and expectations, and in the public domain they are seen as simply 'naughty' or, worse, little criminals. This is hardly surprising when one only has to pick up a newspaper (referred to in Chapter 2) to see how the so-called yob culture is affecting decent, law-abiding citizens who ask for no more than a quiet life. Stories of aggression, theft, vandalism and violence by teenagers in urban areas that result in antisocial behaviour orders, tagging and strict curfews are growing in profile and are increasingly debated. Support, sympathy or solace are properly focused on the many victims of these crimes, but how best to deal with the perpetrators effectively is more of a problem. It appears that this problem has now extended to whole groups of young people and to particular residential areas that emerge as those that are most socially and economically deprived.

Of course, not all 'troubled and troublesome young people' turn to criminal activity, and deprivation is not in itself a reason for criminal behaviour. A recurrent theme of this book revolves around the constructs of self-regulation, nascent resilience and self-efficacy, meaning that everyone has choices to make. Through developing self-awareness and through learning, a young person begins to understand the consequences of those choices. Sometimes the young person will make the wrong choices, setting off a chain of events that ostensibly will ruin their life chances. Perhaps rescuing rather than criminalising is the order of the day for many young people? Conversely, one might deduce that not all those involved in crime necessarily suffer from behavioural, emotional or social difficulties, although there is perhaps a thin divide between the two.

Absurd contradictions abound in our society, where commercial interests promote the drinking of alcohol as a 'cool' leisure activity and do everything possible to 'hook' young people in, and then public opinion condemns the subsequent behaviour of young people who cannot control themselves or their drinking. Getting a little drunk or pushing a boundary has always been part of a learning curve for young people. Lack of shared boundaries on top of economic and social pressures has now inflated the problems of partying and learning from over-consumption.

It appears that groups of young people are becoming more and more criminalised and getting involved in more and more seriously antisocial behaviours, rather than in recognised dissenting or socially active groups. The encouragement of aggressive behaviour in the media and the criminalising of challenging behaviour or expressions (albeit sometimes inappropriate) of disaffection, in contrast to violent or seriously antisocial behaviour, are muddying the waters. Teachers and parents, when establishing blame for misconduct, will often make a distinction as to whether the youngster 'did it deliberately' or whether extenuating circumstances justified the action. For most victims, however, background and circumstances surrounding incidents, especially when they have resulted in personal suffering or loss, are inconsequential. The behaviour and results remain the same. More often than not, knee-jerk reaction and summary retribution are the results. However, approaching the issues and problems in a thoughtful, reflective and perhaps more enlightened way may mean that the outcomes are more beneficial and effective for all concerned. This raises an interesting point in the context of schooling, described by Bennathan (1998: 2) in a passage already quoted in Chapter 4: 'Until schools are confidently in control of most of their pupils it is almost impossible to tell a child with real emotional and behavioural difficulties from a child who could behave well if s/he chose.'

From criminality, control and coercion to cooperation and consensus

Teachers are mentors and facilitators, not prison officers or sergeant majors. The role of mentor, teacher, guide and facilitator is not consistent with that of an iron-hard disciplinarian, and there are not many teachers who see themselves in that role. If anything, they are generators of self-discipline, self-awareness, resilience and self-regulation. Nevertheless, teachers have been encouraged to think exclusively in 'control' terms. This thinking even extends to physical control and restraint. They often have this training in the absence of proper training in preventive avenues of personal interaction, advanced and organisational communication, and interpersonal skills. Short and sporadic training in such techniques without coherent and constant practice and retraining is utterly useless. Controlling actions and even physical restraint are often used before all other avenues have been effectively exhausted. As a result, individual teachers are not trained to avoid 'precipitation' into equally challenging responses and could well escalate situations unnecessarily (Cornwall, 2000). Self-defence and security for teachers are clearly necessary, but there is little need in most schools for control and restraint. When it is needed, this is often because the 'behavioural graffiti', the 'writing on the wall', has been ignored. It takes many years of training and practice to use physical restraint techniques effectively and safely, and such training is neither desirable for, or available to, most teachers. So, it is a half-baked measure in every respect and its place in schools, and particularly mainstream schools, should be seriously questioned.

There is really not much new in the problems faced by young people, their schools and society as a whole. The old solutions are not working and it is time to explore some genuinely new options. In therapeutic education, care and control are not seen as separate components but viewed as a whole. There is little point in controlling young people who do not feel 'cared for' as well. At the same time, young people cannot feel 'cared for' unless the situation they are in is safe and secure. The concepts of care and control are intertwined. There is a delicate balance between them that must be maintained if there is to be a positive outcome for a young person at the point of learning.

One of the key features of the National Curriculum is that all schools, within certain limited parameters, should be delivering a standardised set of subjects and subject content, albeit differentiated to match individual levels of attainment. However, if a school operates outside this sphere, then assessment of these additional and often unique dimensions to school life can become problematic. The UK education system is characterised by the coercive and punitive influences of the inspection system and is still without an appropriately shared foundation for improving the learning environment, rather than just measuring outcomes and limited academic standards. Consequently, inspectors have been faced with something of a dilemma. They have either to pursue their familiar inspection regime but run the risk of failing perfectly adequate schools, or to adjust their criteria to recognise and measure the quality of education in other dimensions of school life.

Interestingly, the most recent OfSTED *Inspection Annual Review* (2004) actually states that a balance needs to be struck by inspectors sufficiently well trained to recognise good practice in whatever form it takes. Without a more transparent and less rigid approach to OfSTED training and inspection, this is unlikely to happen at the moment. However, the danger of some special schools attempting to conform to a rigid and sometimes inappropriate set of standards is still a real issue that may have already severely impaired the overall quality of some provision, and runs the risk of continuing to do so. Tierney (2001) summarises the potential consequences by identifying some key issues. These are:

- failure to resource the development of young people with significant unresolved emotional needs;
- the reorganisation along inappropriate curriculum-based lines of some schools catering for young people with emotional and behavioural difficulties;
- the lack of extended periods with identified teachers at an early age;
- lack of flexibility to acknowledge the central role of self-expression for emotionally underdeveloped young people;
- the failure to offer therapeutic education in small, manageable schools with specially trained staff.

Despite these serious issues, the potential effect on special schools designated for children and young people with behavioural, emotional and social difficulties (BESD) is a matter that raises some interesting points. The majority of young people attending this type of school may have some academic delay but are generally of average intelligence. 'Such children are referred to therapeutic schools not primarily for their failure to achieve academic progress but for their failure to mature' (Tierney, 2001: 37).

A key factor in the development of therapeutic education approaches for young people who are vulnerable and challenging involves the application of a bio-psycho-social paradigm. Some approaches look upon difficult behaviour as a disability or even an illness (e.g. oppositional or defiant disorder, ADHD), ignoring the contextual and interactive factors involved; others describe 'difficulties' of a social, emotional or behavioural origin. The very phrase 'social, emotional and behavioural' is so generalised as to be almost meaningless. It includes young people who are disaffected, challenge authority or are aggressive and violent, through to those who are withdrawn, phobic or simply uncomfortable in regular education provision (for an even wider variety of reasons). There is a new trend in labelling behaviour as disorders or syndromes as if there is a constant set of behaviours independent of context, circumstance and personality. The relatively new term 'oppositional defiant disorder' medically labels anti-authoritarian behaviour. Once the label has been applied, there is the implication of a set 'treatment' to effect change. This is clearly nonsense. Pupils should be active learners, not passive recipients of treatment. Teachers have no remit to label, diagnose or sort children and young people into medical, psychological, cultural or health-related categories in order to teach them. Teaching and assessment for learning have more to do with recognising capability and promoting engagement, motivation and participation than with the more redundant activity of grouping or categorising. Even within the practical constraints of the classroom, teachers are often painfully aware that they are teaching a collection of individuals, as much as homogeneous groups of any kind.

From retribution and recidivism to ecology, relationships and learning behaviour

The early chapters developed a theoretical base centred on a bio-psycho-social paradigm or, more simply, an eclectic approach. In practical terms it behoves us to advance a true multi-agency and multidisciplinary approach that seeks to combine knowledge and principle with theory across professional divides. The development of child-centred services is still a long way off but it has begun, following the publication of *Every Child Matters* (Treasury, 2003). At the moment, practice in UK schools lurches between an individualistic medical therapeutic model and inclusive intentions based purely on a social constructivist paradigm. The case study and research evidence gathered for this study strongly support a combination of approaches to the education of troubled and troublesome young people. This 'eclection' (not collection) of approaches can be seen in the diverse range of interventions used and in relation to the theoretical models in which they are located. Illustrating the strategies and interventions available gives an overarching picture of the level and intensity of positive behaviour and personal support offered. In this way an alternative perception of 'best value' can be ascertained. Table 10.1 illustrates how one might categorise these strategies and interventions within a hierarchy of support across a school specialising in the education of troubled and troublesome pupils. The hierarchy of support shown in the table is reflective of an increasingly differentiated and specialist service, represented by levels 1 to 5. The support is further compartmentalised at each level by commenting on the groups of features that relate to physical or environmental aspects of a school, effective organisation, use of resources and the

Table 10.1 Summary of activities at different levels indicating support in a therapeutic learning environment

Level	Setting conditions/ environment	Operational tools	Knowledge/expertise
1	Comfortable; relaxed; purposeful; friendly; safe	Behaviour policy; code of conduct; daily routine; consistency; structure	Positive attitudes – encouraging; accepting
2	Dynamics; grouping; group size; specialist classrooms	Pastoral system; incentives; rewards; flexibility; time. YP self-regulate and make meaningful decisions	Individual understanding, experience, sense of agency and multidisciplinary assessment
3	Specialist areas of activity (e.g. music, art) with emphasis on self-expression	IEPs; BMPs; Functional analysis; STAR scheme; focused interventions; meaningful incentives and rewards	Proactive, active and positive behaviour support. Pastoral support with a sensitive, reflective approach
4	Study areas; quiet areas; outlets for pent-up emotion and for self-expression	Life-space interviews; teaching new social and emotional skills; finding and using 'teachable moments'	Proactive, active and reactive behaviour support. Personal attitudes, values, beliefs and empathic awareness
5	Shaped environment to encourage calmness and allow for self-expression and self-regulation. A no-blame culture visibly celebrating success, not sanctions	Therapeutic tools and expertise. Responses gauged according to need and positive outcomes. Resources and tools include staff self-regulation of behaviour	Therapeutic awareness and intervention. Greater personal awareness, understanding of nature of needs and responsibility for own actions. CAMHS; counselling

Note: CAMHS, child and adolescent mental health services.

expertise or knowledge base of the staff. In a general sense, one might view each of these groups in the form of a building block, as the features of a particular level tend to be the prerequisites of implementing the features in the next.

Readers will note that all the above features are consistent with the themes that have been explored so far in the book. They relate to the organisation of a therapeutic learning environment that has self-efficacy, self-regulation, participation and engagement as a vein running through the planning process. The importance of drawing out the features described here lies in their careful management and interaction. None is exclusive, and it is not to say that any, none or some features, regardless of level, cannot combine to effect a successful learning platform for a given clientele or group of young people. Indeed, the skill and teamwork that are applied in subtly blending these features together will largely determine the success of the overall strategy. The features can be defined or interpreted in a variety of ways, as can the method or extent to which they might be applied to any given circumstance. For example, implementing a behaviour policy that leads to consistency and a routine that young people can work within is as relevant at level 5 as it is at level 1. Nevertheless, the behaviour policy remains at the foundation of a good system of management and an expression of the management of positive relationships. Its content should be reviewed and updated to take account of other, more sophisticated initiatives as the system evolves.

A number of questions are likely to emerge from any efforts to apply any, some or all of the level features illustrated above. For example, on a practical level some aspects of the content curriculum are more reliant on structure and order than others, and this could lead to conflict in the way pupils need to be taught to ensure success while remaining within the National Curriculum framework. So what are the implications in terms of resources and staff expertise? Are the demands on staff unrealistic and is this flexibility of approach something that additional specialist training can support?

For schools that feel they have the potential to extend their provision in more therapeutic ways, what is the effect of reducing the punitive dimension of school life and replacing this with a greater reliance upon effective staff–pupil relationships, self-regulation and positive behaviour support?

Appendix 2, 'Therapeutic education assessment for shared values', provides a useful starting point for identifying how effectively staff perform in terms of promoting a therapeutic environment. Two crucial features of the 'level 5' support shown in Table 10.1 merit further discussion: namely, a 'shaped environment' and a 'no-blame culture'. There is an assumption here that support of this kind is possibly the most demanding for staff because it requires them to operate at a level that is the most intuitive and empathic. This requirement is emphasised by a number of researchers, including Laslett's 'staff's intuitive approach' (1995: 7) and the discussion by Zarkowska and Clements (1996) of what is involved in a 'therapeutic relationship'. Professionals and adults who work in this context also need to recognise the impact of their behaviour in developing and maintaining a special relationship with each young person in their care. This also means a greater awareness of how their behaviour will influence any given interaction, incident or crisis.

The concept of creating a therapeutic environment is not a process that can be switched on like a light. Achieving an effective educational environment through therapeutic means requires all staff to become increasingly skilled and resourceful in their efforts to manage behaviour in less stereotypical ways. Harder still is to acknowledge the part each of us plays in shaping a crisis and take responsibility for that involvement without automatically casting blame on the young person. A thoughtless or inconsiderate action by a young person that results in an accident or injury will very often have serious repercussions for the young person.

Unfortunately, 'knee-jerk' reactions by bureaucratic or fixed systematised responses rarely take into account all the factors surrounding an incident. The practice of using 'fixed term' or indeed 'permanent' exclusion to combat challenging behaviour will, more often than not, be seen as a punitive measure. It is widespread in schools because it is seen as a quick and easy tactic that removes the responsibility of dealing directly with the issue from the people involved up to that point. The moment at which the problem is passed to a senior member of staff is the moment at which all responsibility for engaging with and supporting that young person is effectively discharged.

Some will argue that a decision to send a young person home might prevent an escalating problem and that a 'cooling off' period is therefore preferable to having to deal with severe aggression and violence. But however the professionals view the arrangement made informally or formally with the home, the fact remains that the school's provision at that moment is deemed inadequate.

The moment can often arise as a knee-jerk reaction to the crisis. The issue may have deteriorated beyond the capacity for staff to deal with it effectively, have been taken personally, or have resulted in an injury or damage to property. Given these conditions, there is usually plenty of justification for exclusion:

- It serves as a direct punishment or 'justice'.
- It enforces a rule.
- It serves as an example to others.
- It serves a purpose for the staff or school.
- It removes the problem from the scene.
- It creates a breathing space.

Any school has the ability to exclude a pupil, but exclusion is understandably unpopular with parents, carers and other professional bodies, who see this action primarily as a 'cop-out'. However, in a school that boasts of being 'inclusive' and 'therapeutic' there is a greater onus on staff to manage crisis situations more effectively using a variety of internal means. At a school that professes to specialise in dealing with severely challenging behaviour, staff have a special duty of care that includes managing a whole range of behaviours that include severe aggression and violence. This is reflected in the huge costs involved in providing this type of service. Proactive, positive behaviour support requires that the young person's education and welfare are paramount regardless of the physical, emotional or psychological impact that this might have. Zarkowska and Clements (1996) refer to this as unconditional positive regard (see Chapter 2).

Clearly, when a member of staff suffers significant physical injury he or she has a perfect right to take legal action against the young person. However, psychological discomfort and difficulty on the part of both adults and young people is often taken far less seriously and yet can result in the exclusion of a young person from mainstream school. How much bearing this action has on the therapeutic relationship very much depends upon a whole host of factors, including the nature and circumstances surrounding the event, the course of action followed by staff and in particular the effectiveness of any remedial or follow-up intervention. If either party feels that the action taken has been unfair or unjust, this can sow the seeds of a further deterioration in behaviour and an inevitable breakdown in the relationship with the school. If people continue to think the worst of a young person because of their history of failure, then even a new environment will merely perpetuate that belief. A therapeutic environment accepts the past and attempts to shape a new environment that will be more engaging for the young person. The environment is shaped by the staff collectively, based on their knowledge of the young person and knowledge of the environment of which the young person becomes part. A school that assumes or expects that a young person will simply conform to a particular regime could well be setting unrealistic and unreasonable conditions that may bring about instant failure. Young people referred to special schools have successively failed in previous situations and often have had substantial periods out of school or repeated failure of both home and school placements. This indicates that their ability to successfully adapt and engage in any similar, albeit new, scenario becomes increasingly unlikely. The downward spiral of failure and rejection will continue unless the cycle of retribution and recidivism is broken. Current overemphasis on attainment and limited standards defined by those with a narrow view of education and personal growth will result in alternative provision becoming less and less available. Ultimately, with no stability and often a deep resentment for existing school environments and ethos, the whole idea of engaging in learning becomes too overwhelming to contemplate. Figure 10.1 shows two flow charts that follow a chain of events, in one case clearly perpetuating a blame culture, but in contrast the other, more therapeutic route maintains a positive and supportive culture. In this way the cycle of retribution and recidivism can be broken.

These events are based on the premise that people have a lesser or greater awareness and understanding of what is meant by a 'troubled and troublesome young person'. The use of terms like 'naughty', 'disturbed', 'difficult', 'disaffected' and 'challenging' is still widespread in professional and domestic circles. Indeed,

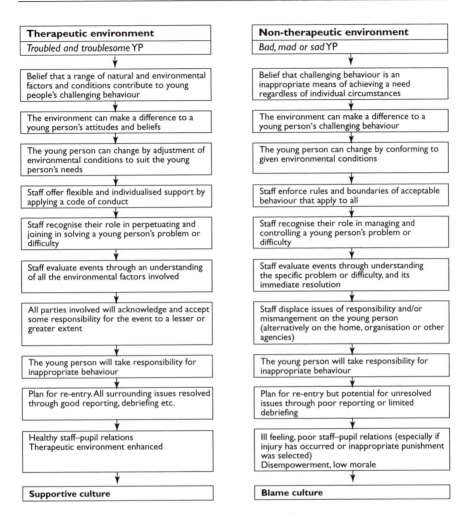

Therapeutic environment	Non-therapeutic environment
Troubled and troublesome YP	*Bad, mad or sad* YP
Belief that a range of natural and environmental factors and conditions contribute to young people's challenging behaviour	Belief that challenging behaviour is an inappropriate means of achieving a need regardless of individual circumstances
The environment can make a difference to a young person's attitudes and beliefs	The environment can make a difference to a young person's challenging behaviour
The young person can change by adjustment of environmental conditions to suit the young person's needs	The young person can change by conforming to given environmental conditions
Staff offer flexible and individualised support by applying a code of conduct	Staff enforce rules and boundaries of acceptable behaviour that apply to all
Staff recognise their role in perpetuating and joining in solving a young person's problem or difficulty	Staff recognise their role in managing and controlling a young person's problem or difficulty
Staff evaluate events through an understanding of all the environmental factors involved	Staff evaluate events through understanding the specific problem or difficulty, and its immediate resolution
All parties involved will acknowledge and accept some responsibility for the event to a lesser or greater extent	Staff displace issues of responsibility and/or mismanagement on the young person (alternatively on the home, organisation or other agencies)
The young person will take responsibility for inappropriate behaviour	The young person will take responsibility for inappropriate behaviour
Plan for re-entry. All surrounding issues resolved through good reporting, debriefing etc.	Plan for re-entry but potential for unresolved issues through poor reporting or limited debriefing
Healthy staff–pupil relations Therapeutic environment enhanced	Ill feeling, poor staff–pupil relations (especially if injury has occurred or inappropriate punishment was selected) Disempowerment, low morale
Supportive culture	Blame culture

Figure 10.1 Breaking the cycle of retribution and recidivism.

it is deliberate, to reinforce the idea that in a non-therapeutic environment it is presumed that, by definition, the young person is the focus of blame. Not only does a therapeutic environment require the staff to shape the environment to the needs of the individual young person, but furthermore, it is likely that as time progresses, the environment will need to be reshaped even further to suit the needs of a shifting and changing clientele.

Interpersonal relationships and human agency in the facilitation of learning

In the United Kingdom and United States, very diverse groups of young people are forced into the same enclosed school and classroom environments and all taught together. Some want to learn in a classroom environment through traditional teaching methods, some can't and some won't. In this book we have taken trouble to keep reaffirming the role of evidence-based practice (also emphasised in the US 'No Child Left Behind' policy of 2004). There is a need for critical reflection on new ideas proffered, from wherever they come. Further to the criticisms of New Age or postmodern approaches to learning rehearsed in Chapter 1 and 9, there are other new approaches that could be thought of as part of therapeutic education. These include recent and past concepts of individual learning styles, which Kingston (2004) sees as making some young people 'fashion victims' in this latest craze to assess young people for their individual learning styles. The article criticises the provenance of some new approaches to learning, and this is appropriate, as too many new initiatives are applied simplistically in the classroom. It is clear from the research involved (Coffield *et al.*, 2004) that there has been a fundamental misunderstanding of the way in which this kind of theoretical base should be applied. In the case of this particular research, Kingston cites some examples of where teachers in further education colleges have attempted to apply tests and assessments of individual learning styles, but the article also develops, without any evidence bases, into a criticism of individual approaches and differentiation of work for individuals. It is true that, as with therapeutic education, many new approaches are contestable; some are flawed and should be looked at critically. The instances found in Coffield *et al.* (2004) and described by Kingston mention teachers applying the results of learning styles tests by adjusting their teaching too closely to each style of learning in turn and inefficiently 'chunking' lessons or courses accordingly. This is a simplistic rendering both of the application of learning styles in multisensory teaching and of the research findings themselves. It is necessary, in multisensory teaching and acknowledging potential learning styles, to work in a multilevel manner.

Part of the problem is that some (usually not teachers) regard teaching (contrary to what skilled and experienced teachers know) as a monochromic activity having only one level. Skilled and advanced teaching requires multilevel delivery. The need for this kind of skilled and advanced teaching depends upon the situation and the group of learners involved and their responses to education. Limited teaching techniques and the construction of discouraging learning environments that are not dynamic (including the curriculum impact) should be severely questioned. Unfortunately, it is only when things go wrong that questions are asked. At the moment, young people still acquire most of the blame.

Another problem lies in the constraints and restrictions placed on teachers (and being subject to constraints is not the same as professional accountability), which deny them the opportunity to be as creative as they could be in dealing with diverse needs within their groups. So, one does not necessarily 'chunk' a lesson to deliver to each individual sequentially, but designs the lessons to work for individuals concurrently. Multisensory teaching (which existed before new concepts about learning styles) is a multilevel activity. This is akin to the simplistic way in which 'literacy' is now supposed to be taught as a result of government diktats. This could also be a multilevel process. Experienced teachers know that 'literacy' (and numeracy and science) can be developed through any curriculum (or other) subject matter, but it cannot be 'judged' simplistically, so it is written off the agenda because teaching has become subservient to a mechanistic accounting exercise. In OfSTED inspection the fixed timetable of rigid subjects still reigns supreme. The interactive curriculum described in this and other chapters is a case in point. It is quite possible to teach a curriculum at one level but at the same time be dealing with cultural, social and emotional factors within a group of young people. In fact, teachers have been doing this for decades, if not centuries or millennia. Teaching is a social and psychological activity, and the transmission of culture and knowledge cannot be divorced from its human interactions and processes.

Teachers are very capable of 'sifting' through good and bad practice, given the opportunity to look at research. The criticism extended to 'protectionist' researchers and education consultants by the example Kingston (2004) mentioned also extends to those who criticise new developments without also using evidence bases, theoretical underpinnings and current research. Educational research should be undertaken by professionals in the field. There is a large 'industry', encouraged by the dishing out of government money (and hence under strict controls), of people researching education. Why is this important in the context of working with young people who are troubled and troublesome? We, the authors, feel that, more than any other area of education, the concepts of 'access' to knowledge, 'participation' in the events associated with learning and 'engaging' with peers and others in the learning environment are poorly understood. The consequence, as we have already underlined, is inappropriate judgements by both the DfES (statistics) and OfSTED (emphasis on standards through the National Curriculum). These have led to misleading statements on what are effective and successful schools and centres catering for young people in trouble.

The terms 'access', 'participation' and 'engagement' are ones that have been extensively used in terms of entitlement to educational opportunity. They are not well-defined constructs in terms of young people who are vulnerable, troubled and challenging. They form the basis of recent research into behaviour for learning (Powell et al., 2004) and are very much related to Carl Rogers's conclusions (discussed in Chapter 2) on the qualities and attitudes that facilitate learning. The first of these has to do with what he terms 'realness', in that the 'real me' of the teacher (McGuiness, 1993) is involved in the learning process. The teacher is not a robot or a machine but is entering into a relationship with the learner. Meeting learners on a person-to-person basis enables the learner to model from the adult and to understand how to learn, to develop more effective social and emotional skills and confidence from the adult model. Denying this opportunity to the learner means the adult *may* have power but no empathy.

Successful learning facilitators care for the learner, but not in a possessive way, where the success of the learner merely reflects the success of the teacher or institution (e.g. academic results). The acceptance of the learner as a separate person, an individual having worth in their own right, involves a basic trust – a belief that this other person is somehow fundamentally worthy, no matter how imperfect or unsuccessful they may be in academic terms. Such acceptance acknowledges that the learner has many feelings but also has many potentialities. A further element that establishes a climate for self-initiated experiential learning is empathetic understanding. If the teacher or adult is able to understand the student's reactions from the inside, with a sensitive awareness of the way the young person sees the process of education and learning, then significant learning is more likely to take place.

From curriculum to relationships, personal growth and lifelong learning

In conclusion, the study has recognised that there is another dimension to education that is vital to the well-being and personal development of every young person and one that teachers cannot ignore. Personal areas of growth such as self-confidence and self-esteem, awareness of interpersonal relations and study skills are all precursors to engaging effectively in the content curriculum (Goddard, 1996). For many young people, educational progress has been impeded because of a failure to address these and other key areas. This has led to disengagement from the learning process and a downward spiral of frustration, anger and disruptive behaviour. Can schools afford to disregard a dimension of education that serves as the foundation upon which the whole of the content curriculum relies and, more importantly, influences a young person's academic success and future prosperity? Special schools that serve troubled and troublesome young people are inherently designed to respond to behavioural, emotional and social difficulties. The approach each school takes will vary depending upon a whole host of factors that will sway, and be swayed by, the location of their theoretical base. The school discussed in this study has followed a therapeutic approach and the evidence presented has demonstrated a marked impact on the quality of teaching and learning, the quality of relationships and the young people's general quality of life. Evidence indicates that developmental work will continue and this will include regular review and refinement of particular techniques and strategies used at an operational level. The therapeutic approach to date has shown much success and is worth pursuing. The range and effectiveness of the features of a therapeutic approach to education exploited by professionals involved will make a difference for troubled and troublesome young people. This book and case study describe some of those features, but none is more important than the attitudes, values and beliefs of the professionals involved. If they remain genuine in their resolve to offer positive, child-centred support, then the quality of relationships, the quality of teaching and learning, and the overall quality of life for each young person must surely be enhanced.

The principle of shared responsibility is also seen as a fundamental part of the re-educative process. By sharing together with the staff full responsibility for the management of their community, young people are thought to share in something much more than exercises in decision making. They learn to be responsible both for (and to) others; to accept the natural consequences of their own acts; and to value themselves as people who have something to contribute to the general good (Wills, 1948). Even though Wills's beliefs were expressed over five decades ago, they have lost none of their relevance and are echoed in the statements currently made about personal, social and health education in 2005 (QCA, 2005: 3):

> Young people demonstrate that they recognise their own worth and that of others (for example by making positive comments about themselves and classmates). They can express their views confidently and listen to and show respect for the views of others. They know how to face new challenges positively (for example the transition to secondary school). They know that there are bodily and emotional changes at puberty, and have ways of dealing with these in a positive way. They can talk about a range of jobs, and understand that they will need to develop skills to work in the future. They know how to look after and save money. Young people can make choices about how to develop healthy lifestyles (for example by knowing the importance of a healthy diet and regular exercise). They have an understanding of what affects mental health (for example exercise or dealing with emotions). They can make judgements and decisions and know ways of resisting negative peer pressure around issues affecting their health and well-being. They know which commonly available substances and drugs are legal and illegal, and are able to describe some of the effects and risks of these. They can identify the risks in different situations and are aware of how to behave responsibly (for example discussing issues connected to personal safety).

It seems that little has changed in aspirations for educating young people, the only difference being that in 1948 perhaps this aspect of education was seen as important. By 2004, personal growth and development had almost disappeared off the agenda in the United Kingdom and have been ignored by those who have had executive responsibility for the design and implementation of a national curriculum over the past fifteen years. It had become an irritation to squeeze on to the timetable in the face of pressures to provide a narrow curriculum. The irony has been that many traditionalists incorrectly assumed that the National Curriculum was a more traditional curriculum. The sentiments expressed by

Wills (1948) and the Education Act 1944 clearly espouse a much broader and more balanced view of education than was encapsulated in the legislation of the 1980s and 1990s. In effect, teachers, schools and young people suffered a parochial narrowing and abuse of the ethos of education in the United Kingdom late in the twentieth century (Kelly, 1994). We sincerely hope that there will now be a resurgence and recognition of the importance of the development of the whole child and young person.

School days should be the best days of our lives. A therapeutic approach to education aims to enable young people who have particular and special needs to look back on their childhood with happy memories of their experience at school. This chapter summarises how the extensive research and development that has taken place within one school can have a wider application in education. Through genuine case studies and real-life experience it becomes apparent that many of the difficulties associated with educating disaffected children and young people can be overcome. The formation of positive human and learning relationships is emphasised as a main foundation for learning throughout this book. The process of creating an effective learning environment will inevitably demand the considerable time and energy of all those who work for or on behalf of any school, centre or therapeutic learning provision. People who work with disaffected and vulnerable young people need to be consistent and persistent in pursuit of their goals. However, once achieved, a subtle blend of child–centred techniques, genuine engagement and procedures delivered within a sensitive and caring environment can have a profound impact on the lives and the futures of young people in difficulty. This book is concerned with the relationships, transactions, transfer of knowledge and cultural transmissions that characterise current practice in educating young people. It happens that the authors have focused particularly on young people who are both challenging and vulnerable and who represent a significant minority who have been excluded or are at risk of exclusion from mainstream education. Our experience is mainly in the United Kingdom and some in the United States, with a modicum of continental European experience thrown in. Notwithstanding the focus on this group of young people, we feel that some of the principles and practices encapsulated in this book are international in scope and should be an integral part of lifelong learning.

It is also argued that incorporation of humanistic and holistic approaches acknowledging the psychological (e.g. emotional) and social mediation of learning could well benefit attitudes and approaches in mainstream education. This book has explored the cultural, social and psychological context of the problems currently encountered and has given a brief perspective of the past four or more decades. We have endeavoured to set the scene for the proposal of a model of therapeutic education which is examined and researched through a case study in the context of current social and educational research in the United Kingdom with some perspectives from the United States. The book also contests and develops the proposed model as befitting the spirit of the action research project from whence it originated. The book started by exploring the theoretical and philosophical underpinnings of an approach to therapeutic education but then advocated, through the research literature and practical evaluation, a model of practice. We cultivated and shared the growth of this model of practice from Chapter 5 onwards. Young people who are vulnerable or highly disaffected severely challenge assumptions about practice and the resources available in the education services. We have had considerable teaching experience and echo the sentiments of Carl Rogers (Kirschenbaum and Henderson, 1990) in saying that young people in difficulty are extremely appreciative (even when they have difficulty expressing this) when they are simply understood (not judged and evaluated). Many adults in the world of a young person are 'teachers' in every sense, and young people do not necessarily see themselves as 'pupils' or even 'students' for much of the time. The spirit of working 'together' is crucial to the development of children's services by professionals in the next decade and to the fostering of better relationships with young people in the future. Teaching is not something done 'to' young people, and learning is a process that teachers and learners undertake together.

Evaluating areas of therapeutic working

Therapeutic approaches and techniques involve all areas of the curriculum and the social environment of the project. This table is simply intended to trigger off your thoughts about where and how you could develop some areas of working in your project. Here are some examples:

	Programme content	Group work	Staff involvement	Learning support	Whole project
Combating school pathology	Positive and encouraging scripts for adults and for clients/ students. Effective teaching starts from where the learner is. Includes ideas of nurture, growth and development with nurturing strategies. Attendance (encouraging environment).	Individualised education programmes, skill development and traditional academic accreditation. Adventure-based activities and outdoor education. Life skills curriculum/independent living, employability skills, and understanding individual responsibilities of citizens.	Securing young persons' motivation and concentration. Makes explicit what skills young people need in order to learn in school settings. Removes the 'threat' involved in learning and develops successful risk-taking behaviour. A willingness to confront in-school factors that promote disruption and disaffection.	Monitor individuals carefully and be open about this and sharing observations. Using appropriate assessment approaches. Setting targets for learning, not performance. Support and counselling for those in difficulty.	Development of positive relationships in project work. A carefully planned learning environment that enables the young person to see his or her own learning in a new and more successful light. Planning procedures, i.e. thinking it through beforehand.
Sociogenic factors	Social skills curriculum in communications, conflict resolution, anger management, drug and alcohol education, and understanding cognitive distortions. Community service work – experiencing positive community activities.	Reading social situations and networks; interacting smoothly; using these skills to persuade and lead, negotiate and settle disputes, for cooperation and teamwork. Give practice in resolving conflicts by generating controlled situations. Role play – make-up of social skills important and opportunities for rehearsal of social skills.	Encouraging social and personal responsibility. Develop cooperation and trust. Encourage partnership with parents. Willingness to improve interpersonal skills of staff and pupils (training).	Effective links with parents/carers and a forum for parents to share views and concerns. Positive regard for young people – encouraging potential – not pushing arbitrary targets.	Prevention of criminal activity and residential. Challenging existing conditions, habits, responses or circumstances. Recognising and evaluating the social dynamics of the school.

continued

	Programme content	Group work	Staff involvement	Learning support	Whole project
Psychogenic factors: emotional intelligence	Handling emotions in relationships well and accurately reading social situations and networks.	Developing emotional literacy through literature and poetry. No pseudo-psychology but genuine sharing of experience including feelings.	Cultivating rapport and 'attunement' with a broad diversity of people. Accepting the EI involvement in learning	Sensing what people are feeling and being able to take their perspective	Using feelings to guide and support decision making.
Psychogenic factors: cognitive	Social and interpersonal skills at work and in learning. Individuals keeping diaries – noting problems *and* good times. Self-awareness of emotional 'patterns' in their life.	Developing more structured group work/ discussion to practise social skills. Increasing awareness re feelings by exploring social stories and situations. Developing the language of personal expression and assertiveness.	Adults modelling effective learning behaviours. Adults develop a skilled, firm but very empathetic response to young people. Adults modelling skilled social and emotional behaviour.	Classroom assistance for learning. A transaction between individuals or in small groups.	Individual and group counselling and individualised treatment plans in a multi-agency framework.
Psychogenic factors: efficacy	Developing useful life skills. Self-regulation and handling emotions so that they facilitate rather than interfere.	Using the client's own expression output to work with and develop or shape. Developing competency in communications. Vocational and cultural field trips.	Values young persons' views and gives them responsibility – helps them to manage. Identified steps and criteria for success. Recognition of the need for 'time out' and privacy (also physical spaces, etc.)	Positive strokes in all areas of the curriculum. Teaching young persons to express anger without directing it at a person.	Fostering maturity and emotional development. Self-assessment and review built into the programme.

Therapeutic education assessment for shared values

Level descriptors for understanding and competency. Level 1 = low; level 5 = high.

	Level 1	✓	Level 2	✓	Level 3	✓	Level 4	✓	Level 5	✓
Knowledge and expertise	I have read and understand the establishment's Statement of Purpose.		I have good knowledge of the children I support. (strengths, preferences, SENs, triggers, etc.).		I use my knowledge and experience to ensure that I remain *child-focused* and *child-centred*.		I have sound knowledge of a wide range of proactive, active and reactive skills and techniques that I can use with confidence.		I have a clear grasp of how my practice relates to known theoretical principles.	
	I have read and understand the establishment's code of conduct for staff and also what I should reasonably expect from the children.		I promote established routines and boundaries of behaviour with confidence.		I am flexible in the way I think about and react to issues and difficulties that arise.		I have developed a sensitive and empathic understanding of the needs of the children I support.		I embrace the expertise of other professionals/agencies in recognition of a *holistic* approach to supporting children.	
Attitudes, values and beliefs	I care about children and wish to help them in being healthy and well-adjusted young citizens.		I act out of genuine concern and respect for the children I support.		I have developed some genuine and positive relationships with the children I support.		I recognise that my response to any given situation is inextricably linked to the behaviour of the children whom I support.		My practice is based upon an *unconditional* positive regard for the child.	
	I generally have a positive outlook on life.		I often use humour to de-escalate a potential problem.		I regularly and appropriately use LSIs to put closure on an event and discuss with the child how to improve the situation.		I *shape* my responses to support the individual and use this effectively to avoid confrontation or conflict.		I maintain responsibility for a situation throughout an event and actively seek closure.	

	Level 1	✓	Level 2	✓	Level 3	✓	Level 4	✓	Level 5	✓
Self-awareness and self-control	I am reasonably perceptive to the needs of, and difficulties experienced by, the children I support.		I am generally confident when in dialogue with others.		I am assertive when it comes to making decisions or making a point during a conversation.		I offer consistent support to the children that they see as being fair.		I understand the need to differentiate my approach to managing a situation based upon individual needs and associated impact factors.	
	I generally appear relaxed and non-threatening to others.		I can keep a cool head in a crisis.		I am resourceful and will actively seek alternatives during an escalating situation with a child/children.		I recognise that my own stresses, anxieties and general emotional state will have an impact on how any situation is managed.		I have heightened self-awareness that relates to my emotional state and physical readiness that helps me manage a situation better.	
Performance/ practice	I often praise and encourage children for their successes.		My practice is essentially non-aversive.		I *actively listen* to the children I support.		I regularly use opportunities to *teach skills* and alternatives to a child on a one-to-one basis.		I can reflect on my own practice and performance without feeling threatened or blameful.	
	I discuss my practice with other staff.		I use incentives and rewards appropriately and effectively to promote good behaviour.		I share experiences with other staff and generally accept positive criticism.		I actively encourage children's participation in contributing to organisational policy and practice.		I take part in formal debriefing to identify changes to my practice and improve performance.	

continued

	Level 1	✓	Level 2	✓	Level 3	✓	Level 4	✓	Level 5	✓
Limiting factor	I often use threatening language or punitive strategies to manage an immediate problem. e.g. 'Do that again and I'll . . .'		Sometimes I knowingly escalate a problem to pursue a 'rule' or make a point, i.e. create a power struggle.		I sometimes respond to a situation without fully understanding the function of behaviour, which can lead to apportioning blame. (i.e. fuelling a blame culture)		My effort to uphold consistency sometimes contradicts action that is in the best interests of the child.		I sometimes seek to discharge my responsibilities without first exploring *all* the alternatives and resources at my disposal.	

Proactive and pro-social management of behaviour

Proactive techniques and skills

1   Being non–confrontational
    Avoiding conflict, remaining calm, adopting non-threatening postures, gestures, etc., using a questioning style of dialogue.
2   Teaching and encouraging self-management
    Teaching self-management skills, opportunity to practise self-management, use of self-recording, self-evaluation, self-cueing and self-talk.
3   Using pre-emptive strategies
    Tutoring, pastoral time, 'time out', redirecting activities, personal challenges, opportunity of expression, personal space and time, etc.

Incentives

1   Praise/encouragement
    This takes place in the classroom, corridor, playground or wherever staff see pupils adhering to our code of conduct.
2   Achieving and celebrating good work
    A special assembly takes place once a week to celebrate good work and achievements. Entries are made in home/school books to keep parents/carers informed of progress.
3   Work certificates
    Stickers and certificates are used to celebrate and record good work. Each child has a portfolio of good work.
4   Points system
    This is a key system for recording and monitoring individual targets. (See Appendix 4.)
5   Curriculum flexitime
    Some additional curriculum time can be created to support particular privileges or cross-curricular projects the pupils are involved in.
6   Games equipment
    The school offers a range of small games and large games equipment that the children can use at break times and lunchtimes.

7   Privileges
Additional privileges are negotiated with pupils, e.g. Year 11 pupils allowed off site at lunchtimes.

8   Attendance raffle
Additional privileges are gained by good attendance at school throughout the week.

Sanctions

- Verbal reprimand/verbal warning: *Any pupil in breach of our classroom rules or pupil expectations may be given a verbal reprimand or warning.*
- Fewer points gained (*see Appendix 4*): *Although a pupil cannot ordinarily lose points, he/she will gain fewer points for unacceptable behaviour.*
- Withdrawal of privileges: *Extra trips and treats may be withdrawn if this action does not appear detrimental to the child's basic academic needs.*
- Detention within school hours: *Break times and lunchtimes may be used when pupils have deliberately flouted the code of conduct or need additional time to catch up with their studies. DETENTIONS ARE NOT PUNITIVE. The enforcement of detentions through and beyond the school day is primarily to ensure satisfactory output of work by the pupils. Detentions are to make up for missed work and constitute the completion of existing tasks (not 'lines' or extra tasks). Detentions take place either at morning break, part of lunchtime or after school. The member of staff who originally set the work will initiate detention during the school day. Other member(s) of staff who are on duty during the following break may offer supervisory support. Homework is an additional means of ensuring the completion of work should the pupil not respond to in-school detentions. An after-school detention takes on a higher profile and is deemed more serious, when other sanctions have failed. This will necessarily involve the headteacher's ratification and require 24 hours' notice to parents.*
- Detention after school hours: *Usually held on Tuesdays and Thursdays with notice given to parents/carers. An after-school (headteacher's) detention may require some negotiation with parents and/or carers owing to transport arrangements. It may be that the school provides/pays for transport in order that the detention can be completed successfully.*
- Time out (preventive/sanction): *This is a period of time in isolation in a quiet area to gather thoughts and prepare for returning to the classroom with suitable staff support.*
- Quiet time in school: *This is a period of time working in isolation in a study room with minimal staff support.*
- Personal challenge in or out of school: *This is a short period of time (usually half a day) in order to unpick a problem with staff when all other means of support have been exhausted. Challenges are in the form of off site visits incorporating additional curriculum work.*
- Fixed-term exclusion: *Used when a deliberate act of violence has resulted in injury to persons or property. The school operates very short periods of exclusion from one*

to five days, as we recognise the importance of maintaining the continuity of the learning process.

- Permanent exclusion: *Used when it is evident that the school is no longer able to support the child's needs and further attempts to make provision for the child would be deemed detrimental to the overall functioning and effectiveness of the school. This could include severe or prolonged periods of abuse or violence but it could also be a result of prolonged absence when a child is intent on breaking the placement down.*

The points system

Description

Westwood School has adopted a system that rewards acceptable and good behaviour and learning effort. The system also incorporates strategies in order to manage challenging behaviour. Staff awards points after each session within the school day. Pupils will gain points for appropriate behaviour as identified later in this document. Pupils are able to exchange their points for a variety of merchandise or privileges.

Rationale

The points system is an example of token economy and operates on the principle that appropriate behaviour is rewarded (reinforced). The approach is that of staged intervention whereby basic rules are featured in the early stages of the programme leading to more specific and individualised targets at more advanced stages. Pupils exhibiting challenging behaviour are automatically withdrawn from the system for a specified amount of time and must earn the privilege of rejoining it.

Structure

All pupils begin on a Yellow Card that highlights the basic school rules:

- being on time and staying on task;
- respect for others and property;
- positive work ethics.

When the staff agree, the pupil is moved to the next level using a Blue Card. At this level, pupils have the opportunity to earn more points targeting specific behaviours in relation to their individual needs in addition to continued reinforcement of basic rules. The ultimate level is referred to as contract status in which the pupil is deemed capable of adhering to a code of conduct without the need for constant sessional monitoring. Pupils on this level are awarded considerably more points and gain access to a range of additional privileges. Overriding these levels is the Red Card procedure. This is put into action when pupils display unacceptable behaviour within the school. The Red Card has three main functions:

1   It outlines and records the antecedents, behaviour and consequences of the pupil's actions.
2   It takes the pupil off the main system.
3   It necessitates the pupil achieving certain targets to earn the privilege of being placed back on to the system.

If any incident is deemed to be exceptionally serious, then pupils are withdrawn from the system entirely and our serious incident procedure is activated.

Serious incident procedure (SIP)

The serious incident procedure (SIP) is intended only for use in dealing with incidents that are deemed more serious than could be dealt with by using the Red Cards within the points system. Such incidents would include acts of aggression or violence to pupils, staff or property, or any behaviour that attempts to undermine good order and discipline in the school.

Following a serious incident:

•   The member(s) of staff involved consult with the Headteacher or Deputy Headteacher to clarify the nature of the incident and discuss the appropriate action.
•   Action may involve isolation, reparation or exclusion or any combination of these sanctions.
•   If immediate action is deemed necessary, then parents/carers are consulted.
•   If the pupil continues to be non-compliant and/or physically violent, police assistance may be summoned.
•   The SIP takes the pupil completely off the points system. No points may be earned and in cases of vandalism all unused points earned will be lost.
•   An incident report will be written and dispatched to parents/carers.
•   Before the pupil returns to school, a meeting between the Headteacher or Deputy Headteacher and parents/carers may be convened.
•   When the pupil returns to school, he/she will be seen by the Headteacher or Deputy Headteacher, at which time individual targets will be set.

The value of the system

Within the school week pupils can earn the following:

- Yellow Card: 850 points
- Blue Card: 1,200 points
- Contract: 1,200 points (automatic) + 75 bonus points

The administration of the points system differs considerably from Key Stage 3 to Key Stage 4, because of the age and capabilities of the children. The older pupils take personal responsibility for their own cards during the day.

The points system

Points are awarded to pupils for acceptable and good learning behaviour. Points are monitored by staff using individual coloured cards and awarded after each period of the day. Targets are specified on the cards corresponding to the level of behaviour expected.

Maximum points per week

Yellow Card   850
Blue Card   1,200
Contract   1,200 (automatic) + 75 bonus points
'Caught Ya' cards   25 points each issued as appropriate

The nominal value of each point earned is 0.1 pence. Points can be cashed in for rewards at a convenient point outside classroom time. However, points cannot be cashed in while a pupil remains on a Red Card. Points earned may be withdrawn following deliberate or malicious damage to property. Points can be 'banked' to provide 'interest' over a period of weeks.

Rewards

200   Small tube of sweets or equivalent.
400   Chocolate bar, soft drink or equivalent
900   McDonald's voucher
2,000 £2 gift/book voucher
5,000 £5 gift/book voucher

Other privileges, including 'personal challenges', may be negotiated upon request on either an individual or a group basis.

Criteria for moving up or down the system

Yellow Card to Blue Card – 2 weeks on 90% points or above
Blue Card to Contract – Exemplary behaviour over half a term.
Contract to Blue – Any sustained unacceptable behaviour. (Reviewed weekly.)
Blue Card to Yellow Card – 2 weeks on 70% points or below.

Breakdown of points allocation on cards

Conduct	Yellow	Blue	Contract*
Attendance/timekeeping	2	2	2
Respect to staff	2	2	2
Respect to pupils	2	2	2
Respect for property	2	2	2
Work achieved	5	10	10
Target I	5	8	8
Target 2	2	4	4
Lesson total	20	30	30
Registration	10	10	10
Break	5	5	5
Lunchtime	10	10	10
Uniform	5	5	5
Daily total	170	240	240
Weekly total	850	1,200	1,200

*Points on Contract are automatic. A pupil achieving Contract in Year 11 gains Prefect status.
A range of privileges and responsibilities are bestowed on a pupil at this level.

Handling difficult and violent situations

Section 1: Guidance, training and information

This section sets out guidelines regarding the use of force to control or restrain pupils. The guidelines fully recognise and embrace the following documents on this matter:

- Circular No. 9/94, *The Education of Children with Emotional and Behavioural Difficulties*, DFEE
- Circular No. 10/98, Section SSOA of the Education Act 1996: *The Use of Force to Control or Restrain Pupils*, DfEE
- NCH Core Policy Document No. 2, Section 1: *Code of Conduct and Practice Guidelines Addressing Acceptable Boundaries and Limits for Children and Young People, Positive Contact and Permissible Forms of Control and Restraint*
- DFEE Circular No. 10/98 on Section SSOA of the Education Act 1996 (July 1998) and Circular No. 8/94 (May 1994)
- DfEE/DOH guidance on promoting positive handling strategies for children with severe behavioural difficulties
- BILD *Code of Practice for Trainers in the Use of Physical Interventions*, 2001.
- BILD *Physical Interventions – Policy Framework* (third reprint), 2000

It is essential that positive approaches be used in confronting difficult behaviour. To this end, all staff supporting pupils at Westwood School are trained and are confident to follow a strict code of practice. Its five main elements include:

1 gaining an awareness of problem behaviour;
2 gaining an understanding of the pupil;
3 gaining knowledge of calming techniques;
4 gaining knowledge of intervention techniques;
5 understanding of prevention of aggressive behaviour.

All staff are trained in Pro-Act SCIP-r UK (Strategies for Crisis Intervention and Prevention) procedures and practice. Pro-Act SCIP-r UK is a programme of staged intervention approved by BILD and recognised by Kent Education Authority and NCH. There are times when specified techniques in escorting and restraining are necessary when dealing with challenging behaviour. These techniques are used when all other options have been exhausted and only if there is a risk of a child committing a criminal offence, harming himself/herself or others, damaging property or engaging in any behaviour prejudicial to maintaining good order and discipline (Section 55A of the Education Act 1996, 10/98).

Section 2: The recovery phase and life-space interview

During restraint, there will be regular dialogue with the child in order to calm and comfort. When the child has regained control to the extent that all staff agree to release the hold, this proceeds with staff gently releasing and 'rolling' away one by one. A transition from Supine to a supported seated Wrap is also a common form of recovery.

With the child 'under control' from the recovery process and accepting directions from staff, a 'life-space interview' should follow. This discussion takes place after a short pause given to the child to have a drink, straighten clothing and gather his/her thoughts. Although 'distance' should be maintained, staff will continue to communicate acceptance and warmth as the discussion begins. The basic aims of the 'life-space interview' are:

- to continue the calming process with the child and allow him/her to regain self-control;
- to explore with the child his/her responsibility for what has happened;
- to identify alternative strategies for the child to use in future;
- to plan for the child's reintegration into school/class.

Stages to the life-space interview

I	Isolate the child	There must be privacy and space for discussion to take place.
E	Explore things from the child's point of view	The child's view of reality must be heard without criticism.
S	Share	Providing a reality from the staff's point of view.
C	Connect	Making links with similar situations that identify how feelings affect behaviour.
A	Alternatives	Ideas from the child as to how they might handle things better next time.

continued

P	Plan	Identify the best course of action for next time, allowing the child to feel fully involved in the decision making process.
E	Enter	Summarise what has been agreed and start the reintegration process.

All staff should complete an entry in the physical interventions/sanctions file and incident book within twelve hours of the event.

Appendix 6

Case-study data and preliminary analysis

Section 1   Range and form of the data gathered over the four-year period
Section 2   Preliminary analysis of pastoral contextual data
Section 3   Preliminary analysis of pupil case studies
Section 4   Preliminary analysis of academic contextual data
Section 5   Restrictive physical intervention analysis
Section 6   Inspection reports analysis
Section 7   Summary and analysis of annual review and business plans
Section 8   Summary and analysis of staff questionnaire
Section 9   Analysis of pupil questionnaire and interviews
Section 10 Analysis of agency questionnaire
Section 11 Analysis of the school behaviour policy

Section 1: Range and form of the data gathered over the four-year period of the research

In this case study the data gathered take the following forms:

School contextual data (pastoral)	Half-termly record of pupil attendance, absenteeism, exclusions, incidents, restraints, injuries, complaints and child protection cases. Sept. 2000–July 2003.
Pupil case-study material	Background and progress material for six pupils. Current pupils. June 2003.
School contextual data (academic)	Academic achievements and pupil destinations. July 1999–July 2003.
Physical intervention analysis	Account of patterns and trends of incidents across the school identifying pupils, ages, staff, time of day and times of year. 1999–2002.
Inspection reports	Adviser's Position Paper 1999, HMI reports 1999–2000, Kent LEA monitoring visit 2000, OfSTED inspection report 2002.

continued

Annual review and business plans	Covering period 1999–2003.
Staff questionnaire	Teaching and non-teaching staff opinions and views surveyed July 2002.
Pupil interviews/ questionnaire	Pupil opinions surveyed September 2003/January 2004.
Agency questionnaire	Agency professionals/representatives opinions surveyed January 2004.
School behaviour policy	Information relating to school philosophy, aims, ethos, structure and management of the school day, incentive systems, sanctions. 2003–2004.

Section 2: Preliminary analysis of pastoral contextual data

The consumer information clearly evidences, among other features, a steady increase in roll towards its capacity of thirty pupils, with the majority of referrals being male. Of greater significance is the generally poor attendance rates shown (66 per cent to 83 per cent), primarily due to *unauthorised* absences, where pupils would abscond from school. Sessions of attendance are also lost through formal exclusions. Although there has been a downward trend in sessions lost by exclusions, the numbers of pupils who have been excluded one or more times over the period has remained relatively constant. Similarly, the number of pupils requiring physical interventions has remained relatively constant despite the actual number of restraints falling slightly over the period. Accidents and injuries recorded have also remained consistent over the period, averaging five reports every half-term.

- The level of pupil attendance must be a significant issue for the school since it is consistently well below the OfSTED threshold of 90 per cent. Absconding from school appears to be something of a fundamental characteristic among the difficulties presented by a large proportion of the pupil population. Coupled with other complex emotional difficulties, and given that the school does not offer the inherent 'twenty-four-hour stability' that residential provision might, is it reasonable to expect overall attendance to improve? Is it feasible to expect more sophisticated internal strategies to be developed in order to improve the situation?
- Formal 'fixed-term' exclusions are used when a pupil causes deliberate injury or damage to property, but they are also used in response to persistent breaches of the school code of conduct, such as placing others at risk, verbal abuse, bullying, drug use and smoking on-site. The exclusion period is generally very short (one to five days) since it serves no useful purpose

beyond this time. The downward trend in exclusions is a healthy sign that the proactive and active measures being developed in the school are having an impact. However, there still seem to be a proportion of children who continue to require this type of sanction in order to successfully engage in school life.

- The use and frequency of restrictive physical interventions (RPIs) is probably the single most significant issue that faces the school. There are now strict guidelines and standards that inform the use of RPIs in schools and residential facilities. These are rigorously enforced to ensure that, wherever possible, staff offer the 'least restrictive environment' when managing an event or crisis. Consequently, the downward trend in physical interventions at the school is a good sign that other, more proactive and active (as opposed to reactive) methods of intervention are making a difference. The question of whether the use of RPIs can be reduced or eliminated altogether is uncertain on the strength of this evidence, and it seems that for a small proportion of (usually younger) pupils, RPIs will remain an important strategy.
- Accidents and injuries appear to be an inevitable result of working alongside pupils who present challenging behaviour, with a significant risk for staff but occasionally for pupils too. Thankfully, the level of injuries here seems reasonably low, given that the figure also includes minor medical attention. Staff are more able to ensure their own safety and the safety of pupils they support by raising their level of self-awareness and gaining greater know-ledge of the pupils. This can be achieved by a system of formal training and good communication among staff.

Section 3: Preliminary analysis of pupil case studies

This section compares six children who, as of July 2003, were all on roll at the school. The children were chosen at random in order to show a cross-section of referrals, their background circumstances and particular difficulties. Without any intent to lessen the importance of individual needs, it is apparent that these cases have common elements that can be used to establish a typical profile of a child most likely to be referred to the school. A logical starting point is to view the child's statement of special needs, highlighting the nature of difficulties experienced and identifying the most appropriate educational provision. The very fact that the statement exists means that a number of agencies have been involved in the formal assessment process. These may include psychological services, health and clinical services, the social services department or child and family services.

Two cases here are of children whose home lives have been so traumatic that a care order has been sought, while others refer to relationship difficulties at home, especially with siblings and other local children. At school, all have strug-gled academically with the added difficulties of poor communication skills, lack of concentration and disaffection. Two cases have been identified as having clinically diagnosed conditions, one having an autistic spectrum disorder (ASD) and another with attention deficit hyperactivity disorder (ADHD). All documents refer to behavioural difficulties at school showing anger and sometimes violent behaviour that has led to such inevitable consequences as permanent exclusion. Additionally, this pattern of events has continued, with some statements referring to several school placements and subsequent breakdowns.

Not surprisingly, the most common feature in all cases is the demand for a supportive educational environment with access to small group work and individual programmes of study while setting clear and consistent boundaries for behaviour. While these conditions appear reasonable, to apply them successfully when so many similar situations have failed is clearly the biggest challenge. The children themselves will undoubtedly feel that the system has failed them and feel a certain sense of failure themselves. The reports generally indicate a low level of self-esteem, which is why a supportive environment is so important. Although all the children have been assessed as having average intelligence, most are reported as having an academic delay, usually in areas of literacy. The need for more individualised programmes of study geared to specific National Curriculum levels is as important as a balance of subjects to ensure that pupils remain engaged and focused. Making the National Curriculum accessible and relevant through small units of work is a key strategy that virtually all the SEN statements and progress reports make reference to. As all the children described have had difficulties forming and maintaining positive relations with others, one of the most crucial aspects of the work is the development of positive relations between staff and pupils based upon trust and mutual respect. Clearly, class size is a major factor in enabling good working relations with other children and adults, as well as ensuring that sufficient support is available when needed.

Section 4: Preliminary analysis of academic contextual data

A variety of basic contextual data are collected about the school each year, covering the period 1999–2003, and show attendance rates, Standard Attainment Test (SAT) results, formal examinations achieved and pupil destinations. The figures reveal the following trends and patterns:

- The school is populated by a predominance of boys. Although such a predominance is common in schools of this particular designation, it clearly raises issues regarding the appropriate support of any minority group in this situation.
- Rates of attendance by national standards have been poor but some improvement is shown across the period. Poor attendance may be attributed to a number or combination of factors, such as the nature of the children's difficulties – that is, disaffection and general unwillingness to engage in school life. It may be the fact that the school offers day provision in an urban

district (and so has less control over environmental conditions), but more serious is the possibility that the school is failing to offer an appropriate environment for the children's needs.

- The Year 9 tests show very similar academic levels in terms of both the subject and the cohort. The average attainment of Year 9 pupils appears to be National Curriculum level 3–4 in all core subject areas. Although attainment is low by mainstream standards, it is probably more realistic to judge achievement based upon progress while at the school and set this against previous individual records.

- Most pupils in Years 10 and 11 achieve some academic success at roughly the same levels as indicated by the SAT results. Since the school admissions policy allows pupils to enter the school at any age and time of year, the timing of their entry, coupled with the quality and success of their previous education experience, will heavily dictate their effective engagement in any formal academic courses. The opportunity to achieve more formal qualifications has improved over the period, and figures suggest that pupils have generally responded well to this.

- The majority of leavers have shown a preference to take up college courses upon leaving the school. This is most likely due to the recommendations made by the school and careers service, which advises pupils to continue their formal education post-16 whenever possible or appropriate. However, there have been some successful transitions to formal employment through apprenticeships. In each of the years in question a small minority leave the school without any identified progression routes but these cases are pursued by the Connexions officer allocated to the school.

Section 5: Restrictive physical intervention analysis

This is a summary of the analysis of restrictive physical interventions (RPIs) at the school reported over the period 1999–2003. The statistics give an important indication as to the effectiveness of the school even though they report on but one aspect of the work of the school and are reflective of only a small selection of the interventions used on a day-to-day basis.

- Some people argue that *any* need for physical intervention in a school setting can never be considered either appropriate or therapeutic, as previous chapters debate. However, there remains a strong case for its use when supporting children who present severe behavioural difficulties. RPIs are used only as a last resort to challenging behaviour when all other strategies have been exhausted and any other course of action is likely to result in personal injury or damage to property. The school would always aim to manage challenging behaviour in more proactive ways, but, historically, a degree of physical intervention has been needed from time to time with some individuals. The overall purpose of RPIs is to stabilise a crisis situation and allow the young person to regain self-control as soon as possible.

- Any increase or decrease in incidents requiring RPI across an extended time frame may be indicative of a number of possibilities, including the effectiveness and use of specific proactive, active or reactive strategies to manage challenging behaviour. The shifting needs of the client group or a change in the beliefs, attitudes and values of staff may also have a significant bearing on the situation.

- Separate statistics for each year identify some common trends that are particularly pertinent here. Perhaps the most significant of these is the fall in the number of physical interventions used over the period by some 40 per cent. One would like to think that this is attributable to the school's capacity to offer an increasing range of proactive and therapeutic strategies, although a number of other factors and variables are bound to impact on this figure. It is a healthy trend, nevertheless, and one that links to a key development target for the school.

- Another common feature of these statistics is the lower number of RPIs used across the 14- to 16-year-old age group (Key Stage 4) when compared to the 11- to 13-year-olds (Key Stage 3). These figures accurately reflect a different approach to supporting the older pupils by allowing them greater capacity to self-advocate in times of crisis. This is based on the notion that older pupils will utilise the greater freedom of movement around the school grounds when dealing with personal difficulties without placing themselves at risk. Although pupils at Key Stage 3 are offered a range of 'outlets' in times of stress, it is less likely that they would be given such freedom of movement and they are more likely to be restricted to the main school building.

- The statistics have revealed that learning support assistants (LSAs) have shown a significantly higher involvement in RPIs than any other group of staff. This has been consistent over the three years, and is not at all surprising since the remit of the LSAs has evolved into extensive involvement with pastoral and welfare matters. It is therefore most likely that in times of crisis LSAs would manage a situation or support others in that capacity. In an everyday classroom situation this would leave the teacher free to maintain continuity with the other pupils. Interestingly, this policy has effectively shifted the responsibility of classroom management from the shoulders of the teachers despite remaining a key requirement under teachers' terms and conditions.

- Another pattern that has emerged is the time of day when RPIs most often occur. This appears to be shortly after arrival at school and shortly after the lunch break. If these are potentially stressful times for children, then this clearly spells out the need for investigating the way the school day is structured in order to alleviate this effect as much as possible. Put simply, the less intense and demanding these times can be made for the pupils, the less likely it is that aggressive outbursts will ensue.

- Finally, it was recognised that the time of year has a bearing on the number of RPIs, with the data revealing that a higher percentage of interventions occurred shortly into each term, with a gradual reduction as the term progressed. This suggests that as children become accustomed to the environment, staff, regime, rules, etc., there is less reason to respond aversively. With each new term this pattern will recur as the child becomes re-accustomed to school life. Additionally, it is likely that new pupils will begin at the start of a new term rather than mid-term and therefore require some time to adjust to a new environment, with a greater possibility of displaying inappropriate behaviour.

Section 6: Inspection reports analysis

The reports derive from various sources and are useful in highlighting key milestones in the development of the school from year to year. Over the four years covered in this study there was at least one inspection or external monitoring visit per year. The Position Paper by a local education adviser provides some background and an initial overview, while the three HMI reports and county advisory feedback highlight some important steps in the school's aim to develop a more therapeutic environment. The OfSTED report from January 2002 is particularly significant as it helped to secure the school's status as a non-maintained special school in addition to offering some key development points that were subsequently built into the next School Improvement Plan (SIP). All reports contain sections that measure the quality of teaching and learning. The conclusions documented by all advisers/inspectors were reached using a combination of examining professional documents such as policies, schemes of work, lesson plans, etc., formal teacher (lesson) observations and formal interviews.

- The first inspection report from an HMI visit in February 1999 identifies a number of serious weaknesses across the school, including weaknesses in curriculum, staffing, accommodation, resourcing and behaviour. Indeed, the report indicates that a full inspection at this time was likely to result in the school being the subject of special measures. At this time, all the areas mentioned above were under review and development, with a priority on staff recruitment. The quality of provision overall at this time was considered very poor.
- The advisers' report (Position Paper, July 1999) explains the school's desire to shift what was a very rigid and confrontational regime to a more proactive and systematic approach to managing behavioural difficulties. The reference to Del Goddard's model 'the interactive curriculum' (1996) when planning and shaping the ethos, environment and curriculum provided a crucial focus that has remained at the very core of the developmental work of the school.
- Lessons observed at this time were generally sound, although it was clear

that at this stage planning, content and delivery methods were not well refined or consistent, and this resulted in some children disengaging from the lessons. Staff development recommendations focused upon:

- establishing good relations with pupils through consistent adult responses, setting clear boundaries;
- generating a more stimulating learning environment;
- reducing pupil anxieties by offering consistent and positive support;
- using appropriate incentives and rewards.

Overall, there was a positive feel to the report, but with many good ideas and strategies in their infancy, it highlighted a need for more 'joined-up thinking'.

- The second HMI visit in November 1999 focused heavily on accommodation in relation to an extensive building and refurbishment programme that would be launched the following summer. However, there was also recognition that planning for an appropriately broad, balanced and relevant content curriculum was well under way and it was noted that a sound behaviour policy had been installed and was taking effect.

- The next HMI visit to the school in June 2000 provided a more detailed report on the quality of provision. Lessons were observed and were all deemed to be at least satisfactory. Various aspects of behaviour management were acknowledged, including the use of an incentive scheme, the use of withdrawal in avoiding crisis situations and the techniques and methods used in RPIs. Areas for development at this time included ensuring consistency in the quality of teaching and learning, improving attendance levels and providing more focused support for literacy difficulties.

- In October 2000, Kent LEA inspectors reported on some key areas of the school, but made some particularly useful comments regarding the quality of pastoral and behaviour support offered. The following points were made:

  - The curriculum provides opportunities for the development of self-esteem through promoting self-advocacy, decision-making skills, risk awareness and communication skills.
  - Relationships are characterised by openness, respect and the promotion of dignity.
  - There are clear and appropriate policies for behaviour management and bullying.
  - Children's rights are fully respected and embedded in practice.
  - Children have a nominated adult for support and guidance.
  - The school actively promotes independence skills and manages the transition to the next phase of education/adult life.

- In January 2002 the school received its first OfSTED inspection by a team of HMIs. A total of twenty-two lessons were observed, of which fifteen were deemed satisfactory or better. Unsatisfactory lessons were attributed to the work being insufficiently stimulating or some children's acute anxiety and stress over-spilling into the classroom. The quality of teaching and learning at Key Stage 3 was to be a key action point for the school. Even so, it was noted that while the younger pupils still had some way to go to establish good attitudes and behaviour patterns, they had all made steady and in some cases marked improvements since joining the school. In Key Stage 4 classes the pupils' behaviour was good and their attitude to study was at least satisfactory and often good.

- In terms of the pupils' welfare it was noted that staff worked hard to establish and maintain good relationships with the pupils and to foster a secure and caring learning environment. It was also recognised that staff knew the pupils well and were sensitive to their social and emotional needs. Interestingly, this was the only comment that referred specifically to these key areas of development.

- In the parents survey, most expressed positive views about the work of the school and in particular expressed a belief that the school promotes the personal and social development of the children.

- The reports as a whole provide evidence of some significant steps in the development of the school and highlight the transition that has been made over four years to regenerate the school based on very different philosophical and organisational constructs. The reports identify a steady improvement in terms of the quality of teaching and learning, and this was key in achieving non-maintained special school status, gained soon after the final inspection. However, of particular interest here are the comments that were made regarding the quality of therapeutic care offered. Given the emphasis and significance on the management of children's emotional, social and behavioural difficulties, it was odd but not entirely surprising that inspectors should make only passing or general comments such as 'good behaviour patterns' and 'good relationships with pupils'. Little or no reference was made to the interactive curriculum, intervention strategies or PSHE profiles that had been devised and developed within the same time frame. The most significant observations came from the LEA advisers, who seemed to have a better understanding and interest in these matters and realised their significance and central role in a school like this one.

Section 7: Summary and analysis of annual review and business plans

The annual review and business plans serve as useful reference points as they further track the development of the school over the period 1999–2003. There are three documents used, each reviewing the previous year and planning for the forthcoming year. The information contained within each document was the result of a systematic and detailed survey of staff opinion followed by whole staff discussion. These discussions, coupled with other local and corporate factors and issues, generated the establishment targets for the forthcoming year. The business plans focus on all aspects of school life, including buildings, premises, accommodation and resources, management and organisation, staff and pupils, curriculum, and welfare and support. The range of topics and themes is extensive and many overlap issues that have been discussed in other sections of this chapter. Consequently, in order to avoid unnecessary duplication, the focus of this section is on key issues that have remained common threads throughout this whole period and continue to be important areas of discussion, review and development within the school. As 'working documents', all the material within the business plans can be used to provide further insight as to how effective staff have been in progressively applying and managing new therapeutic strategies within a rapidly changing culture and environment. The following targets drawn from the plans have particular pertinence here, as they are all measures of the quality of service that the school offers:

- increase the pupil roll (financial sustainability);
- improve pupil attendance and reduce level of absconding (pupil engagement);
- reduce the need for exclusions and RPIs (effective proactive strategies in place);
- review and refine the behaviour policy to ensure that existing strategies used are appropriate for the pupils' needs (ability to adjust to a changing clientele);
- address areas of inconsistency when managing challenging behaviour (clear, coherent and consistent approach to managing behaviour);
- further develop proactive strategies to more readily support young people (ability to offer a range of therapeutic strategies);
- improve the physical environment to make sure that it is welcoming, safe and comfortable (non-aversive setting promoting a good working protocol);
- ensure that staff are trained using accredited programmes to ensure confidence and competence when dealing with challenging behaviour (reflective of good professional knowledge and expertise and continuing professional development);
- investigate ways in which other professionals may work with the school to strengthen its provision (offer a multi-agency approach);
- improve the profile of the school by raising awareness of its work within the local community (establish the school as a centre of excellence).

Section 8: Summary and analysis of staff questionnaire

The survey was administered during June and July 2002 and distributed to all staff working directly with children at the school. The questionnaire yielded a 92 per cent return. A number of overarching themes were embodied in the five sections of the questionnaire.

- **Segment 1** begins to explore the school's working environment and the philosophy upon which operational practice is based. Do staff feel that their particular brand of education makes a difference to the lives of the children they support?
- **Segment 2** explores the nature of pupils' difficulties and needs and identifies how they are manifested in a school context. What are staff's perceptions of the children's difficulties?
- **Segment 3** explores how staff perceive and determine their roles individually and collectively.
- **Segment 4** introduces the concept of therapeutic education and seeks staff views on its application within a special school for young people with behavioural, emotional and social difficulties (BESD).
- **Segment 5** explores staff understanding and views on the special school curriculum and introduces the concept of an 'alternative curriculum' for use in special BESD schools.

The following highlights and summarises the responses to each of the above segments prefaced with an introductory statement:

Segment 1: What makes your school so special?

Staff appear generally confident in explaining why the school is here, the service it offers and the value of that service. They also feel that, on the whole, other professionals, parents and carers are aware of the nature of the school's provision. However, staff are less confident that the pupils themselves fully understand what the school provides for them. Staff feel that the general public/community has little understanding or knowledge of the school or the nature of its provision.

The school's aims and objectives, among other documents, are well publicised in the school brochure and behaviour policy. Despite this, all staff commented on what they felt were the school's aims using their own interpretation and description for this purpose. The results highlight a number of common phrases and statements such as 'to educate disaffected children', 'to develop abilities to function in society' and 'to develop individual potential'.

Common phrases were evident when describing the underlying philosophy of the school such as 'caring', 'therapeutic', 'safe', 'secure', 'nurturing' and 'sensitive'. The terms 'firm', 'consistent' and 'structured' were also frequently used in this context. Interestingly, the consistency issue is one that has been echoed in school business plans as an area for development.

Staff were then asked to describe what they felt were 'special features' of the school. Features that were considered particularly significant included a strong, experienced and qualified team and a positive, caring and proactive ethos with a family-oriented approach to school life. Operational features identified included the high staff : pupil ratio and the high level of support available, the size of each class and the size of the school generally. Good, clear structures, procedures and policies were also felt to be important, in particular an effective behaviour policy. It was felt that the school was able to offer a relevant curriculum and one that was enjoyable yet challenging for the pupils.

In the wider context, staff felt that the school had developed strong links with parents and carers and shared common goals. There was also a feeling that being part of NCH, one of the United Kingdom's largest childcare charities, was a clear strength.

Segment 2: How do you define troubled and troublesome children?

It was generally felt that pupils want to come to school and want to learn. This is actually a prerequisite of the pupil entering the school and is discussed as a condition at the outset. It was also felt that although pupils enjoyed freedom of expression and generally wanted to feel empowered, these feelings are tempered by their wish for clear boundaries and guidelines. It is interesting to note here that despite the very overt 'specialness' of the school, staff considered that pupils had relatively little awareness of their own special needs.

Staff were asked why, in their experience, pupils might be referred to the school. A range of responses were given beyond the obvious 'challenging behaviour', including mainstream schools being unable to respond appropriately to the needs of the pupil, trauma in early childhood or difficult social or family issues.

Similarly, staff were asked for their opinion as to why pupils might want to come to, or enjoy being at, school (presuming that they want to in the first place). The responses were an interesting spread ranging from the more positive reasons such as pupils responding to the friendly atmosphere, or seeing the placement as a fresh start with new opportunities. Less preferred reasons included examples such as when a home placement depended upon school attendance, or where the school is simply offering better provision than elsewhere. Obviously, it is the hope that pupils want to learn and enjoy the curriculum activities that the school offers, but this is not always the case.

When staff were asked what the biggest fear or anxiety might be for the staff when receiving a new pupil, the most common response was the lack of prior information. Inevitably, this will have an impact on other uncertainties such as whether the pupil is appropriately placed, and the dynamic effect of the child on other pupils and, conversely, other pupils on the child. Another significant concern is the degree of home support that the school can expect, which cannot easily be determined until the placement is well under way. This has proved to be a crucial factor for the placement to be successful.

The next segments within this part of the questionnaire looked specifically at the nature and degree of difficulties presented by the pupils as perceived by the staff from a personal perspective. They were then asked to consider the same difficulties from a whole school point of view. Those pupil difficulties/ characteristics that were of greatest concern to staff on a personal level included aggression and violence, poor social skills, disaffection, disrespect and destructiveness. In contrast, of least personal concern were lack of confidence, academic delay and attendance.

When compared to the staff's perception of the school's current difficulties, aggression and violence and poor social skills are once again highlighted as most significant, along with immaturity and low self-esteem. Of least significance were attendance, criminal activity and destructiveness. There are obvious similarities here, but these last results seem inconsistent, given the recent HMI report that identified attendance as an issue for the school. Similarly, the school has always taken wilful damage to property with the utmost seriousness. The results suggest that these areas are not problematic for the school, which, statistically, is untrue.

Segment 3: What constitutes an effective staff team and what do you think characterises a good team member?

Staff were asked to identify what, in their opinion, are the most and least important characteristics of an effective staff member. Of those listed, the characteristics that appeared to be most important were resourcefulness, flexibility and the ability to be a good team player. Of less importance was physical strength, having a strong personality and liking children, although none of these characteristics was ruled out as unnecessary.

Much work has been done within the school to ensure that staff are fully aware of the relationship between intervention techniques and established theory. Not surprisingly, then, when asked about their own personal theoretical perspective there was equal emphasis placed upon each of the four commonly known models: behaviourist, cognitive, ecosystemic and psychodynamic (listed in descending order). The descending order of the models can be seen as a predictable result since it corresponds well to the likely degree of their practical knowledge of these models and their application within the school context.

Staff were asked to comment on work style, first by identifying descriptors that they felt matched their own approach and then, in contrast, identifying a style that would prove ineffective in the current working environment. The responses suggested that a work style that was consistent, supportive, caring, empathic and assertive would be most effective. The least effective was considered to be controlling, authoritative and dominant. However, in practice it is not so easy to compartmentalise work styles since so much depends on a whole range of environmental factors. As mentioned earlier, the most effective practitioners should be flexible, and this may mean using a variety of styles to suit particular circumstances.

Segment 4: Is a therapeutic approach to education a feasible and effective vehicle for establishing an 'alternative curriculum' in a school of this designation?

Views on the effectiveness of a therapeutic approach to education and its exclusivity in a BESD school have revealed some interesting, if not conflicting, thoughts from staff. All agree that a therapeutic approach can be linked to education and that it 'fits' the school's general philosophy and approach in creating an 'alternative curriculum'. It is also generally recognised that education at the school is about more than simply performance and outcome.

However, there is a view that the essence of therapeutic education is contained in the school's 'content' curriculum and 'hidden' curriculum. This implies a restricted view of the process and its potential for extended and enhanced intervention programmes.

The use of physical intervention techniques was generally considered to be therapeutic, yet some staff suggested that removing the use of physical intervention techniques would result in the loss of a power base.

Descriptors separately identifying therapeutic and educational approaches were used in order to best summarise the school's particular slant to its work. Not surprisingly, the vast majority of descriptors chosen by staff were educational rather than therapeutic in nature. The raises the question of their compatibility in what must still be considered essentially an educational setting. There were high levels of response (over 50 per cent) to the following descriptors:

- maintains and raises self-esteem and self-awareness;
- values pupils' views and gives them responsibility – helps them to manage themselves;
- gives staff and pupils the confidence to engage with one another and the curriculum;
- challenging to existing conditions, habits, responses or circumstances.

The following statements are practical examples of how the staff see therapeutic education operating in their particular field of work:

- 'The use of time on a "Personal Challenge" – giving them personal attention, building rapport and enabling them to understand that with help they can achieve, no matter what their circumstances, background, etc.'
- 'Enabling the young person to develop strategies and tools for them to become an individual with their own thoughts, feelings and emotions. Giving them self-empowerment through LSIs and one-to-one support in their learning and social communication.'
- 'One pupil has trouble being in school. He has always truanted and his stock response is to swear and knock tables and chairs over. I brought a hand puppet into school – a small cat. The pupil has a cat at home called Honey.

I introduced the puppet in a non-threatening way and the pupil imme-diately put it on and 'became' Honey. Honey could then write out spellings, dance to French tunes and do maths and enjoy school – without the pupil losing face. After a while, Honey was just left on the pupil's desk but is used in times of stress to "do the pupil's work". Honey is always praised highly for good work but the pupil now does good work and is praised as well as, or instead of Honey.'

- 'The use of the PSHE profile and hence target setting in order to modify and put into place strategies is often a useful tool. This method of negotiation with the pupils in order for them to arrive at solutions can prove to be effective.'

- 'Making tasks and environment clear and defined, so as not to allow the child to become upset or dwell upon problems, not allowing opportunity for adverse behaviour.'

- 'A pupil was having trouble with being able to resist the peer pressure to abscond (mainly first thing in the morning). Plants were bought for the classroom and the pupil was given the opportunity to take responsibility for the care and watering of the plants. This took place first thing in the morn-ing. The pupil knocked on the door every morning voluntarily, to come into the school. He enjoyed the one-to-one attention and his absconding was not such an issue, even after the activity stopped.'

- 'Verbalising the students' feelings for them; confirming that it's OK to be angry and setting out ways of dealing with feelings appropriately. Then repeating this process as necessary.'

- 'Maintaining and raising self-esteem and self-awareness – with one particular child who was also trying to go against authoritative ruling. He is now able to self-talk and give explanations about behaviour.'

- 'Students now show an enthusiasm for personal/imaginative writing. Previously, poor spelling skills and lack of confidence to attempt work prohibited this. Word banks created on the whiteboard by brainstorming ideas – fluency and self-esteem gradually improved.'

Segment 5: What constitutes an 'alternative curriculum' and can it sit comfortably alongside other statutory obligations of the school?

- Staff were asked what, in their opinion, constituted an 'alternative curriculum'. The majority considered that it was a critical feature of a BESD environment and not a 'cop-out' for not tackling the content curriculum effectively. Staff on the whole also believed that the 'alternative curriculum' can sit alongside the National Curriculum and is fully embodied in the pastoral time and personal, social and health education (PSHE) lessons. This suggests that there is no scope for enhancement outside the confines of the content curriculum and thus limits its application.

- Staff considered that on the whole there is a good work ethic in the school, and although pupils may sometimes manipulate a situation to avoid tasks, this would not present a barrier to implementing an 'alternative curriculum'. It was felt that a day school (as opposed to residential provision) would be in a less favourable position to deliver an 'alternative curriculum', but having the appropriate quality and number of staff was an overarching factor.
- When asked to define the 'alternative curriculum', over 50 per cent of staff favoured descriptors such as 'individual', 'child-focused', 'relevant', 'interactive' and 'positive'. The 'interactive curriculum' was sited as the best model for implementing an 'alternative curriculum' as it:

   - incorporates all aspects of personal development;
   - is a live tool monitoring performance and establishing patterns of behaviour;
   - is a means of feeding key reporting documents in the school;
   - utilises an assessment system that identifies specific behaviours and targets.

   Staff considered that all of the above statements were valid and useful in the workplace but the majority of staff considered the latter statement particularly relevant to the school.
- Overall, the staff were 80 per cent confident about the direction the school was taking with regard to supporting pupils with emotional, behavioural and social difficulties.

Section 9: Analysis of pupil questionnaire and interviews

A pupil questionnaire was designed for the purposes of the school annual review procedure and launched in January 2004. The survey was analysed in such a way that an overall response of 60 per cent or more would be considered generally positive, while a figure between 40 per cent and 60 per cent would be considered an area of weakness. A figure between 20 per cent and 40 per cent suggests that the respondent is unsure of the question and would most likely need more information to answer accurately.

- The pupils' responses were largely positive. Most felt valued, listened to and welcomed in the school and they thought staff showed care and consideration for all pupils. There was a strong sense of feeling safe both in the school building and around the school site. However, they felt that some people did not treat others with respect and were equally concerned that rules and punishments were not effective in curbing the behaviour of some children.
- Pupils expressed a clear sense of what to do to behave well at the school and felt that their efforts to improve behaviour were recognised. Pupils also

felt strongly that they knew where to get help when needed and that staff would help to sort out problems fairly.

- Pupils were less content with the school's efforts to involve all parties in school development and that the organisation as a whole worked in partnership with all parties to help the pupils.
- A series of interviews made by a school governor with Year 11 pupils in September 2003 has provided additional information. Although brief, the report is significant as it offers some insight into the feelings and opinions of young people who have attended the school throughout its period of transition and development and who are therefore in an ideal position to comment on some aspects of school life. They also provide a strong measure of the quality of relationships in the school and the overall quality of provision.
- The pupils were generally positive about the school. They liked the teachers and appreciated the incentive systems in the school. Although they felt that overall the regime was fair, one pupil commented on disliking the security around the building and felt that greater access to places where they could cool off would be beneficial. The same pupil also commented on disliking change in the school (or change generally).

Section 10: Analysis of agency questionnaire

The agency questionnaire was distributed in January 2004 to all partnership authorities, external services and other professionals that work on behalf of the children in the school within the health, social services or education sectors. This survey was the first of its kind and formed part of the school self-evaluation and monitoring procedure.

Overall, there was an excellent rate of return and some positive points made. Respondents generally felt that the school made them feel welcomed and valued, people treat each other with respect and staff show care and consideration for all pupils. However, there appeared to be a strong feeling that agencies should have greater opportunity to be involved in school life and in making decisions about the school and its development. This was also reflected in the number of respondents who were unable to answer some questions owing to lack of knowledge or information.

Overall there was a positive response regarding the level of service received from the school, and some additional comments made about the school were particularly favourable.

Section 11: Analysis of the school behaviour policy

The 'aims and objectives' section of the policy succinctly describes how the school sets about its purpose of supporting children in a proactive way, and this is a thread that runs throughout the whole document. Proactive support is exemplified in a number of ways, including the use of a flexible incentive system, the use of teaching skills on a routine basis and recovering from a crisis situation. The 'life-space interview' technique is used in a variety of situations to offer active support to a child who may show signs of distress or anger. That this and other active techniques are so prevalent is a mark of the good rapport and trust that staff and pupils are able to develop in the school environment. The policy also describes the routine of the day and the additional mechanisms that have been installed to shape the environment around the needs of the children. The policy describes the 'interactive curriculum' and further indicates the school's commitment to planning the management of challenging behaviour on an individual level through the use of individual education plans (IEPs), STAR analysis and the formulation of behaviour management plans (BMPs).

A schedule for observing and assessing a therapeutic approach

Teaching and managing processes, the teacher, support assistant or other professional:

☐ offers lots of encouragement to students focusing on their social and emotional, as well as academic, achievements;

☐ encourages students to set goals for themselves and understand and accept reasonable limits and boundaries based on understanding the present;

☐ include in their plans an assessment of individual educational and emotional need, including recognising 'triggers' to challenging behaviour;

☐ places a greater emphasis on spiritual, moral, social and cultural dimensions;

☐ uses modelling techniques to illustrate focus on appropriate behaviour;

☐ models 'foresightful behaviour' by explicit planning techniques and engaging students in the planning processes;

☐ integrates social skills training by rehearsing social and conversational skills and making them explicit in everyday conversations;

☐ influences change and management through credibility and skilful planning, not formal power

☐ uses non-aversive approaches to behaviour management and behaviour change;

☐ maintains a relaxed approach and uses relaxation techniques (breathing, calming exercises) when necessary;

☐ focuses on teaching functional skills to eliminate the need for negative behaviour;

☐ utilises a range of skills, including listening, empathising, problem solving and information giving;

☐ engages in a minimal use of negative consequences and punishments;

☐ is comfortable with a multi-element approach involving several interventions implemented simultaneously;

☐ gives young people the opportunity to discuss their work with others;

☐ plans activities that foster motivation, interest and the ability to concentrate;

☐ encourages 'self-cueing' (finding conditions that trigger a more appropriate response);

☐ plans for self-reinforcement (providing positive outcomes for appropriate behaviour).

Learning experiences empower a young person to:

☐ take control of triggers that set off their inappropriate behaviour
☐ reflect upon 'actions' (observable behaviours and interactions with others);
☐ use strategies to reduce arousal and generally increase control over their own environment;
☐ cooperate with adults and peers and work productively;
☐ develop motivation, interest and the ability to concentrate;
☐ become confident in posing questions and solving problems;
☐ develop strategies for reflection on meaning and intention in social and emotional encounters;
☐ engage in self-cueing (finding conditions that trigger a more appropriate response);
☐ engage in self-reinforcement (finding more positive outcomes for appropriate behaviour);
☐ critically examine their own personal beliefs and develop independent self-belief.

The curriculum encompasses:

☐ comprehensive assessment of social, interpersonal and emotional interactive skills in real situations (i.e. performance in life, not just the classroom);
☐ comprehensive assessment of behaviours and events that identify 'setting conditions' and 'triggers' for individual and group behaviour;
☐ processes for identifying and working on specific areas of focus for certain individuals;
☐ a framework for learning about the society a young person lives in and their relationship with this society in terms of rights and responsibilities;
☐ a course or courses that develop a young person's awareness of themselves, their interpersonal, social and emotional skills and the possibilities of learning;
☐ pre-planned resources that will enable teachers to rehearse and simulate social and emotional scenarios for use with young people;
☐ materials that will enable a young person to use self-regulatory processes and mechanisms, develop 'foresightful behaviour' and cultivate self-awareness.

. . . and provides opportunities for:

☐ knowing right from wrong or learning the differences and perspectives (e.g. victim and attacker);
☐ developing respect for persons, truth and property;

- ☐ exercising responsibility – including making reasoned and responsible judgements;
- ☐ cooperative and productive participation in work with others when possible;
- ☐ developing good observation of events and accurate information skills;
- ☐ structured and supported self-expression and communicating ideas;
- ☐ putting into effect and encouraging relationships based upon trust and respect;
- ☐ discussing rights and responsibilities with adults and with peers in a properly structured way (e.g. school council, PSHE lessons).

School or environmental considerations should include systems that:

- ☐ sustain and monitor a safe and secure environment for adults and young people alike;
- ☐ define and monitor quality of relationships in the school or centre;
- ☐ can cope with changes to the physical or social environment, providing more personal space or adjusting structures, routines and schedules;
- ☐ encourage an alliance based upon equality and mutual respect between teacher/assistants/carer/adult and troubled individual;
- ☐ enable the young person to apply and evaluate what has been learned in social and community-based situations;
- ☐ support an appropriate physical, social and occupational climate in which 'triggers' (stimuli that set off actions) and 'results' (events that follow) are automatically evaluated and discussed regularly;
- ☐ emphasise the importance of, validate and sustain good adult role models;
- ☐ provide opportunities for young people to talk and be listened to without being judged.

Behaviour and PSHE profile

Notes

It has to be remembered that assertive skills are relative to the situation and that being assertive, reasonable and controlled does not apply to *every situation* that comes along. The purpose of applying a *'personal and social skills' approach* to behaviour management is to give the young person *choices about their behaviour.* This is to replace impulsive, aggressive and negative behaviour that so often results in conflict, punishment and problems for the young person.

This profile is a level 3 response to pupils' individual needs.
LEVEL 1 – Whole school approaches and strategies
LEVEL 2 – Group and interlinked curricular activities
LEVEL 3 – Individual profile and behaviour programme

- The underlined statements are based on observations of behaviour and linked to the behaviour management framework and policy.
- The statements in *italics* are positive developments and are linked to the interactive (PSHE) curriculum and to pastoral care.
- The statements in brackets represent an attempt to translate the observations/ behaviours into pupil-oriented expressions. Users will no doubt develop their own versions of 'pupil-speak'.
- The emphasis is on pupils taking responsibility for themselves and their own behaviour – through self-management, direction, organisation, etc.
- Statements pertinent to an individual are noted and prioritised in the adjacent columns (labelled A (autumn), S (spring), and S (summer)) on a scale of 0–5, denoting the level of importance.
- These sheets are reviewed informally on a regular basis and formally each term along with IEPs – using daily/weekly data.

BEHAVIOUR AND PSHE PROFILE for _____

Date _____

PERSONAL GROWTH				LIFESKILLS				LEARNING TO LEARN		
Relationships	A	S	S	Acceptance of authority	A	S	S	In the classroom	A	S	S
Physical abuse of peers *Expresses anger appropriately – uses self-talk* (To stop and think before you lash out)				Physically abuses the teacher/adults *Exhibits self-control through self-talk supporting* (Respect adults' personal space)				Does not stay in seat *Able to maintain an interest and motivation within himself or herself* (Ask when you want to move from your seat)			
Physical abuse of adults in the school *Exhibits self-control through self-talk* (To stop and think and talk to staff)				Verbal abuse of teacher/adult *Controls impulse – uses reason/argument* (Speak appropriately to adults)				Does not sit appropriately in seat *Able to maintain an interest and motivation within himself or herself* (Beware of the dangers of not using chairs properly)			
Verbal abuse of peers in class or school *Controls impulse – uses reason/argument* (Think about what you're about to say)				Lies to teacher/adult *Sufficiently confident to tell the truth and know or accept the consequences* (Be honest)				Does not stay in class *Maintains focus on work objectives* (Ask permission before leaving class)			
Verbal abuse of adults in class or school *Uses more assertive/moderate language* (Express your feeling to teachers without shouting, talk to us)				Argues regularly with teacher/adult *Has confidence in own opinions and can be objective – not reactive* (Stop arguing!)				Does not stay in school *Is able to find someone to talk to when he/she feels they must leave* (Ask permission before leaving school or find someone to talk to rather than leave school)			
Provokes peer conflict physically *Shows restraint in conflict situations and is able to express feelings verbally* (Hold yourself back and talk about your anger)				Does not follow instructions or directions *Accepts reasonable direction or asks questions when unsure* (Follow reasonable instructions)				Late to lessons *Works on organisation skills and knows where s/he should be – timetable* (Be on time for school and lessons)			

BEHAVIOUR AND PSHE PROFILE for

Date

PERSONAL GROWTH	A	S	S	LIFESKILLS	A	S	S	LEARNING TO LEARN	A	S	S
Relationships				Acceptance of authority				In the classroom			
Provokes peer conflict verbally *Uses reasonable language and self-control. Finds other ways to express frustration or anger* (Do not tease or/and criticise others)				Tries to manipulate teacher/adult *Expresses opinions honestly and openly. Has confidence to be seen to have opinions/needs* (Say honestly what you need)				Does not attend required lessons *Attends or explains reasons for absence. Is able to discuss reasons why.* (Attend all lessons)			
Does not handle disputes with peers appropriately *Recognises potential conflict – acts appropriately with self-control* (Sort your problems out by talking and not fighting)				Does not trust or accept intentions of teacher/adult *Develops some trust and accepts work with focused intentions* (Develop some trust about work given)				Does not enter classroom appropriately *Arrives ready to focus on work objectives – is prepared and organised* (Come into classroom calmly and ready to work)			
Tries to dominate or otherwise manipulate peers *Can ask clearly and directly for things he or she needs and give reasons for wanting things* (Treat everyone with respect)				Does not accept sanctions or consequences of actions *Talks about reasons for actions and the need to comply/modify or reasons why not* (Understands the need for sanctions)				Does not leave classroom appropriately *Remains focused until the end of the lesson and checks task completion and prepares for next lesson/activity* (At the end of lessons tidy away and leave calmly)			
Fights with peers or adults on a regular basis *Talks out problems and frustrations. Able to handle differences in people/opinions, etc.* (Learn to listen to other people's opinion)				Refuses to discuss problems *Able to express opinions, fears and discuss problems* (Talk things through)				Does not have required materials *Prepares for lessons – developing planning skills* (Check your timetable and bring to school all you will need)			

Relationships	A	S	Acceptance of authority	A	S	In the classroom	A	S
Spits at peers to express disagreement or anger *Maintains self-control through self-talk and finds more acceptable ways to defuse anger/feelings* (Do not spit)						Abuses school equipment *Shows respect for school property – understands others' need to use it* (Treat school equipment as if it was your own)		
Rejected by peers on most occasions *Increased awareness of own behaviour and language – of the feelings of others* (Think about how you make people feel)						Talks inappropriately in class *Exhibits self-control and feels able to ask questions in class* (Use polite and appropriate language when others are not speaking)		
			Self-responsibility and problem solving	A	S			
Uses intimidating tactics towards peers/adults *Talks out problems and frustrations. Able to handle differences in people's opinions etc.* (Do not pick on people)			Does not learn from experience *Is able to review their work/actions successively . . . with help* *without help* (Learn from experience)			Tries to copy the work of others *Develops confidence in own abilities* (Rely on your own work, not others')		
Non-trusting of peers without discrimination *Expresses insecurities or misgivings about situations and can say 'no' appropriately. Begins to select circumstances and individuals to trust* (Try trusting someone sometimes!)			Not aware of acceptable behaviour *Is working on social skills curriculum and has achieved appropriate level for daily contact/age* (Understand which behaviours are unacceptable)			Does not raise hand when requiring help *Recognises need for working atmosphere in class* (Put hand up when you need help)		

BEHAVIOUR AND PSHE PROFILE for _____

Date _____

PERSONAL GROWTH				LIFESKILLS				LEARNING TO LEARN			
Relationships	A	S	S	Self-responsibility and problem solving	A	S	S	In the classroom	A	S	S
Not willing to share on most occasions *Begins to make mutual transactions or mini-contracts with others* (It's good to share, give it a go!)				Does not describe problems or feelings *Expresses problems or feelings to specific/trusted individuals* (Find someone to talk to)				Interrupts teacher when talking *Exerts self-control through self-talk and has developed active listening skills* (Only speak when the teacher has finished speaking)			
Does not help peers/others at all *Explores/understands mutual self-interest – later social rewards/friendships* (Help someone, and they might help you back)				Does not anticipate consequences for own behaviour *Aware of/begins to discuss consequences of actions* (Talk through problems in quiet times)				Verbally inappropriate to teacher/adult *Uses more assertive/moderate language* (Speak calmly and appropriately to adults)			
Does not resist any peer pressure to behave badly *Develops a degree of self-belief and self-reliance* (Do not get drawn into bad behaviour)				Does not try new behaviours *Is aware of own self-concept and has developed sufficient confidence and self-esteem to be wrong sometimes* (Accept it is OK to be wrong sometimes)				Physically inappropriate to teacher/adult *Exhibits self-control through self-talk and is aware of personal and social distance/space* (Recognise personal space of adults)			
Does not cooperate with peers in play or unstructured situations *Moving from self-interest to mutual self-interest to sharing* (Join in and be a team player)				Does not participate in planning own work or programmes *Is able to discuss programme sensibly with adult* (Plan your work with an adult)				Overactive in class *Learns to move about more quietly when necessary and finds appropriate time/ways to discharge physical needs* (If you need to move around the classroom, remember others are working)			

Relationships	A	S	S	Self-responsibility and problem solving	A	S	S	In the classroom	A	S	S
Does not cooperate with peers/others in task situations *Becoming aware of teamwork and success through cooperation* (Remember the classroom rules)				Does not attempt to deal appropriately with own problems *Is able to express own problems and has the required language of emotions/ personal matters* (Attempt to deal with own problems appropriately)				Throws/flicks objects in class *Understands his/her disruptive behaviour – moderates in response to external cues/sanctions (then internal)* (Understand the problems of throwing objects around the class)			
Does not accept any help from peers or others *Has confidence and self-esteem, coupled with appropriate listening skills to consider advice* (To understand that you need help sometimes)				Does not cope with less or unstructured situations *Developed sufficient self-direction to maintain behaviour and organise own activities* (Organise own activities . . .)				Lethargic, tired or apathetic in class *Is able to monitor own physical conditions (e.g. fatigue, bedtimes). Discuss reasons for tiredness* (Be aware of the importance of regular sleep and meals)			
Does not relate to peers when no adult present Does not try to form relationships with peers *Is able to talk to adults about own problems and explore fears and anxieties.* (You are a great person. Learn to like yourself!)				Unable to get self to school regularly *Explores/explains reasons for this with appropriate adults* (Improve time keeping and attendance)				Seeks teacher/adult attention inappropriately/too often *Solves problems that are appropriately focused to his/her understanding* (Try sometimes to work by yourself without asking for adult help)			
Does not consider feelings of peers or others *Is able to talk about situations from another viewpoint and 'live in' other people's experience (e.g. through stories, etc.)* (Treat others as you would like to be treated. Think of others!)				Does not offer help to others or adults *Offers to help others or willingly helps when asked* (Be helpful!)				Needs constant supervision *Is developing self-direction, self-organisation and self-talk to reduce impulsiveness* (Try sometimes to work by yourself)			

BEHAVIOUR AND PSHE PROFILE for _____   **Date** _____

PERSONAL GROWTH

Relationships	A	S	S
Does not consider the effects of behaviour on peers or others *Understands immediate consequences through behaviour programme and is able to talk about own and other's behaviour with adults* (Do not be cruel; put yourself in their shoes)			
Exhibits age-inappropriate/immature behaviour towards peers and others *Recognises the social value of appropriate speech/language, etc.* (Act your age!)			
Does not make allowances for peers or others *Appreciates others' situation and/or capabilities* (Think of other people's feelings)			
Does not protect peers when able to *Acts in a positive and supportive way with peers* (Learn to look after each other)			

LIFESKILLS

Self-responsibility and problem solving	A	S	S
Does not control use of bad or offensive language *Tries to correct himself/herself using self-talk* (Think before using bad language)			
Damages others' property *Shows respect and consideration for others' property.* (Take care with others' property)			
Steals others' property *Recognises ownership and respects other people's property* (Do not steal!)			
Does not manage personal anxieties from outside school, within school *Communicate issues and concerns with staff as appropriate in order to manage* (Talk to staff about problems at home)			

LEARNING TO LEARN

In the classroom	A	S	S
Does not contribute to class discussions *Expresses opinions honestly and openly. Has confidence to be seen to have opinions/needs* (Have your say in class discussions)			

Task orientation	A	S	S
Does not start on time/when asked *Enters the classroom in an organised manner and prepared to work* (Start straight away when asked)			
Does not complete on time *Able to plan their work schedule – with/without help* (Try to get all your work done in lesson)			
Unacceptable level of errors *Reviews their work – able to set improvement targets* (Check your work for mistakes when finished)			

Relationships	A	S	S	Self-responsibility and problem solving	A	S	S	Task orientation	A	S	S
Lies to peers and to others *Is truthful and tactful towards others* (Tell the truth)				Acts out problems within the school environment *To verbalise needs and issues with staff and/or peers.* (Talk to staff about problems at school)				Badly presented/organised work *Plans time to complete – takes pride in presentation* (Always try to make your work look as good as you can)			
Inappropriate sexual behaviour *Understands customs of social and sexual behaviour – accepts conventions* (Remember to keep your private parts private!)				Largely unaware of inappropriate behaviours and consequences of actions *Learns to regulate behaviour based upon foresight* (Recognising own inappropriate behaviour)				Badly organised desk/materials *Learns ways to manage resources and recognises the reasons why* (Keep your desk tidy)			
Seeks inappropriate attention or approval of peers *Contributes to class conversations and discussions* (Act sensibly, not the clown)								Easily distracted by others or external events in class *Recognises external cues to attend and later uses self-talk (internal monitoring)* (Ignore others' poor behaviour)			
Does not ask to borrow materials appropriately *Uses appropriate protocol and accepts the response* (Ask before you take things)								Easily distracted by internal events/ thoughts *Recognises external cues to refocus and later uses self-talk* (Find the right way to deal with outside problems within school)			

BEHAVIOUR AND PSHE PROFILE for _____

Date _____

PERSONAL GROWTH	A	S	S	LIFESKILLS	A	S	LEARNING TO LEARN	A	S	S
Emotional control				**Self-responsibility and problem solving**			**Task orientation**			
Easily reduced to tears or seriously upset on a regular basis *Begins to recognise external 'triggers' to his/her feelings/problems* (Talk over your problems)							Lack of interest/motivation towards the work *Motivated to participate and complete work* (Think of the benefits school/education offers)			
Not willing to try new situations *Finds and celebrates own successes – regularly* (Give it a go! You will be surprised what you can do)							Lacks confidence in tasks *Approaches work with a positive attitude* (Have a go at all tasks)			
Unable to refuse a request appropriately *Says 'No' without anger* (Say 'No' without anger)							Regularly refuses to work *Motivated to participate and complete work* (Understand that all pupils are expected to work)			
Cannot express feelings appropriately *Learns language of feelings and uses in non-personal situations first* (Try to express your feelings nicely)							Lacks confidence in ability to complete tasks *Motivated to participate and complete work* (Have confidence in yourself and attempt everything that is given to you)			
Cannot protect self or own rights in any way/appropriately *Respond to or discuss problems/issues following correct protocol* (Do not allow others to spoil your day)										

Emotional growth	A	S	Self-responsibility and problem solving	A	S	Task orientation	A	S	S
Cannot cope with social frustration *Removes self from situation – later explains problem(s)* (Take time out if you need it. Don't forget to ask first!)						Does not cope with task frustration *Able to communicate difficulties following correct protocol* (Ask if you need help)			
Physical self-abuse or self-harming *Becomes aware of external or internal 'triggers'* (Talk to others before you do it!)						Not willing to try new work *Motivated to participate and complete work* (To give everything a go)			
Abuses own property and work *Appreciates and values own property* (Take pride in your work and possessions. They must be good because they are yours!)						Regularly requires too much help *Develops confidence to work independently* (Try to do some work on your own)			
Self-esteem (or Self-worth)						Does not accept help from teacher *Recognises that a degree of help will ensure better progress.* (Accept help from teacher when offered)			
Lacks confidence in social situations (either shy or over-strident) *Feels confident/comfortable in the company of peers/adults* (Relax and enjoy yourself!)						Does not ask for help when needed *Recognises that a degree of help will ensure better progress.* (Ask for help when you are struggling)			

BEHAVIOUR AND PSHE PROFILE for _____

Date _____

PERSONAL GROWTH			LIFESKILLS			LEARNING TO LEARN		
Self-esteem (or Self-worth)	A	S	Self-responsibility and problem solving	A	S	Task orientation	A	S
Negative about self and own capabilities _Recalls successes with/without help_ _(Remember all the good things you've done!)_						Avoids work regularly (e.g. by loss of work or materials) _Motivated to participate and complete work_ _(Always complete set work)_		
Cannot accept peer criticism _Listens for 'good' bits – picks out positive points before 'bad' bits_ _(Listen for good bits before the bad bits; advice isn't always criticism)_								
Magnifies problems out of all proportion _Uses problem-solving steps to start looking at parts of a problem_ _(Don't make a mountain out of a molehill!)_								
Attributes blame for events wholly to self _Discusses events rationally with others and can unpick problems with help_ _(Everyone makes mistakes!)_								
Attributes blame for events wholly to others or outside events _Discusses events rationally with others and can unpick problems with help_ _(Recognise it's your fault sometimes!)_								

Self-esteem (or Self-worth)	A	S	S	Self-responsibility and problem solving	A	S	S	Task orientation	A	S	S
Cannot accept peer praise *Enjoys sharing success and achievement with peers and adults* (Celebrate together!)											
Cannot accept adult praise *Enjoys sharing success and achievement with peers and adults* (Take praise when you deserve it!)											
Shows no pride in achievements *Enjoys sharing success and achievement with peers and adults* (Be proud and share your achievements)											

Score diagnostically next to target. 5 = High priority problem. 0 = No problem

Notes

1 Introduction: the 'human face' of education

1 Cited as unpublished research carried out by Stephen Scott for the Home Office, 2002.
2 Recent guidance for primary schools in the United Kingdom actually uses Maslow's triangle but does not properly acknowledge either the psychology behind it or even the reference to his life's research (i.e. a reference to his authorship). It seems to be merely a superficial tool to give the impression of a theoretical base. Teachers are capable of exploring, and willing to explore, properly referenced and cited evidence and theoretical bases for their practice, rather than accept such thinly disguised diktats masquerading as guidance.

2 Behavioural graffiti: ignoring the writing on the wall

1 'Victory in fight to bar violent pupils', *Times Educational Supplement*, 13 April 2001; 'Unholy children', *Times Educational Supplement*, 22 December 2000; 'Family is costing taxpayer £43,000', *Daily Mail*, 25 April 1996; 'Yob of the form', *Sun*, 23 April 1996.
2 'Zero tolerance: how to banish bad behaviour at your school', *Secondary Teachers* no. 38, May 2005; 'Staff turn to police to subdue unruly pupils', *Times Educational Supplement*, 13 April 2001.
3 Paraphrased from the *Occupational Outlook Handbook*, US Department of Labor, April 1991.

3 Education: adventure or nightmare?

1 This refers to the very latest (as this is being written) and sudden idea (seemingly of Ruth Kelly, the UK Secretary of State for Education) to have a panel of headteachers and teachers to act as a guiding light in moving 'discipline' in schools forward on a national basis. The authors are not convinced that this selectionist and minority-generating strategy will have the desired effect; nor will using 'discipline', rather than 'self-discipline', as the central plank.

7 Measuring the effectiveness of holistic and ecosystemic interventions

1 This quotation also cites National Center for Innovation and Education (1999) and is also supported by the work of Carl Rogers (e.g. Rogers, 1967).

9 Achievement and lifelong learning: a 'principled' approach

1 At the time of writing, the UK Secretary of State for Education, Ruth Kelly, has proposed setting up a working group of teachers and headteachers to consider the problems of behaviour in schools as a reaction to public debate prior to the election.

References

Antidote (2001) *Manifesto for an Emotionally Literate Society*. London: Antidote.

A.R.T.I.S.T. website. http://www.graffiti.org/ (accessed February 2004). Or visit the A.R.T.I.S.T. website http://www.openair.org/alerts/artist/nyc.html.

Aspen Education Groups Walkabout Therapeutic Expeditions. http://www.khnl.com /Global/story.asp?S=2323535 (accessed December 2004).

ATRA (American Therapeutic Recreation Association) (2005) www.atra-tr.org (accessed May 2005).

Ayers, H., Clarke, D. and Murray, A. (1995) *Perspectives on Behaviour: A Practical Guide to Effective Interventions from Teachers*, London: David Fulton.

Bandura. A. (1977a) 'Self-efficacy: toward a unifying theory of behavioral change'. *Psychological Review*, 84: 191–215.

Bandura, A. (1977b) *Social Learning Theory*, Englewood Cliffs, NJ: Prentice Hall.

Bandura, A. (1986) *Social Foundations of Thought and Action: A Social Cognitive Theory*. Englewood Cliffs, NJ: Prentice Hall.

Bandura, A. (1991) 'Self-regulation of motivation through anticipatory and self-reactive mechanisms'. In R.A. Dienstbier (ed.) *Perspectives on Motivation: Nebraska Symposium on Motivation*, 38. Lincoln: University of Nebraska Press.

Bandura, A. (1996) *Social Learning Theory*, Englewood Cliffs, NJ: Prentice Hall.

Bandura, A. (1997) *Self-Efficacy: The Exercise of Control*. New York: Freeman.

Bandura, A. (2001) 'Social cognitive theory: an agentic perspective'. *Annual Review of Psychology* 52: 1–26.

Bannister, A. (2002) 'Setting the scene: child development and the use of action methods'. In A. Bannister & A. Huntington (eds), *Communicating with Children and Adolescents*. London: Jessica Kinglsey.

Bannister, D. & Fransella, F. (1986) *Inquiring Man*. London: Croom Helm.

Barrett-Lennard, G. T. (1998) *Carl Rogers' Helping System: Journey and substance*. London: Sage.

Barron, A. (1969) 'What is therapy – what is training?'. *Therapeutic Education*, Autumn, p. 35.

Bennathan, M. (1998) 'Meeting the needs of all children'. *AWCEBD Newsletter*, May, p. 2.

Bennathan, M. and Boxall, M. (2000) *Effective Intervention in Primary Schools: Nurture groups*. London: David Fulton.

Berghman, J. (1995) 'Social exclusion in Europe: policy content and analytical framework'. In G. Room (ed.), *Beyond the Threshold: The Measurement and Analysis of Social Exclusion*. Bristol: Policy Press.

Berman, D. S. & Davis-Berman, J. (1995) 'Outdoor education and troubled youth'. http://www.aee.org (accessed January 2005).

Bertalanffy, L. von (1950) 'An outline of general systems theory'. *British Journal for the Philosophy of Science* 1: 139–164.

Bertalanffy, L. von (1969) 'Evolution: chance or law?'. In A. Koestler and J. Smithies (eds), *Beyond Reductionism*. London: Hutchinson.

BILD (British Institute of Learning Disability) (2001) *Code of Practice*. London: BILD.

Blaxter L., Hughes, C. & Tight M. (1996) *How to Research*. Buckingham, UK: Open University Press.

Bowlby, J. (1973) *Attachment and Loss*. Volume 2. *Separation: Anxiety and Anger*. New York: Basic Books.

Bowlby, J. (1979) *The Making and Breaking of Affectional Bonds*. London: Tavistock/ Routledge.

Bradshaw, J., Kemp, P., Baldwin, S. & Rowe, A. (2004) *The Drivers of Social Exclusion: A Review of the Literature*. Summary of the Report for the Social Exclusion Unit of the Office of the Deputy Prime Minister. York: Social Policy Research Unit, University of York.

Bridgeland, M. (1971) *Pioneer Work with Maladjusted Children*. London: Staples Press.

Bull, K. (1994) AWCEBD Conference Paper Lecture 1, St Albans Centre, London. 7 June.

Charlton, T. and David, K. (1993) *Managing Misbehaviour in Schools*. 2nd edn. London: Routledge.

Chess, S. & Thomas, A. (1992) 'Interactions between offspring and parents'. In B. Tizard and V. Varma (eds), *Vulnerability and Resilience in Human Development*. London: Jessica Kingsley.

Ciarrochi, J., Forgas, J. & Mayer, J. (2001) *Emotional Intelligence in Everyday Life: A Scientific Enquiry*. Hove, UK: Psychology Press.

Clough, P. & Barton, L. (1995) *Making Difficulties: Research and the Construct of SEN*. London: Paul Chapman.

Coffield, F., Moseley, D., Hall, E. and Ecclestone, K. (2004) *Should We Be Using Learning Styles?* http://www.lsrc.ac.uk/ (accessed 2005). London: Learning and Skills Research Centre.

Cole, E. & Visser, J. (1998) 'How should the effectiveness of schools for pupils with EBD be assessed?'. *AWCEBD Journal* 3 (1): 40.

Cooper, P. (2004) 'Nature and nurture: understanding the interaction between biological, social and psychological factors in emotional and behavioural difficulties'. In E. Haworth (ed.), *Supporting Staff Working with Pupils with SEBD: A Handbook*. Lichfield, UK: QEd.

Cornwall, J. (2000) 'Violence in schools: a perspective from the UK'. Public presentation at Fontbonne College of Higher Education, St Louis, MO. Participation in the 'special educators' postgraduate programme and St Louis's 'Action on Violence' programme.

Cornwall, J. (2001) 'Enabling inclusion: is the culture of change being responsibly managed?'. In T. O'Brien (ed.), *Enabling Inclusion: Blue Skies – Dark Clouds?* London: The Stationery Office.

Cornwall, J. (2004) 'Therapeutic approaches to education: working with the curriculum'. In E. Haworth (ed.), *Supporting Staff Working with Pupils with SEBD: A Handbook*. Lichfield, UK: QEd.

Cornwall, J. (2005) 'Re-constructing threat and the pathway to violent behaviour using personal construct psychology'. Unpublished doctoral thesis. Canterbury: Canterbury Christ Church University.

Cornwall, J. (2005b) 'Travailler avec les enseignants à la mise au point d'un programme d'études adéquats et d'un environnement pédagogique favorable pour les élèves à risque ou exclus'. In D. Zay (ed.), *Prévenir l'exclusion scolaire et sociale des jeunes*. Paris: Presses Universitaires de France.

Cornwall, J. & Tod, J. (1998) *Individual Education Plans: Pupils with Emotional and Behavioural Difficulties*. London: David Fulton

Dewey, J. (1897) 'My pedagogic creed'. *School Journal* 54 (3): 77–80.

Dewey, J. (1938) *Experience and Education*. New York: Macmillan.

DfEE (Department for Education and Employment) (1998) *Excellence for All Children: Meeting Special Educational Needs*. Green Paper. London: DfES Publications.

DfEE (2001) *Promoting Children's Mental Health within Early Years and School Settings*. Guidance Document. Nottingham: DfEE Publications.

DfES (2002a) *Special Educational Needs in Schools in England*. January (provisional). London: National Statistics (Education & Training). http://www.dfes.gov.uk/statistics/DB/SFR/.

DfES (2002b) *Guidance on the Use of Restrictive Physical Interventions for Staff Working with Children and Adults Who Display Extreme Behaviour in Association with Learning Disability and/or Autistic Spectrum Disorders*. Circular LEA 0242 2002.

DfES (2003) *Every Child Matters*. Presented to Parliament by the Chief Secretary to the Treasury.

DfES (2004) *Behaviour and Attendance Training Materials: Core Day 2*. Key Stage 3 National Strategy. London: The Stationery Office.

DfES and OfSTED (2002) *Best Value in Schools*. London: DfES Publications.

Diamond, M. (1988) *Enriching Heredity*. New York: The Free Press.

Ecclestone, K. (2003) 'Lifelong learning: education or therapy? A lecturer assesses the demoralisation of post-16 education in the UK'. Reprinted from http://www.spiked-online.com/Articles/00000006DC18.htm.

Eisenberg, L. (1995) 'The social construction of the human brain'. *American Journal of Psychiatry* 152: 1563–1575.

Elias, M., Hunter, L. & Kress, J. (2001) 'Emotional intelligence and education'. In J. Ciarrochi, J. Forgas and J. Mayer (eds) *Emotional Intelligence in Everyday Life: A Scientific Enquiry*. Hove, UK: Psychology Press.

Elton (1989) *The Elton Report: Discipline in Schools*. London: HMSO.

Falconer-Hall, E. (1992) 'Assessment for differentiation'. In special edition, 'Differentiation: Ways Forward'. *British Journal of Special Education* 19 (1): 20–23.

Fish, J. (1985) 'Educational opportunities for all? A report to the committee reviewing provision to meet SEN'. ILEA.

Florian, L., Tilstone, C. & Rose, R. (1998) *Promoting Inclusive Practice*. London: Routledge.

Forlin, C., Douglas, G. & Hattie, J. (1999) 'Inclusive practices: how accepting are teachers?'. *Support for Learning* 14, (4): 155.

Franklin, M. (1968) *Studies in Environmental Therapy* 1: 27–30.

Freud, A. (1946) *The Ego and the Mechanisms of Defence*. New York: International University Press.

Furedi, F. (2003) on the Limbicnutrition website, *The Psychological Turn of Public Policy*

(2 December 2003). (Posted by Limbic on 10 December 2003 11.21 a.m. Accessed 12 May 2005).

Gardner, H. & Hatch, I. (1989) 'Multiple intelligence goes to school: educational impact of the theory of multiple intelligence'. *Educational Researcher* 18 (8): 4–9.

Garner, P. (2001) 'Goodbye Mr Chips: special needs, inclusive education and the deceit of initial teacher training'. In T. O'Brien (ed.), *Enabling Inclusion: Blue Skies, Dark Clouds*. London: The Stationery Office.

Gillham, J. & Seligman, M. (1999) 'Footsteps on the road to positive psychology'. *Behaviour Research and Therapy* 37: 163–173.

Goddard, D. (1996) *Children and Students as Lifetime Learners*. Report of ATL (Association of Teachers and Lecturers) Conference, October 1996. London: ATL.

Goertzel, B. (2004) 'Patterns of awareness: dynamical psychology'. http://www. goertzel.org/dynapsyc/2004/HardProblem.htm (accessed January 2005).

Goleman, D. (1998) *Working with Emotional Intelligence*. London: Bloomsbury.

Gore, C. *et al.* (1995) 'Introduction: markets, citizenship and social exclusion'. In G. Rodgers *et al.* (eds), *Social Exclusion: Rhetoric, Reality, Responses*. Geneva: International Labour Organisation.

Greenhalgh, P. (1996) 'Behaviour: roles, responsibilities and referrals in the shadow of the code of practice'. *Support for Learning* 11 (1): 17–18.

Grossman, D., Neckerman, H., Koepsell, T. & Rivara, F. (1997) 'The effectiveness of a violence prevention curriculum among children in elementary school'. *Journal of the American Medical Association* 277 (20): 1605–1611.

Hattie, J., Marsh, H., Neill, J. & Richards, G. (1997) 'Adventure education and Outward Bound: out-of-class experiences that make a lasting difference'. *Review of Educational Research*, 67 (1): 43–87.

Haworth, E. (ed.) (2004) *Supporting Staff Working with Pupils with SEBD: A Handbook*. Lichfield: QEd.

Hobcraft, J. (2000) *The Roles of Schooling and Educational Qualifications in the Emergence of Adult Social Exclusion*. CASE Paper 43. London: Centre for Analysis of Social Exclusion.

ILRTA (Illinois Recreation Therapy Association) (2003) University of St Francis, 500 Wilcox, Joliet, Illinois 60435, Attn: Ann Zito (815) 740–3691. www.iltra.org (accessed May 2005).

Innocenti Report Card No. 4. (2002) *A League Table of Educational Disadvantage in Rich Nations*. Innocenti Report Card. Issue No. 4, November. Florence: UNICEF.

Kay, K. (2000) 'What are we going to play today?' The effects of computer based education as an intervention in the behaviour disruptions of emotionally/ behaviourally disabled students. http://mrkay.org/therademics/research/play/text. html#top (accessed November 2004).

Kelly, A. (1994) *The National Curriculum: A Critical Review (1994 Update)*. London: Paul Chapman.

Kelly, G. (1955) *The Psychology of Personal Constructs*. New York: Van Nostrand.

Kemmis, S. (1988) 'Action research'. In J. Keeves (ed.) *Educational Research Methodology and Measurement: An International Handbook*. Oxford: Pergamon Press.

Kingston, P. (2004) 'Could tests to diagnose "learning styles" do more harm than good?' *Guardian* (London), Tuesday, 4 May.

Kirschenbaum, H. and Henderson, V. (eds) (1990) *The Carl Rogers Reader*. London: Constable.

Kolb, B. & Whishaw, I. (1998) 'Brain plasticity and behavior'. *Annual Review of Psychology* 49: 43–64.

Kolb, D. (1984) *Experiential Learning*. Englewood Cliffs, NJ: Prentice Hall.

Laslett, R. (1977) *Educating Maladjusted Children*. London: Crosby Lochwood Staples.

Laslett, R. (1995) 'Beliefs and practice in early schools for maladjusted children'. *Therapeutic Care and Education* 4 (1): 5–9.

Lederman, R. (2005) *It's All Under Control*. from the A.R.T.I.S.T. web site: http://www.openair.org/alerts/artist/nyc.html (accessed May 2005).

Levine, M. D., Lindsay, R. L. & Reed, M. S. (1992) 'The wrath of math: deficiencies of mathematical mastery in the school child'. In E. R. Christophersen & M. D. Levine (eds), *Development and Behavior: Older Children and Adolescents*. Philadelphia: W. B. Saunders.

Levitas, R. (1998) *The Inclusive Society? Social Exclusion and New Labour*. London: Macmillan.

Lindsay, G. & Thompson, D. (1997) *Values into Practice in Special Education*. London: David Fulton Publishers.

Lloyd, S. & Berthelot, C. (1992) *Self-Empowerment: How to Get What You Want from Life*. London: Kogan Page.

Locke, E. & Latham, G. (1990) *A Theory of Goal Setting and Task Performance*. Englewood Cliffs, NJ: Prentice Hall.

Long, R. (2004) *Emotional Literacy: The Rhetoric and the Reality*. In E. Haworth (ed.), *Supporting Staff Working with Pupils with SEBD: A Handbook*. Lichfield: QEd.

Long, R. & Fogell, J. (1999) *Supporting Pupils with Emotional Difficulties*. London: David Fulton Publishers.

Lund, R. (1991) 'Towards the establishment of a curriculum model for working with children with emotional and behavioural difficulties'. *Therapeutic Care and Education Journal* 1 (2): 83–91.

McGuiness, J. (1993) *Teachers, Pupils and Behaviour: A Managerial Approach*. London: Cassell.

Margerison, A. & Rayner, S. (1999) 'Troubling targets and school needs: Assessing behaviour in the classroom context'. *Support for Learning* 14 (2): 87–92.

Maslow, A. (1968) *Towards a Psychology of Being*. New York: Van Nostrand.

Mayer, J. & Salovey, P. (1993) 'The intelligence of emotional intelligence'. *Intelligence* 17 (4): 433–442.

Mayer, J. & Salovey, P. (1997) 'What is emotional intelligence?'. In P. Salovey & D. Sluyter (eds), *Emotional Development and Emotional Intelligence*. New York: Basic Books.

Mills, C. (1943) 'The professional ideology of social pathologists'. Reprinted in J. Beck *et al* (eds) (1970) *Worlds Apart: Readings for a Sociology of Education*. London: Collier-Macmillan.

Molnar, A. & Lindquist, B. (1989) *Changing Problem Behavior in Schools*. San Francisco: Jossey-Bass.

Mongon, D., Hart S., Ace, C. and Rawlings, A. (1989) *Improving Classroom Behaviour: New Directions for Teachers and Pupils*. London: Cassell.

Morris, L. (1994) *Dangerous Classes: The Underclass and Social Citizenship*. London: Routledge.

Murray, C. & Phillips, M. (2001) *Underclass + 10*. London: CIVITAS – Institute for the Study of Civil Society.

National Center for Innovation and Education (1999) *Lessons for Life: How Smart Schools Boost Academic, Social and Emotional Intelligence*. Bloomington, IN: Hope Foundation. www.communitiesofhope.com.

NCC (National Curriculum Council) (1989) *A Curriculum for All*. York: National Curriculum Council.

NfER (National Foundation for Educational Research) (2003) *Annual Survey of Trends in Education: Digest No. 14*. Slough: NFER.

Norwich, B. (1994) 'Differentiation: from the perspective of resolving tensions between basic social values and assumptions about individual differences'. *Curriculum Studies* 2: 293

O'Connor, J. & Seymour, J. (1990) *Introducing Neuro-Linguistic Programming: The New Psychology of Personal Excellence*. London: HarperCollins.

Oettingen, G., Hönig, P. & Gollwitzer, P. (2000) 'Effective self-regulation of goal attainment'. *International Journal of Educational Research* 33: 705–732.

Office for Standards in Education (OfSTED) (2004) *OfSTED Inspection Annual Review*. London: Crown Publications.

OMRDD (New York State Office of Mental Retardation and Developmental Disabilities) (1998) *SCIPr-UK Handbook. Unit 2.1*. Albany, NY: OMRDD.

O'Sullivan, D. (1980) 'Teachers' views on the effect of the home'. *Educational Research*, 22 (2): 138–142.

Papert, S. (1993) *The Children's Machine: Rethinking Schools in the Age of the Computer*. New York: Basic Books.

Parsons, C. (1996) *Exclusion from School: The Public Cost*. London: Commission for Racial Equality.

Parsons, C. (1999) *Education, Exclusion and Citizenship*. London: Routledge.

Parsons, D., Hayden, C., Godfrey, R., Howlett, K. & Martin, T. (2002a) *Outcomes in Secondary Education for Children Excluded from Primary School Research Report*. London: DfES.

Parsons, C., Denman, S., Moon, A. & Stears, D (2002b) *The Health Promoting School: Policy, Research and Practice*. London: RoutledgeFalmer.

Parsons, C., Godfrey, R., Annan, G., Cornwall, J., Dussart, M., Hepburn, S., Howlett, K. and Wennerstrom, V. (2004) *Minority Ethnic Exclusions and the Race Relations (Amendment) Act 2000*. London: The Stationery Office.

Patterson, G., Reid, J. and Dishion, T. (1992) *Anti-social Boys*, vol. 4. Eugene, OR: Castalia.

Paugam, S. (1993) 'La Dynamique de la disqualification sociale'. *Sciences Humaines*, May.

Phillips, P. & Jones, R. (1983) 'Individual maladjustment or systems failure? A process of negotiation and redefinition'. *AEP Journal* 6 (2).

Piaget, J. (1928) *Judgement and Reasoning in the Child*. London: Routledge & Kegan Paul.

Pilling, D. (1992) 'Escaping from a bad start'. In B. Tizard and V. Varma (eds), *Vulnerability and Resilience in Human Development*. London: Jessica Kingsley.

Polsky, H. (1965) *Cottage Six*. New York: Wiley.

Powell, S., Tod, J. & Cornwall, J. (2004) *A Systematic Review of How Theories Explain Learning Behaviour in School Contexts*. London: TTA (EPPI) Systematic Review.

Priest, S. (1999) 'Introduction'. In J. Miles & S. Priest (eds), *Adventure Programming*. State College, PA: Venture Publishing.

Pritchard, J. (2004) 'An introduction and overview of the management of children with emotional, social and behavioural difficulties'. In E. Haworth (ed.), *Supporting Staff Working with Pupils with SEBD: A Handbook*. Lichfield, UK: QED.

QCA (Qualifications & Curriculum Authority) (1999) National Curriculum online. http://www.nc.uk.net/inclusion.html (accessed 2004).

QCA (2005) *End of Key Stage Statements for PSHE (Including Citizenship at Key Stages 1 and 2): Draft Guidance*. London: QCA.

Quicke, J. (1999) *A Curriculum for Life: Schools for a Democratic Learning Society*. Buckingham, UK: Open University Press.

Raven, J. (1991) *The Tragic Illusion: Educational Testing*. Oxford: Oxford Psychologists Press.

Rogers, B. (1991) *You Know the Fair Rule*. London: Pitman.

Rogers, C. (1967) 'The interpersonal relationship in the facilitation of learning'. Reprinted in H. Kirschenbaum and V. L. Henderson (eds) (1990) *The Carl Rogers Reader*. London: Constable.

Room, G. (1995) 'Poverty and social exclusion: the new European agenda for policy and research'. in G. Room (ed.), *Beyond the Threshold: The Measurement and Analysis of Social Exclusion*. Bristol: Policy Press.

Rosier, M. (1988) 'Survey research methods'. In J. Keeves (ed.) *Educational Research Methodology and Measurement: An International Handbook*. Oxford: Pergamon Press.

Rutter, M. (1992) *Nature, Nurture and Psychopathology*. In B. Tizard & V. Varma (eds), *Vulnerability and Resilience in Human Development*. London: Jessica Kingsley.

Salmon, P. (1976) 'Grid measures with child subjects'. In P. Slater (ed.), *The Measurement of Intrapersonal Space by Grid Technique*, vol. 1. London: Wiley.

Salzman, A. (2005) 'No Child Left Behind? Hardly!' *The New York Times*, 1 May.

Sanders, J. (1997) 'Linking the past to the future'. *Residential Treatment of Children and Youth* 15 (2): 1–16.

Scottish Executive (2001) *Better Behaviour – Better Learning: Report of the Discipline Task Group*. Edinburgh: Scottish Executive.

Seligman, M. (2001) 'Positive psychology, positive prevention, and positive therapy'. In C. Snyder & S. Lopez (eds) *Handbook of Positive Psychology*. Oxford: Oxford University Press.

Seligman, M. & Csikszentmihalyi, M. (2000) 'Positive psychology: an introduction'. *American Psychologist* 55: 5–14.

Sharp, P. (2001) *Nurturing Emotional Literacy*. London: David Fulton Publishers.

Silver, H. (1994) 'Social exclusion and social solidarity: three paradigms', *International Labour Review* 133: 5–6.

Sparkes, J. (1999) *Schools, Education and Social Exclusion*. Case Paper 29. London: Centre for Analysis of Social Exclusion.

Sperry, R. W. (1993) 'The impact and promise of the cognitive revolution'. *American Psychologist* 48: 878–885.

Stanley, J. (1994) AWC/EBD Conference Paper Lecture 5. St Albans Centre, London. 7 June.

Stratling, R. & Saunders, L. with Weston, P. (1991) *Differentiation in Action: A Whole School Approach for Raising Attainment*. London: HMSO.

Suttle, I. (1952) *The Origins of Love and Hate*. London: Kegan Paul.

Tierney, J. (2001) 'Solving the crisis in child education'. *The Teacher*. April: 37.

Tizard, B. and Varma, V. (1992) *Vulnerability and Resilience in Human Development.* London: Jessica Kingsley.

Tod, J. (2005) 'Including all the Kellys . . .' Inaugural presentation by Professor Janet Tod at Canterbury Christ Church University (unpublished).

Townsend, P. (1979) *Poverty in the United Kingdom.* London: Allen Lane.

Treasury (2003) *Every Child Matters.* White Paper presented to Parliament by the Secretary of State for the Treasury. London: HMSO.

Vygotsky, L. (1962) *Thought and Language.* Edited and translated by E. Hauptman and G. Vakar. Cambridge, MA: MIT Press.

Vygotsky, L. (1978) *Mind and Society: The Development of Higher Mental Processes.* Cambridge, MA: Harvard University Press.

Waldfogel, J. (1999) *Early Childhood Interventions and Outcomes.* CASE Paper 21. London: Centre for Analysis of Social Exclusion.

Walker, R. (1995) 'The dynamics of poverty and social exclusion'. In G. Room (ed.), *Beyond the Threshold: The Measurement and Analysis of Social Exclusion.* Bristol: Policy Press.

Weiner, B., Frieze, L., Kukla, A., Reed, L., Rest, S. & Rosenbaum, R. (1971) *Perceiving the Causes of Success and Failure.* New York: General Learning Press.

Weston, P. (1992) 'A decade of differentiation' from 'Differentiation: ways forward'. *British Journal of Special Education* 19 (1): 6–9.

Wills, W. (1948) 'Shared responsibility'. In *Problems of Child Development.* London: New Education Fellowship. (See also *Evacuation in Scotland.* SCRE Publication 22, p. 199. VLP 1944.)

Wilson, J. (2000) *Key Issues in Education and Teaching.* London: Cassell.

Witcher, S. (2003) *Reviewing the Terms of Inclusion: Transactional Processes, Currencies and Context.* CASE Paper 67. London: Centre for Analysis of Social Exclusion.

Wuerthele, G. (1997) 'A therapeutic education? A last dying gasp from the suburbs of the Woodstock Nation'. *Coshocton Tribune,* 29 June.

Zarkowska, E. & Clements, J. (1996) *Problem Behaviour: The STAR Approach.* London: Chapman and Hall.

Zimmerman, B. (1990) 'Self-regulating academic learning and achievement: the emergence of a social cognitive perspective'. *Educational Psychology Review* 2: 173–201.

Index

Page references for notes are followed by n

action research 93
adventure programmes 14, 15, 33–4
agency 54, 55, 70, 110–11; forethought
    113–14; intentionality 112–13;
    management of fortuity 115–16;
    moral, social and emotional 61–5; and
    self-efficacy 55–61; self-reactiveness
    114; self-reflectiveness 111–12
American Therapeutic Recreation
    Association (ATRA) 34
Antidote 120
antisocial behaviours 157–8
Aspen Education 15
Ayers, H. 77

Bandura, Albert 8, 26, 56, 58, 59, 60,
    62, 77, 111; agency 57; foresightful
    behaviour 114; fortuitousness 115;
    intentionality 112; self-belief 64;
    self-efficacy 51, 52, 121, 150;
    self-regulation 65–6
Bannister, A. 66
Bannister, D. 8
Barrett-Lennard, G. T. 31
Barron, A. 11
Barton, L. 148
behaviour 20–2; challenging 42–8, 50;
    holistic theories and realities of
    schooling 22–8; and interactive
    curriculum 124, 210–21
behaviour for learning 30
behaviour policy: case study 127–8, 130;
    handling conflict and potentially
    violent situations 137–9;
    implementation and management
    132–4; operational procedures and
    methods 134–7, 207–9; points system

74, 182–5; proactive and pro-social
    74, 179–81; theoretical and legislative
    precursors 130–2, 186
behavioural, emotional and social
    difficulties (BESD) 42, 88–9, 160;
    nature and scope of provision 77–83;
    number of children 47–8; and
    therapeutic education 72–4
behaviourist models 77
Bennathan, Marion 11, 50, 68, 158
Berghman, J. 41
Berman, D. S. 15, 33
Berthelot, C. 5, 62
best value 83, 88, 108, 109
BILD (British Institute of Learning
    Disability) 83, 131
Bowlby, John 50, 77
Boxall, M. 11, 50
Bradshaw, J. 5
Bridgeland, M. 9, 11
Bull, K. 73, 84–5

case study 90–4, 105–6, 168; behaviour
    policy implementation and
    management 132–4; behaviour and
    PSHE profile 142, 210–21; data sets,
    synthesis and analysis of data 94–105,
    189–206; demonstrating effectiveness
    of therapeutic education 108–10;
    handling conflict and potentially
    violent situations 137–9; interactive
    curriculum 76, 124, 125; operational
    procedures and methods 134–7,
    207–9; statement of purpose 124,
    125, 126–30
Charlton, T. 86
Chess, S. 68

child and adolescent mental health services (CAHMS) 3
Children Act 1989 130
Children's Social Adjustment Society 9–10
Ciarrochi, J. 59, 118
Clements, J. 75, 77, 80, 81, 83, 150, 162, 164
Clough, P. 148
Coffield, F. 166
cognitive models 77
Cole, E. 84, 87
Columbine High School 21
Connecticut 3–4
Cooper, P. 47, 49, 50
Cornwall, J. 5, 28, 35, 42, 43, 72–3, 74, 83, 158
crime 5, 157
Csikszentmihalyi, M. 68, 107–8
curriculum 75–6, 92, 103, 124, 125, 134, 167, see also National Curriculum

David, K. 86
Davis-Berman, J. 15, 33
Dewey, John 13, 18
DfEE 47, 68, 151–2, 155
DfES 35, 131, 167; BESDs 47; best value 83; Excellence for All Children 41; Primary Behaviour Strategy 30; restrictive physical intervention 82; statementing 84
differentiation 78–9
discrimination 66–7

Ecclestone, K. 14–15
ecosystemic models 60, 77
education 71; negative experience 38–9; one size does not fit all 41–2; predictability, flexibility, coherence and values 39–40; young people's problems 146–8, see also therapeutic education
Education Act 1944 170
Eisenberg, L. 59
Elias, M. 119
Elton Report 14, 22, 30, 131
emotional intelligence 118–20, 121–2
emotional skills 117–21
empathy 119
Every Child Matters 2–3, 7, 13, 24, 34, 35, 73, 88, 150, 160
Excellence for All Children 41, 131

exclusion 24–5, 27, 41
externalising difficulties 49–50

Falconer-Hall, E. 79
Fish Report 48
Fogell, J. 47, 81
forethought 113–14
Forlin, C. 41
fortuity 115–16
France 13, 34
Franklin, Marjorie 9–10
Fransella, F. 8
Freud, Anna 11
Freud, Sigmund 77
Furedi, F. 143

Gardner, H. 119
Garner, P. 31
Gillham, J. 107–8
Giuliani, Rudolph 19
Goddard, D. 54, 75, 92, 124, 168
Goleman, Daniel 56, 114, 117, 118
Gore, C. 24
graffiti 19–20, 21–2
Greenhalgh, P. 48
Grossman, D. 115

Harborview Injury and Prevention Research Center, Seattle 116
Hatch, I. 119
Hattie, J. 14, 15, 28
health-promoting schools (HPS) 12–13
Henderson, V. 171
Hobcraft, J. 7, 8, 12
human agency see agency
human currency 5–7

identity 51, 55, 67–8
inclusion 2, 6–7, 15, 24, 25, 41–2
Innocenti Report Card 12
intentionality 112–13
interactive curriculum 75–6, 92, 103, 124, 125, 134, 167
internalising difficulties 49, 50

Jones, R. 23, 68

Kay, K. 4
Kelly, A. 149, 170
Kelly, George 8, 31–2, 57, 113–14, 118
Kelly, Ruth 222n, 223n
Kemmis, S. 93

Kent Education Authority Special Needs Audit 83–4
Kingston, P. 166, 167
Kirschenbaum, H. 171
Klein, Melanie 77
Kolb, B. 55
Kolb, D. 55

Laslett, R. 48, 73, 81, 162
Latham, G. 62
learning styles 166
Lederman, R. 19
Levitas, R. 25
life-space interview 135, 136, 139, 187–8
Lindquist, B. 23, 60
Lindsay, G. 78, 83
Lloyd, S. 5, 62
Locke, E. 62
Long, R. 47, 48–9, 81
Lund, R. 86

McGuiness, J. 22, 23, 24, 25, 28, 38, 72, 143, 146, 167
maladjustment 10
Margerison, A. 86
Maslow, A. 9, 18, 30, 49, 222n
Mayer, J. 119
medicalisation 10, 11, 20
Mills, C. 24
Molnar, A. 23, 60
Mongon, D. 86
moral agency 62–4
Morris, L. 25
motivation 119
Murray, C. 5

National Curriculum 73, 76, 84–5, 142, 149, 159, 169–70
National Curriculum Council 78, 79
NCH (Action for Children) 91, 101
NfER (National Foundation for Educational Research) 2
No Child Left Behind (NCLB) 3–4, 24, 166
Norwich, B. 78
nurture movement 11

O'Connor, J. 9, 58, 75, 144–5
Oettingen, G. 113
Office of Mental Retardation and Developmental Disabilities (OMRDD) (New York State) 50, 81, 82, 88

OfSTED 83–4, 107, 143, 159, 167
O'Sullivan, D. 24

Parsons, C. 5, 12–13, 23, 146
Pasteur, Louis 115
Patterson, G. 50
Paugam, S. 25
Pavlov, Ivan 77
personal responsibility 46
Phillips, M. 5
Phillips, P. 23, 68
Piaget, J. 48
Pilling, D. 7
planned environment therapy 9–10
Polsky, H. 87
Pompeii 19
positive psychology 54, 68, 107–8
Powell, S. 21, 30, 48, 51, 149, 167
Priest, S. 17, 33
Pritchard, J. 41
Promoting Children's Mental Health within Early Years and School Settings (DfEE) 151–2, 155
PSHE 82, 124, 210–21
psychodynamic models 77
psychogenic effect 25–6, 143

QCA (Qualifications & Curriculum Authority) 31, 117, 169
quality of life 87–8
Quicke, J. 28

Raven, J. 4
Rayner, S. 86
recidivism 164, 165
reiprocal determinism 77
relationships 13–14, 27, 53, 72–3, 74–7, 162–3
resilience 54, 69, 70, 150–2, 154–5
restrictive physical interventions (RPIs) 82–3; case study 97–8
retribution 164, 165
Rogers, B. 7, 11
Rogers, Carl 27, 42, 167, 171, 222n
Room, G. 24
Rosier, M. 93
Rutter, M. 69

Salovey, P. 119
Salzman, A. 69
Sanders, J. 15, 33
Saunders, L. 78
SCIP (Strategies for Crisis Intervention and Prevention) 82

Scottish Executive 2
Second Step curriculum 115–16
self-awareness 119
self-belief 64–5
self-development 65
self-efficacy 51–2, 53, 110–11, 150;
    forethought 113–14; and human
    agency 55–61, 70; intentionality
    112–13; management of fortuity
    115–16; moral, social and emotional
    agency 61–5; self-reactiveness 114;
    self-reflectiveness 111–12
self-esteem 49
self-reactiveness 114
self-reflectiveness 111–12
self-regulation 65–6, 113, 119, 150
Seligman, M. 54, 68, 107–8, 111
Seymour, J. 9, 58, 75, 144–5
shared responsibility 169
Sharp, P. 81
Silver, H. 41
Skinner, B. F. 77
social cognitive theory 8–9
social skills 117–18, 119, 120–1
sociogenic effect 24
Sparkes, J. 5, 28
special educational needs (SEN): audit
    83–4; inclusion 41–2; teachers'
    qualifications 2
Special Educational Needs and Disability
    Act 2001 41
Sperry, R. W. 57
Stanley, J. 83–4
Stratling, R. 78
Suttle, I. 11

TCI (Therapeutic Crisis Intervention)
    82
TEAM TEACH (Techniques that are
    Effective with Aggression
    Management utilising Therapeutic,
    Educational Awareness,
    Communication, Handling strategies)
    82
therapeutic education 28–32, 36–7, 152,
    156, 160, 168–71; assessment for
    shared values 39–40, 175–8; and
    BESD 72–4; BESD provision 77–83;
    case study 90–106; challenging
    academic tradition and social norms
    7–8; contesting and developing
    notions 11–18; demonstrating
    effectiveness 108–10; effective and

empowering practices 148–50;
    holistic theories and reality of
    schooling 22–8, 172–4; introducing
    empowerment concepts 144–6;
    mapping on to current practice 32–6;
    measuring quality 83–8; new
    solutions to old problems 141–4;
    relationships 74–7; resilience 150–2,
    153–5; roots, principles and
    paradigms 8–11; strategies and
    interventions 161–2
Thomas, A. 68
Thompson, D. 78, 83
Tierney, J. 72, 73, 78, 159, 160
Tizard, B. 51, 147
Tod, J. 5, 30, 61
Townsend, P. 41
Treasury 2–3, 7, 24, 34, 88, 160

unconditional positive regard 75, 80–1,
    164
underclass 5
United States: adventure programmes 14,
    15; education and affluence 18;
    health-promoting schools 13; No
    Child Left Behind 3–4, 24, 166;
    Second Step curriculum 115–16;
    special education 2, 42; therapeutic
    education 33–4, 35
urban art 19–20

value added 83, 109–10
values 39–40, 135, 175–8
Varma, V. 51, 147
Visser, J. 84, 87
vulnerability 68–9, 70, 150, 152, 153–4
Vygotsky, L. 48

Walker, R. 41
Weiner, B. 50
Weston, P. 78, 79
Whinshaw, I. 55
Wills, W. 169, 170
Wilson, J. 47
Winnicott, D.W. 11
Witcher, S. 6, 66, 67
Wuerthele, G. 16

Young People's Fund 3

Zarkowska, E. 75, 77, 80, 81, 83, 150,
    162, 164
Zimmerman, B. 65